D1564213

Growing Up
in a Divided Society

Growing Up in a Divided Society

The Influence of Conflict on Belfast Schoolchildren

Sean Byrne

Madison • Teaneck
Fairleigh Dickinson University Press
London: Associated University Presses

Associated University Presses
440 Forsgate Drive
Cranbury, NJ 08512

Associated University Presses
16 Barter Street
London WC1A 2AH, England

Associated University Presses
P.O. Box 338, Port Credit
Mississauga, Ontario
Canada L5G 4L8

The paper used in this publication meets the requirements
of the American National Standard for Permanence of Paper
for Printed Library Materials Z39.48–1984.

Library of Congress Cataloging-in-Publication Data

Byrne, Sean, 1962–
    Growing up in a divided society : the influence of conflict on
Belfast schoolchildren / Sean Byrne.
        p.   cm.
    Includes bibliographical references and index.
    ISBN 0-8386-3655-1 (alk. paper)
    1. Children—Northern Ireland—Belfast—Social conditions.
    2. School children—Northern Ireland—Belfast—Social conditions.
    3. School children—Northern Ireland—Belfast—Attitudes.
    4. Children and violence—Northern Ireland—Belfast.   5. Belfast
(Northern Ireland)—Social conditions.   I. Title.
HQ792.N67B96   1997
305.23′09416—dc20
                                                             96-28842
                                                             CIP

PRINTED IN THE UNITED STATES OF AMERICA

This book is dedicated to my parents, Michael and Patricia Byrne, my wife, Jessica Byrne, and my brother and sister, Niall and Jennifer Byrne, whose basic respect and love for people transcend distinctions of politics, nationality, creed, wealth, and social standing.

I do not know of any measures which would prepare the way for a better feeling in Ireland, than uniting children at an early age and bringing them up in the same school, leading them to commune with one another and to form those little intimacies and friendships which often subsist through life.

—Dr. Doyle, the Roman Catholic Bishop of Kildare and Leighlin, 1826

The founders of Lagan College believe that it was to say the least unfortunate that the division in the existing schools with very few exceptions mirrored a divided community. They believed that the purpose of education was not simply to mirror back to society its divisions but to seek to heal those divisions. This they believed a school could do by bringing together young people in their formative years and by educating them in a practical environment of respect and tolerance for a variety of religious, political and cultural points of view. Not with the end in view of removing from the young person their religious or political or cultural identities but rather of helping them to see that their own identity is of necessity linked to those from whom they differ as a matter of birth and, that their own is not diminished by day-to-day contact with others but rather enhanced by it.

—Mr. Terry Flanagan, former Principal, Lagan College, integrated all-ability coeducational second-level school, Belfast, 28 November 1991

Contents

Tables

Acknowledgments

THIS research project was developed over several years, and I am grateful for the support and guidance of many people during this time.

First, I wish to acknowledge my academic indebtedness to the International Relations Program and the Program on the Analysis and Resolution of Conflicts (PARC) at Syracuse University's Maxwell School of Citizenship and Public Affairs, where this manuscript began to take shape as a doctoral dissertation. The support and encouragement of my dissertation committee chair, Stuart J. Thorson, director of the Global Affairs Institute, greatly influenced my life and career. I am also grateful to the other members of my dissertation committee, whose guidance and mentorship was invaluable, including Kristi Andersen, Stephen Koff, Louis Kriesberg, and Thomas Patterson. I am also grateful to other faculty who provided advice and guidance with this project, including John Agnew, Donna Arzt, Michael Barkun, Sari Knopp Biklen, Thomas Boudreau, Richard Braunguart, Richard Grant, Neil Katz, Marie Provine, and the late James Laue (visiting professor from George Mason University).

This project was also made possible by the generous support of the Theodore Lentz Post-Doctoral Research Fellowship in International Peace and Conflict Resolution, sponsored by the Center for International Studies and the Department of Political Science, The University of Missouri-St. Louis, and the Theodore Lentz Peace Research Association. I thank Robert Baumann, Ellie Chapman, Bill Chapman, Miranda Duncan, Joel Glassman, Thomas E. Jordan, George McCall, and J. Martin Rochester for their encouragement and guidance during this time. I am especially grateful to Bud Deraps of the Lentz Peace Research Association and peace activist, whose fine cooking and stimulating conversation provided pleasant companionship during this year away from home.

During its final stages, this work was supported by the Department of Dispute Resolution at Nova Southeastern University in Ft. Lauderdale, Florida, where I benefit from my association with colleagues who are devoted to research, education, and practice in the field of conflict resolution. I thank Ronald Chenail (Dean), Nora Femenia, Loraleigh Keashly, John Lande, Brian Polkinghorn, Bill Warters, and Cathie Witty.

I have also been influenced by my professors at the University of Limerick—John Coakley, Brian Faloon, Evelyn Mahon (now at Trinity College, Dublin), Edward Moxon-Browne, and the late Frank Wright, as well as professors at Queens University in Belfast—Paul Bew, Vince Geoghegan, and Adrian Guelke.

A special word of appreciation is also due some very special family members and friends who kept my spirits up during my years as a student and greatly influenced who I am—my parents, Bernard, Kay, Anna-Rose, Frank, Jimmy, Ester, Anne, and Brendan; both my grandmothers; Captain Robert Laver; Winnie, Davey, and Peter Toner; Vincent O'Brien; Alan Conlan; Yaovi Nuto; and Teddy and Til Tuliszewski. I thank my wife and soulmate Jessica Senehi Byrne, for proofreading and editing this work and for always being a sharp intellectual sounding board for me. The love and humor of my brother and sister, Niall and Jennifer Byrne, and my cousins north and south of the border is an invaluable resource. I thank my parents, Michael and Patricia, for their love, support, and wisdom.

My cousin, Paula Clear, and Mrs. Margaret Melenik-Carney, assisted in typing some of the interviews. I thank Aimeé Delman, Michael Geraghty, and Rick Reed for reading and indexing this book. Their time and effort is greatly appreciated.

Finally, let me thank the pupils, parents, teachers, and staff at both Belfast schools without whom this study would not have been possible. Also, the many fine scholars and grassroots peace activists cited throughout this book have influenced my work. May their efforts continue to encourage others to pursue paths to create a better society for everyone.

Growing Up
in a Divided Society

1

Children in a Global Context

Introduction

HUNDREDS of thousands of children throughout the world live in war-torn, partitioned, and segregated societies like Northern Ireland (Coles 1986; Dodge and Raundalen 1987, 1991). Despite considerable work on children's experiences of war, a neglected area of study has been the psychological and emotional effects of political violence and sectarianism on children who live in fragmented societies where long-standing political conflict is the norm (Bilu 1989). How does living in conflict-ridden environments affect the development of these children's attitudes and perceptions, and ultimately the societies they grow up in?

Political violence has traumatized the political world views of children living in conflict regions (Dawes 1990; Garbarino et al. 1991; Punamaki and Sulieman 1990; Yogev and Ben-Yehoshua 1991). All children in Northern Ireland have grown up against this background of political violence. Today's children are tomorrow citizens. How Protestants and Catholics born into the strife grow up in Northern Ireland has implications regarding the bases of their world views and their political understandings about citizenship, political institutions, and intergroup tensions. Thus, insights into the political world views of children have implications for policy intended to affect intergroup tolerance and the process of participatory democracy. Because the conflict is intergenerational, an approach focusing on the perceptions of children may shed new light on the ethnic conflict and "the troubles" in Northern Ireland.

Strife and intercommunal conflict have rarely been absent from Northern Ireland's affairs since Ireland was partitioned by the 1920 Government of Ireland Act (Keogh and Haltzel 1994). The Belfast riots of 1920 and 1935, the Irish Republican Army's (IRA) crossborder insurgent campaign of 1956–1962, the violence and counter-violence prompted by the civil rights movement of the late 1960s, and the emergence of the Provisional IRA and Loyalist paramilitary groups demonstrate a continuing struggle over the legacy of partition and the continuing difficulty in resolving the conflict (O'Leary and McGarry 1993). Both ethnic groups seem to hold hardened, diametrically opposed political positions over issues of national identity (Agnew 1989; Douglas 1989).

Every initiative by the British and Irish governments to improve the Northern Ireland situation has been stubbornly and effectively resisted by one side or the other. After more than twenty-four years of direct rule from London, a new and more vibrant structure of devolved government has not been instituted by the British government (McGarry and O'Leary 1990). There is intransigence and suspicion of any involvement by a southern Irish government in the internal affairs of Northern Ireland, coupled with a lack of trust in Britain's long-term intentions toward the region (Bew et al. 1995). Also, overall British policy has indeed exacerbated tensions and escalated sectarian conflict, driving an iron ideological wall between both communities (Bew and Patterson 1990; Byrne 1995). In the event of a breakdown in current ongoing negotiations between Republicans, the Combined Loyalist Military Command (CLMC), and the British and Irish governments, a paramilitary backlash could sabotage the peace process. Thus, any movement towards enduring peace and conflict resolution must involve all parties and organizations, even the paramilitaries, in a process that will, one, initiate policies from the grassroots up and, two, that will not be imposed or enforced by either or both governments (Byrne 1994a, 1995). Such movement toward bridging the sectarian divide would be a process of social change.

One avenue of movement away from a segregated society chosen by some Northern Ireland families at the grassroots level is integrated education. There is an increased demand for integrated schools throughout Northern Ireland (NICIE 1991a, 1991b, 1991c, 1991d, 1991e, 1991f). Seventeen primary and five second-level integrated schools already exist in the region (Moffat 1993). While eventually supported by the 1989 Northern Ireland Education Reform Act and opposed by many social groups (the Catholic Church, the Free Presbyterian Church, and paramilitary groups, among others), integrated education represents a conscious choice by a segment of society for an alternative to Protestant-only or Catholic-only education for their children. This study seeks to explore how Belfast schoolchildren in a nonintegrated and integrated school think and feel about politics and the Northern Ireland conflict.

This study is based on original data gathered during fall 1991 from interviews with Belfast schoolchildren. Twelve secondary schools in Belfast were requested to participate in a study on the political behavior of schoolchildren. An escalation of political violence during this period limited the study to two schools, a predominantly Protestant grammar school and an all-ability co-educational integrated religious school. In this climate of violence, school authorities and parents in the ten other schools were unwilling to permit their children to take part in this research project because of the possible consequences for their children, themselves, and their schools. While it would have been desirable to interview children from more schools, including a predominantly Catholic school, this was not possible. However, the children at the two schools had new and interesting things to say about the Northern Ireland conflict. I believe it is important for their voices to be heard.

Education, Socialization, and Development

Many writers agree that how children view politics and conflict determines their support for democracy and political institutions. Scholars agree that children should be a focus of study because their attitudes, perceptions, and behavior are important in maintaining and reproducing society. Further, children are good subjects because of their imaginative, blunt, and outspoken political opinions, and are insightful about the political world about them. However, there have been few comprehensive attempts to synthesize these notions and to compare empirically the perceptions and attitudes of children in a particular conflict region.

To date, while excellent case studies have been done on international political development research on children in conflict zones (Bilu 1989; Cairns 1987; Garbarino et al. 1991; Straker 1992; Yogev and Ben-Yehoshua 1991), only Coles (1986) and Dodge and Raundalen (1991) have brought together a number of case studies in their works. Similar types of research on children in Northern Ireland has been limited (Cairns 1987; Fields 1976; Fraser 1973; Harbinson 1983; Heskin 1980; Irwin 1991, 1994). Hence, this study aims to add to our understanding of regional, ethnic, and international conflicts from a children's political development perspective.[1] This study builds on the tradition of studying children's political development.

Children's political development researchers extend the writings of Jean Piaget (1969, 1972, 1976), Fred Greenstein (1960, 1961, 1965), and Laurence Kohlberg (1981). In this study, I adopt the theoretical framework of children's political development theory and Whyte's (1990) theoretical framework for classifying and interpreting the conflict in Northern Ireland. Theoretical concepts, such as attitudes to authority, affective and cognitive learning, and choice of role models are examined in detail. In the discussion of schoolchildren's political behavior, this study also takes into account the necessity of political change (Byrne 1994a, 1995; Keogh and Haltzel 1994; Wright 1991). Several researchers argue that school days are the most formative years in children's political learning and development (Connell 1971; Field 1975; Greenstein 1965; Irwin 1991; Murray 1985; Tolley 1973). Schools are important agents of political socialization especially regarding the civic education of children. Education influences the way children perceive events and this in turn can affect their understanding and development of sensitivities toward their political environment. All over the world, children today are living in a changing culture of communication, information, and increasing violence—all of which are brought into the classroom. These forces must impact on children's perceptions of themselves, their relationship to others, and their position in society. For children, these understandings will underlie their social and political behavior and their approach to conflict at interpersonal, intergroup, and institutional levels. Integrated, rather than nonintegrated, education may play an important part in increasing children's self-esteem, mutual respect, and understanding of complex social problems.

Whyte (1986) concluded that segregated education is one of the most important political socialization instruments in keeping Northern Irish society clearly dichotomized. Clearly, segregated education can influence, affect, or determine the way Northern Irish children perceive the reality of everyday life (Darby and Dunn 1987; Dunn 1986; Fraser 1973; Murray 1985). The revival of interest in integrated education in Northern Ireland to date has been very significant and substantial (Dunn 1989; Dunn and Smith 1989; Flanagan and Lambkin 1991; Graham 1991; Hughes 1994; Irwin 1991, 1994; McEwen 1990; Moffat 1993; Smith and Dunn 1990; Stephen 1990; Wilson and Dunn 1989; Wright 1991).

Therefore, I attempt to respond to Spencer's (1987) call for extending the research agenda of segregated education on the cultural and structural developments of Northern Irish society. In the process, I contribute to a new politics of children's behavior which is cognizant of a much wider range of factors (political, psychological, and educational) than the traditional educational approach (Darby et al. 1977; Murray 1985). Drawing from children's political development theory, this study examines integrated and nonintegrated schoolchildren's political attitudes and perceptions toward social change in a protracted conflict situation. The study includes a comparison of age groups in both educational structures in Belfast, Northern Ireland. Political behavior studies of children to date in Northern Ireland have focused on a single school (Russell and Schellenburg 1976) or a comparison of schools within the segregated school system (Darby et al. 1977; Darby and Dunn 1987; Murray 1983, 1985) or the comparison of an integrated primary school with some nonintegrated primary schools (Irwin 1991). In this study, the attitudes of children from integrated and nonintegrated secondary schools are compared to ascertain whether differences exist in the way these children perceive their political milieu.

Segregated education may be responsible for escalating tensions between both ethnoreligious groups because it does not neutralize stereotypes and prejudicial behavior (Akenson 1973). Integrated education, on the other hand, may permit the evolution of a social situation and atmosphere that can teach pupils new social interaction patterns which can foster friendly relationships with children from the other side, breaking down the crude sectarian and prejudicial stereotypes that exist (Irwin 1991, 1994; Moffat 1993; Wright 1991). The study of integrated school children's political behavior also provides a means of assessing differences in the cognitive and affective attitudes and perceptions of these children. It is possible that the integration of children from Catholic and Protestant communities in the education process could go a long way in reducing prejudice and stereotyping by curtailing the levels of mistrust and suspicion that exist between communities and by promoting a readiness to give and take through communication and understanding the perspectives, fears, and wants of others (Whyte 1990).

The Swiss and Dutch governments, for example, use integrated education systems to foster social harmony between children from various religious and linguistic groups by maximizing contact at a time when impressions are being formed. Likewise, in the case of schools for Jews who had come to Israel from various countries, Amir et al. (1984) noted that direct contact changed psychosocial attitudes and behaviors because each group saw the other in effect to be quite similar to its own group. However, an integrated school system in Northern Ireland would have to be bolstered and reinforced by other stratagems promoting and encouraging cooperation and contact at the local level (Byrne 1994ab, 1995).

What is the potential of Northern Irish research findings for other war-torn, segregated societies? If integrated education can influence political attitudes among children in Northern Ireland, then analogous types of civic education can be engaged in, for example, Bosnia, Sri Lanka, Rwanda, Cyprus, and Lebanon as a stratagem to emphatically reconcile the attitudes and perceptions of opposing ethnoterritorial communities. Integrated education may be part of a process through which antagonistic communities redefine themselves and their culture to promote a shared identity and end the regenerative cycle of sectarian violence.

How the Book Is Organized

Chapter 2 reviews and discusses in historical and cultural perspectives the literature regarding the nature and causes of the Northern Ireland conflict and the roles of both the British and Irish governments in ameliorating or exacerbating the tensions between Protestant and Catholic communities. The complex Northern Ireland conflict has generated interests, goals, and historical processes that perpetuate it. The historical overview outlines why the Northern Ireland conflict is so difficult to resolve. It also introduces the historical and cultural frame within which Northern Irish society operates.

In chapter 3, a bibliographic essay reviews the literature. Theoretical frameworks in the study of political behavior are outlined, and problems with existing theoretical frameworks are reviewed.

Chapter 4 explains the empirical method applied in this book, that is, a series of semiprojective interviews to discern schoolchildren's orientations to conflict and political authority. It describes the procedures of the overall design and explains the methodology used in the study. The school environments in Belfast are described, and the data are classified into appropriate categories to allow measurement of children's images of conflict and political authority.

Chapter 5 examines causes, responses, and possible solutions to the ethnoregional conflict in Northern Ireland and attempts to add an understanding of political aspects to children's political development theory. Findings are conceptually organized by age and school in order to discover and reveal any differences among age and school groups. These children put forward viable solutions to the conflict in Northern Ireland and also suggest where they fit into the conflict by outlining their prospects for the future. Three main questions are examined: How do the children explain the Northern Ireland conflict, how do they fit into the conflict, and what do they suggest can be done about it?

Chapter 6 describes and analyzes similarities and differences of schoolchildren's images of political authority. We see how these children, through their stories, illuminate how they think and feel about public figures. Some of the key theoretical ideas of Greenstein and Tarrow (1970a, 1970b) are examined, including cognitive and affective learning and attitudes toward authority. An important question asked is what are the similarities or differences in children's political imagery toward authority figures?

The conclusions review the significant findings of the study. After reporting the empirical findings, I discuss what I have learned from this interaction with these young Northern Irish children. What the children said is placed into the broader context of possible political possibilities for bringing about peace in Northern Ireland. I discuss how integrated schooling and the European Union may be important factors in extending the identity pie among both cultural traditions in Northern Ireland.

I briefly examine how these forces may provide social change in Northern Irish society and promote and sustain the integrated educational sector in the process. If the integrated sector is to grow, it must be supplemented and supported by other strata of contact and cooperation in the politico-economic arena.

2

The Historical World of Children in Belfast, Northern Ireland

Introduction

SINCE the end of the Cold War, the world has woken up to the phenomenon of ethnic conflict (Gottlieb 1993; Gurr 1993). Pundits now compete to paint a gloomy future of "The New Tribalism" or "The Clash of Civilizations." The conflicts in the former Yugoslavia and Rwanda, not to mention the former Soviet Union, capture the headlines and give credence to these pessimistic diagnoses.

While the clash of ethnic identities has led to brutal battles between neighbors in Bosnia and Herzegovina, Rwanda, and East Timor, recent developments in Northern Ireland have encouraged hopes for the just resolution of the conflict that has plagued this deeply divided society. Temporary yet proactive steps taken by the Provisional Irish Republican Army (PIRA) and the Combined Loyalist Military Command (CLMC) have done much to reduce fatalities from the political violence that has consumed this society over the past quarter of a century. Even though the PIRA broke its cease-fire February 9, 1996, the peace process may yet be salvaged by grassroots protesters in Northern Ireland seeking to get the cease-fire restored.

Much has been written about the long and complex local history of strife, grievances, conflicting national identities, historical claims to sovereignty, and political violence that has helped to shape sectarian and extremist behavior between Protestants and Catholics within Northern Ireland (Rose 1971, 1976). Historical biases, oppressions and hatreds, strong group loyalties and core ethnic identities, collective memories of past glories, traumas and grievances have caused physical and emotional injuries to the Protestant and Catholic communities. For example, Bloody Sunday, Enniskillen, Greeysteel, and the Shankill Road massacres are ingrained in the memories, culture, and folklores of people in Northern Ireland (Northrup 1989; O'Leary and McGarry 1993). The redundant past, symbolizing ethnoreligious identity issues that have not yet been resolved (Lyons 1973), is worked over. These historical images are embedded in people's minds from an early age. A unique political culture has developed, therefore, as children in Northern Ireland live their everyday lives in a conflict situation.

Children's political awareness and inclinations toward conflict and political authority have a historical and cultural basis. They see members of the other community through a particular, separate conceptual historical lens. It is important to trace the historical forces separating the two ethnoreligious groups if we are to understand the political world Northern Irish children experience, feel, and absorb. The historical context in which Catholic and Protestant traditions, perspectives, and behaviors occur must be described if we are to comprehend why the roots of the present conflict in Northern Ireland are so deep. As O'Malley (1983) notes, the Northern Ireland problem is rooted in historical interpretations—myths of siege, massacre, rebellion, and victory.

Historical Overview of the Nature of the Community Divide

Saints, Scholars, and Sinners

The history of volatile relations between Protestants and Catholics in Northern Ireland can be traced back to the Norman invasion and subsequent conquest of the island during the twelfth century. Before the 1171 Norman invasion, the inhabitants of the island were mainly Gaels and marauding Norsemen of Scandinavian descent. The Gaels had their own clan system bolstered by the Brehon laws, in which group identity superseded that of the individual in the overall society (Kelley 1982). The Brehon Gaelic system persisted from the fifth to the twelfth century, when the Normans arrived.

Norman feudalism effectively erased local Gaelic customs, traditions, music, and literature. The Norman expansionist foray into Ireland, led by Strongbow, changed the socioeconomic and political structures of the indigenous population. The Normans solidified their conquest of the island by constructing fortified castles throughout the countryside, destroying Gaelic communal practices in the process.

There were many English settlements prior to the colonization of Ulster, in which many of the "old English" intermarried with the native Gaels and became Irish. However, the Anglo-Irish settlers around "the Pale" in Dublin remained aloof from the local population. All rebellions, such as the 1641 uprising in which local Protestant settlers were put to the sword by the rampaging native Irish nobility, were crushed by local noblemen with the aid of English arms. Many "planters" were massacred during the 1641 rebellion by the native Irish, and these historical images of siege and massacre are enshrined in the traditions, cultural symbolism, and folklore of present-day Northern Irish Protestants, who see themselves as a besieged minority on the island of Ireland (Kelley 1982).

Most of the Gaelic inhabitants of Dundalk and Drogheda were put to the sword by Cromwellian soldiers in the seventeenth century. This act of warfare by Cromwellian soldiers was perceived as genocide by the Irish people and remains important in the Irish nationalist repertoire. Cromwell, who regarded the Gaels, or native Irish, as a racially inferior people, quashed the insurrection in 1649 by driving the militant Irish Gaels toward the barren and desolate West of Ireland with the cry of "to hell or to Connaught," in the process expropriating land and parcelling it out to the remnants of his army, who remained in Ireland.

In 1601 the English parliament perceived Ulster in the North as the most militant part of the island because most of the insurrections started there; it decided to squash the rebel forces that presided in the region (Kelley 1982). Unable to convert the Irish-Gaels to the English language and culture, the English monarchy decided to crush once and for all the indigenous Ulster rebels by planting predominantly Scottish settlers in the northern part of the island beginning in 1608. The Gaelic chieftains from Ulster, O'Neill and O'Donnell, and all their clansmen were forced by the king to flee the country in 1607 and seek employment as mercenaries in the service of continental monarchs.

There are two interpretations of the motives for Scottish settlement in Ulster. Some scholars believe that the Scottish were sent to Ulster because they were Calvinists and therefore would not intermarry with the native populace (Miller 1978). Others believe that the Scots were sent to Ulster because they were ethnically different from the Irish Gaels (Bruce 1986, 1992; Stewart 1977). I concur with the latter; the fact that the Scots were Calvinists was merely coincidental. What was important was that they were lowland Anglo-Saxons who spoke English, were experienced in counterinsurgency warfare with the highland Gaels[1], and would be an important contribution to English colonial expansionist foreign policy of that time—*divida et conquista*.

The failure of the Spanish Armada in 1569 to invade England via Ireland clearly demonstrated the strategic importance of Ireland to the English monarchy. The English government would not allow Ireland to be used by either France or Spain as a springboard to attack England, which had undergone the Protestant Reformation under Henry VIII. Lowland Scots would be used in this foray to crush the spirit of Gaelic militancy in the North of Ireland. We must therefore focus on the relationship between lowland and highland Scots for a better understanding of what actually occurred in Ulster in the seventeenth century and how this has affected the relationship between the two tribes ever since.

The Highland-Lowland Connection

Previous invaders were either repelled or integrated into Gaelic society. Lowland Scottish Calvinists were planted in Ulster in the late sixteenth and early seventeenth centuries on the properties of displaced native Gaelic chieftains. Between the eighth and tenth centuries, the Anglo-Saxons and Danes integrated the Breton Welsh-speaking Scottish lowlanders into Anglo-Saxon society, replacing Welsh with the English language. The upper-class descendants were, therefore, of Danish and Anglo-Saxon origin. When William the Conqueror's Normans defeated the Anglo-Saxons under King Harold at the Battle of Hastings in 1066, the Anglo-Saxon nobility fled to the Scottish lowlands, since it was standard Norman procedure to exterminate the local nobility. Consequently, the ethnic division of Scotland receded in importance as the highlanders and lowlanders, out of fear and hatred of the invading Normans, came together to oppose a common foe. However, the Normans failed to subjugate the Scots who lay behind Hadrian's wall toward the north of the isle.

By the turn of the sixteenth century the power of the Stuart dynasty held sway in the lowlands of Scotland. The work-ethic experience of the Reformation, the importance of Glasgow and Leith as ports, and commercial trading and contact with the rest of Europe turned the lowland Scots into sophisticated, modern, and Europeanized citizens, while their highland neighbors to the north eked out a frugal existence. However, a mutual respect existed between these ethnic groups, with the lowlander viewing the native highlander as distinctively primitive but friendly.

How important were the Scottish wars between lowlanders and highlanders? The lowland Scots were part of Europe and its ecclesiastical setup. A struggle for power, however, arose in the lowlands between the Reformation dissenters and the Catholic lowlanders; the latter solicited support from the Catholic highlanders, and the former viewed the highlanders with disdain and suspicion. In 1606, under the Stuart monarchy, the English-Scottish Union came into existence, and as law and order began to slowly evolve in Europe and the threat of war began to subside, the necessity of having backward and violent highland Gaels in the English armies decreased. The highlanders were now seen as a liability and were subdued and conquered in a series of battles; efforts were made to settle the hamlets of Lewis and Kintyre in the highlands. The 1745 uprising by Bonnie Prince Charlie Stuart was supported by the highland Gaels, while the lowland Anglo-Saxons provided two regiments in the English army to crush the revolt.

The Ulster Plantation

In 1641 the Irish-Gaels rebelled against the English parliament and the Ulster planters. In 1689 they were siding with the Catholic British monarch, James II, as he rallied to defend his throne against the Dutch Protestant pretender King William of Orange (Hill 1970). The subsequent defeat of James II at the hands of William of the House of Hanover at the 1690 Battle of the Boyne ushered in a new era of Scotch-Irish dominance that pushed the native Gael outside the margin of socioeconomic and political relevance (Coakley 1985).

Why were the lowlanders sent by the English monarchy to colonize Ulster? The newly crowned James I of England chose Ulster for resettlement precisely because the region was so fiercely opposed to the English presence in Ireland and the population had been reduced in recent wars with England. These Scots lowlanders were largely Presbyterian and loyal to the crown (Perceval-Maxwell 1973). As the lowland Scots were experienced and conditioned in dealing militarily with the highland Scots Gaels, they would find a common enemy in Ulster. Their knowledge of counterinsurgency and guerrilla warfare, tested and modified in their skirmishes with the highlanders, was put to good use in displacing the native Irish from their lands, sending them to the mountains in droves, as they had done to the hated highlander Gaels (Hill 1970).

Because the English parliament could not pay the predominantly lowland Scottish soldiers with money, the incentives given to settle the northern part of Ireland were land. These planters arrived in Ulster with an attitude of superiority in which the indigenous populace were viewed as culturally, socioeconomically, and religiously inferior, and unredeemingly so. They established a siege mentality to ensure little or no contact between the ethnic groups, with events like the 1641 and 1689 massacres demonstrating the barbarity of the Irish Gaels. This policy differed from that of the French Canadian and conquistador policies in the "New World," where colonizers intermarried with the native indians and integrated them into society. The communal identity of the Irish-Gaels differed from the rugged individualism and frontier mentality of the Protestant settlers.

Hence, James Connolly's hibernicization of marxist thought posits that the clans of the Irish-Gaels lived in an initial golden age of primitive communism (Connolly 1973; Morgan 1980). This is why the Irish-Gael Brehon Law was abolished and efforts were made to stamp out all vestiges of an Irish-Gaelic culture. On the other hand, the lowlanders brought with them the Calvinist work ethic (Weber 1968), whose style of capitalism was bound to produce inequalities between the settler and the indigenous Gaelic population. The religious sentiments of Calvinism—that all men were equally sinful before God—also assisted in uniting the poor and rich planters (Bruce 1986).

The geographic proximity of Scotland to Ulster meant that contact and migration between the two regions were frequent. Hence, highlanders were drawn to Ireland in the thirteenth century to fight as mercenaries for Irish chieftains and became interwoven into the very fabric of Irish society (Perceval-Maxwell 1973). In the struggle between the Stuart monarch James II and King William of Orange for the English throne, Ulster Protestants sided with the Dutch pretender to the throne of England against the Stuarts (who promised the Irish-Gaels their land in return for military service in the Stuart army). As recent colonizers Ulster Protestants would be killed and their land confiscated by the crown if James II prevailed. At the 1690 Battle of the Boyne in County Westmeath, the forces under King Billy routed the royalist and Jacobin French forces of the Stuart monarch. In the context of international politics, the political interests of the Vatican were better served supporting the Dutch Protestant king than the Catholic king James II (Kelley 1982).

The Dissenting or Penal Laws introduced in 1692 discriminated against such social outcasts as Catholics, Methodists, and Presbyterians, since Calvinism did not have a good representation with the established church. It is an irony of Irish history, therefore, that the great nationalist leaders of the eighteenth and nineteenth centuries were Irish Dissenters. A Dublin Dissenter, Henry Grattan, for example, promoted in 1779 the mercantilist interests of the Irish bourgeoisie. Also, the United Irishmen rebels of 1790, influenced by the ideals of the French Enlightenment, were radical deists and anticlericalists who wanted to abolish the dichotomous labels Protestant and Catholic in favor of the more egalitarian labels Irishmen and Irishwomen, and to throw off English rule by establishing an independent Irish Republic (O'Brien 1986). The insurrection, aided by the French, who landed troops on the west coast of Ireland, was crushed by British military forces. However, it can be argued that Theobald Wolfe Tone and the United Irishmen did not want to share power with the existing Gaelic-Irish elite. The rebellion led by Robert Emmett in 1803 was also put down by force of English arms.

Furthermore, it is interesting to note that a parallel Catholic insurrectionary structure, in the form of the Fenians and the Irish Republican Brotherhood (IRB), which had links in the United States among Catholics who had fled the Great Famine of 1844–1848, also existed in Ireland in the eighteenth and nineteenth centuries (Jordan 1994). They drew sustenance from the political examples of Tone and Emmett, extolling their use of physical force to shake off English rule. The uprisings carried out by these organizations were crushed in a ruthless, heavy-handed way, the survivors usually being exported as convicts to Australia (Jordan 1993).

The New Departure, Separate Nationalism, and the War with Britain

The mass electoral nationalist mobilization of the small tenant farmer class under the auspices of both the Land League[2] and the Home Rule[3] parties in the 1870s and 1880s brought about the development of a Catholic nationalist movement that sought to win autonomy and political freedom for Ireland. The island began to be divided between the agrarian south, whose political agenda differed from that of the industrial north, where the industrial magnates and working-class Protestants had commercial and political attachments to Britain. The institutions of government in Ireland were too centralized to deal with the calamity of the famine, while the absentee landlords used the economy based on potato growing to keep the dependent masses in a static situation, producing large families to work on their estates. Much of the landlord-tenant relationship in the decades before the famine, therefore, could be classified as a noncooperative game, in which each side disregarded the interests of the other side while trying to do as well as possible for itself (Bew 1979).

The land question became the most important political question in Ireland in 1879, since it was the continuing campaigns of Irish peasants for land reform that led to the upsurge in Irish nationalism and developed the ethnoreligious cleavage as the most important division in the Irish political arena (Bew 1979). The absence of nonagricultural employment with paid wages and the desire of the Irish peasant to hold land contributed to the wave of rural unrest that engulfed most of the country. The lack of a buffer middle class in Ireland would play its own part in the stagnation of a rural economy lacking an entrepreneurial spirit that would have provided a much-needed source of hard currency (Bew 1987). Furthermore, the woolen and linen mills of England and Ulster tended to wipe out the small cottage-based indigenous spinning and weaving industries in the rural areas of the highlands of Scotland and Ireland by mass-producing cheaper goods for the global economy (Lyons 1971). The uneven concentration of industrialization in the northeast of Ireland led to a distinct political formation in Ulster— Unionism, which sought the integration of Ulster within the British industrial machine and its strategic economic markets (Gibbon 1975; Stewart 1967, 1977).

Thus, when the peasant farmers in the South began to agitate for land reform, they received scant sympathy from the Protestants residing in Belfast, who had begun to feel threatened by the large influx of Catholics leaving the countryside for the city in search of work (Stewart 1977). This exodus of Catholics from the land had the effect of escalating sectarian conflict and politicizing the Catholic masses (Lee 1973). For example, Daniel O'Connell's successful movement for Catholic emancipation in 1829 and his futile agitation for repeal of the Union with Britain in the 1830s and 1840s gave peasants their first practical experience of modern democratic politics. However, the mobilization of Catholic peasants alienated and alarmed the vast majority of Irish Protestants. O'Connell's appeal to a Catholic Irish nationalism was matched with Protestant upper-

class efforts to enflame the Protestant working class (Kelley 1982).
Thus O'Connell's contribution to the involvement of Catholicism
as an institution in Irish nationalism was immense and would influence later nationalists such as Patrick Pearse.

However, religious affiliation came to be seen as a "natural"
national difference as a result of the peculiar course of modernization and development in Ireland—industry in the North and agrar-
ianism in the South (Gibbon 1975; Stewart 1967). Many tenants
found themselves unable to pay their rents. A widespread agitation
for the abatement of the rent burden ensued, and, significantly, the
agitation of the Land League became linked to the parliamentary
movement for home rule (Lyons 1973).

The New Departure was an amalgamation of the Irish Land
League under Michael Davitt, the Irish Parliamentary Party (IPP)
under Issac Butt and Charles Stuart Parnell, and the Irish Republican Brotherhood (IRB) or the Fenians. This coalition of moderate
and radical forces, organized locally by priests, sought to mobilize
the peasantry with the support of the Catholic hierarchy (Bew
1987). In symbolic terms, at least, the national question and the
land question as posed by the Land League were one (Stewart
1967). Landlordism upheld British sovereignty in the Irish countryside, so that the twin ideas of land for the people and Ireland for
Irish Catholics fused into a distinct political framework for action
(Stewart 1977).

The Irish peasant had by now intermeshed the concepts of religion, nationalism, and land into his or her politico-psychological
consciousness. The peasant's resistance to landlordism became the
Catholic resistance to foreign subjugation by absentee landlords
(Bew 1979). Consequently, it was impossible for the Protestant tenant farmers to be part of a land war–home rule movement that
promoted Catholicism and sought to break the total union with the
rest of the United Kingdom (Bew 1987). In the years 1878 to 1886,
the Irish nation, composed of the Catholic population on the island
of Ireland, forged a distinct, exclusive ethnoreligious identity that
did not include Ulster Protestants (Stewart 1967, 1977).

The first major success of the Land League was the Secret Ballot
Act of 1832, by which landlords were prevented from coercing
their tenants to vote for them during elections. This was quickly
followed by the three Fs (fixture of tenure, fair rent, freedom of
sale) that the Whigs under Prime Minister William Gladstone
granted to the Irish tenant farmer in 1885. The Ulster Custom
guaranteed the three Fs to most tenant farmers of Ulster, who were

permitted the luxury of being exempt from participating in this political conflict (Kelley 1982).

It is important to bear in mind that most of the members of the IPP were the landed aristocratic ascendancy, who used the land issue to mobilize the peasantry to protest for Home Rule for Ireland. Parnell's quest for home rule nearly succeeded but for his extramarital affair with Kitty O'Shea, which became public knowledge and led to the fall of "the Uncrowned King of Ireland" and the subsequent demise of the New Departure, along with the eventual schism of the IPP into a faction led by John Dillon and the main body under John Redmond (Bew 1987).

Why did Ulster Protestants turn away from the concept of home rule? First, it is interesting to note that Irish tenant farmers' support for the Liberal Party waned as they embraced the Home Rule Party, and traditional Protestant support for the British Liberal Party switched to the pro-union Conservative Party as Ulster Protestants realized that a home rule parliament protected and maintained by British power would not be under their dominant leadership (Jackson 1989; Loughlin 1987). Second, the Protestants did not want to be a minority in Ireland ruled by the Catholics. The British Liberal Party's attempts, therefore, to initiate home rule by presenting bills to parliament in 1886, 1893, and 1912 only caused both communities to become more polarized. In 1886, and again in 1893, Ulster Liberals to whom Prime Minister Gladstone had been an important political ally were infuriated by his "conversion" to home rule (Jackson 1989; Loughlin 1987). To counteract the political movement for home rule for Ireland, the Protestants of Ulster began to organize politically (Stewart 1977).

The northern Protestant elites could see in home rule only their political elimination from the Irish political spectrum, and therefore they constructed a Unionist ideology to protect the union with Britain that was the only guarantee of their endangered geopolitical position and property (Stewart 1977). Protestants feared Catholics more than they disliked the English, and once the land question showed Protestants that the Catholics would not be grateful and happy followers, they had to preserve their autonomous, distinct culture and ethnoreligious identity from the native Catholic Gaels (Stewart 1967, 1977). The Methodists and Presbyterians disliked the Church of Ireland, but a common language, ethnicity, and ideology—Unionism—enabled all three groups to band together.

The English ignored Northern Irish Protestants during the eighteenth century, an attitude that assisted in reinforcing the Protestants' distinctiveness from both the English and Catholics.

Protestants in the northeast of Ireland now found it expedient to turn toward England again to preserve their ethnocultural autonomy, political power, and economic privileges against the native Catholics (Lee 1973). The Protestant elite of Ulster were already sharing in the affluence of industrial Britain and simply could not or would not abandon the union (Bew 1987).

There were, however, Protestant tenant farmers in Ulster who had agrarian grievances quite similar to those of their Catholic neighbors, and this factor could have laid the basis for undermining the ethnoreligious cleavage in Irish society (Wright 1987). The Unionist elite also depended on Britain for cheap resources and an export outlet for their industrial goods, necessitating the promotion of sectarian divisions (Kelley 1982). Indeed, Presbyterian tenant farmers had taken the lead in land reform agitation since the 1850s and had been quite willing to join forces with Catholic agitation for similar purposes in the South of Ireland (Stewart 1967).

With the advent of the Land League, however, the different connotations of land reform within the two communities became apparent. The goal of Protestant tenant farmers' land agitation had been to defend, consolidate, and extend the Ulster custom of tenant rights such as fixity of tenure (Bew 1979; Lyons 1973; Stewart 1967). Protestant tenant farmers believed that James I had granted certain proprietary rights not only to the landlords, but also to their tenants (Munck 1985). Protestant tenants were claiming, therefore, something they believed the crown had bequeathed their ancestors in the seventeenth century, whereas Catholic tenants, under Land League and IPP auspices, were fighting to regain land they believed the crown had commandeered from their forefathers during the seventeenth century (Stewart 1977).

Not surprisingly, in the early 1880s, when Protestant tenants found that they could not join Land League agitation without implicitly sanctioning the native Irish's national goals, thereby promoting a Catholic Gaelic culture in the process, they simply left the organization (Bew 1979). While Protestant tenant farmers rejected an Irish Catholic nationality, despite some apparent identity of their economic interests with those of Catholic tenants who were the backbone of the national movement, Catholics simply embraced Irish nationalism to sustain what they saw as a basic need—access to the land (Stewart 1977).

Hence, there was at least the possibility for the conflict in the northern part of Ireland to assume a socialist dimension to the Protestant and Catholic ethnoreligious antagonism which arose (Morgan 1980). However, whether aggravation is due to ethnoreligious identities or ethnoterritorial identities makes very little difference to the development of national antagonisms. Reciprocal violence inevitably occurs, and everyone is held equally responsible for the actions of those in its group (Wright 1987). In such conditions, Loyalist extremists such as the Reverend Ian Paisley will always rise to prominence and representative violence will occur, creating some form of ideology as its justification (Boal and Douglas 1982; Wright 1987). In this case, Unionism became the ideology of Ulster Protestants.

The demise of the old Irish Nationalist party and the rise of the new Sinn Fein (SF) party under Arthur Griffith in 1905, also changed the political landscape in Ireland. Further, the development of cultural nationalism created a distinct Catholic/Gaelic psychocultural consciousness peculiar to the Catholic population. For example, the formation of the Gaelic Athletic Association (GAA) by Archbishop Croke in 1884 to promote the Catholic sports of hurling and football, and the efforts by the Gaelic League to reinvigorate Celtic culture and language under W. B. Yeats and the Countess Markievicz in 1893 worked to this end. This type of nationalist ideology further demonstrated to the Protestants in the northeast of Ulster that their position as leaders of Irish nationalism had been usurped and bombasted by the Irish Catholic political elites (O'Brien 1972).

Also, the 1916 Rising in Dublin by members of the Irish Volunteers and the Irish Citizens Army led by James Connolly and Patrick Pearse of the Irish Republican Brotherhood (IRB) and the 1918 by-election in which the Irish independence movement SF had a sweeping victory throughout the country were the final blows to any Protestant form of Irish nationalism (Nelson 1984). Indeed, the Ulster Solemn League and Covenant, pledging the loyalty of the Protestants of Ulster to the British monarch, was signed by more than 500,000 Ulster Loyalists in Belfast city hall in 1912 in protest of the proposed third Home Rule Bill (Stewart 1967, 1977). Lord Carson may also not have realized it at the time, but one immediate result of his movement was to break the growing working-class threat to his Ulster capitalist allies (Morgan 1980).

In 1912 the Ulster Volunteer Force (UVF) was formed as a defense force to prevent and resist any attempts to place Ulster in a "home rule" Ireland and to demonstrate its loyalty to the Crown. In April 1914, 35,000 rifles and 5,000,000 rounds of ammunition were landed by the UVF in Larne and other ports in northeastern Ulster (Stewart 1967, 1977). All attempts at negotiation and compromise failed, and it was only the outbreak of World War I that averted a potential civil war in Ireland (Stewart 1977).

Consequently, the original political problem of who would lead Irish nationalism—the Protestant or the Catholic—had turned to a possible separation of Ulster from the rest of Ireland. Sectarian politics would become a new political panacea to allow the Protestant elites to divide the working class in Ulster and legitimate the creation of two geopolitical entities on the island (Garvin 1987; Stewart 1967, 1977).

The original political role of the Protestants of Ulster to protect the British mainland had become redundant, and a role reversal was occurring in which they looked to Britain for the protection of their ethnoreligious identity and economic privileges (Wright 1987). The Protestant unionist bourgeoisie had not yet envisioned the physical breakup of the island and this position existed right up until the IRA's 1919–20 War of Independence, in which turmoil and naked violence rocked and shook the very foundations of Irish society (Fraser 1986; Garvin 1987). By this time, the Protestants in Ulster began to realize that the IRA was fragmenting the military and political rule of the British government in Ireland (Buckland 1981; Lyons 1973).

The west of Ireland, because of its infertile land and lack of any natural resources, was unable to pull itself out of its preindustrial economy to play a role in the industrial revolution that swept across the rest of Europe in the nineteenth century (Munck 1985; Probert 1978). Because the northeastern industrial sector was the backbone of industrialization in Ireland, it was only logical that the Protestants would want to keep control of it. Finally, in 1919 the War of Independence against the British government was initiated by the militant IRA.

In 1919 the guerrilla warfare carried out by the leader of the IRA, military strategist Michael Collins, forced British Prime Minister David Lloyd George, popularly known as the Welsh wizard, to initiate peace proposals and a cease-fire. The resulting 1920 Government of Ireland Act partitioned the island. A Boundary Commission was established in an attempt to reconcile the political aspirations of Irish nationalists, by appearing to foster Irish unity, with the apprehensions of Ulster Unionists, who would not be coerced into a united Ireland (Buckland 1979, 1981). The 1920 Government of Ireland Act was superseded by the Anglo-Irish Treaty of 1921, which conferred dominion status on the southern Irish Free State. The ratification of the subsequent treaty polarized and split the southern Irish parliament into opposing pro- and antitreaty forces, and the resulting civil war made permanent the separation of the island. The Boundary Commission's cosmetic report of 1925 sought no substantial change to the north-south border. It is important to bear in mind that when Ireland was divided by the Government of Ireland Act in 1920, Northern Ireland was not made an integral part of the United Kingdom. The question remains why the Northern Irish state was not integrated into the United Kingdom on the same basis as Scotland and Wales.

Northern Ireland's experience in the interwar years indicated some of the causes of hostile relations that at present beset the ethnoreligious communities locked in sectarian strife. The solidification of a Protestant populist alliance between the Unionist proletariat and bourgeoisie molded the autonomous Northern Irish state into a specific sectarian form (Bew et al. 1979; Buckland 1979, 1981; Farrell 1980, 1983; Patterson 1980).

Populism and the Crisis of State Formation

The interwar period, however, clearly demonstrated that Unionists were not a monolithic cohesive bloc but were instead torn apart by internal dissension. The bloc divided into populists and antipopulists who vied with each other to influence which government policies were to be adopted (Arthur 1987; Bew et al. 1979, 1995). The split within the Unionist Party was between those who sought to maintain the Protestant shape of the region (populists) and others who wanted to reform it to include the minority population (antipopulist) (Bew et al. 1979, 1995).

The two groups within the Unionist Party had different strategies for maintaining the state of Northern Ireland. On the one hand, the populist faction wanted to maintain the Protestant class alliance through high expenditure and sectarianism (Bew et al. 1979, 1995; Buckland 1979). The antipopulist group, on the other hand, sought to bring about a long-term harmonious situation in Northern Ireland by balancing the budget and by including Catholics in the participation and running of the state (Bew et al. 1979, 1995; Whyte 1983).

The populists, who represented the traditional form of Unionism, worked to increase the standard of living for Northern Irish Protestants and to maintain as broad a political support base as possible, and this strategy necessitated implementing sectarian policies (Bew 1983; Bew et al. 1979, 1995; Nelson 1984; Whyte 1983). Because the Unionist Party embraced such a wide spectrum of class opinion, which included the extreme right, unity could be preserved only by using such symbolic tools as conditional loyalty to emphasize the issues which united them—opposition to a United Ireland and any kind of rapprochement with the nationalist community (Miller 1978).

Antipopulists, on the other hand, strived to secure the union, preserve national security, and to create a state which would have the support of all members in the society (Shea 1981; Wilson 1989). They realized that because the state needed the support of Catholics in order to survive, it was important to address their grievances and to balance the budget in order for the Northern Irish government to prove its political strength and economic viability to Whitehall (Bew et al. 1979, 1995). Such conflicting views demonstrate the importance of intra-Protestant leadership divisions. The populists predominated within the Unionist Party, while the anti-populists tried to control the political behavior of the populist group (Bew et al. 1979, 1995; Buckland 1979).

Consequently, much political tension existed in the interwar period over which strategy within the Unionist Party was to prevail. The state retained its sectarian characteristics, failing to compromise with its Catholic minority. This is rather surprising, considering that the Catholic nationalist threat to the stability of the state was dormant and noninterested (Lyons 1973; Whyte 1980). The populists resorted to sectarian policies in order to obviate any link between the Protestant working class and the Northern Ireland Labor Party (NILP), excluding Catholics in the process (Bew 1983; Bew et al. 1979, 1995; Nelson 1984). The antipopulists tried to curtail expenditure as much as possible and integrate the Catholic minority into the political system (Bew et al. 1979, 1995).

O'Neill, Reconciliation, and Sectarianism

The Northern Irish economy began to stagnate as the decade of the fifties approached. The international decline in the textiles industry in 1951 led to a serious recession in the Northern Irish economy with massive unemployment (Bew et al. 1979). From 1958 to 1962 discontent arose over the government's economic policies as unemployment increased. The linen industry survived in spite of the fact that some of the smaller firms folded during this period (Bew et al. 1979, 1995). In the 1958 general election, the Ulster Unionist Party lost four of its seats to the NILP (McAllister 1977). In 1961 the loss of 8,000 jobs at Harland and Wolf shipyards led to massive demonstrations by workers and formation of the Northern Ireland Joint Unemployment Committee (NIJUC) by the local trade unions and the NILP (McAllister 1977).

The very fact that Protestants might have to leave their homes and families in search of employment in mainland Britain was unacceptable and was, therefore, an important factor in working-class Protestants turning toward the NILP (McAllister 1977; O'Dowd et al. 1980). The continuing disenchantment of the Protestant working class with the Unionist government and the growing electoral threat from the NILP forced Lord Brookeborough into retirement in 1963. A new style of politics was marked by the entry of the great liberal reformer, Terrence O'Neill, who ushered in a new era in Northern Irish politics. Captain O'Neill became prime minister of Northern Ireland in 1963. In his early speeches, O'Neill announced his intentions to change the political situation within Northern Ireland by eliminating the sectarian image of the Unionist Party (Buckland 1981; O'Neill 1969).

O'Neill realized that the unemployment situation would take on a dangerous political mantle if the Protestant proletariat came under the political influence and control of the NILP (Bew et al. 1979; Boserup 1972; MacAllister 1977). Working-class Protestants politically supported the NILP during this period. Hence, the managerial capitalism of O'Neill competed with the clientelist brokerage sectarianism of the Orange Order to win the hearts and minds of the Protestant working class (Bew et al. 1979, 1995; Farrell 1980; O'Dowd et al. 1980).

O'Neill tried to formulate a centrally planned economy. He was a strong advocate of regional policy and attracted such international corporations as Michelin and ICI to set up business in Northern Ireland. Guelke (1991) maintained that the reforms were merely empty rhetoric because O'Neill's modernization program was trying to entice to the Province foreign investment and MNCs who would not tolerate sectarian labor policies. However, MacLaughlin and Agnew (1986) contended that the reindustrialization of Northern Ireland ensured that replacement industry went to Protestant areas east of the river Bann to patronize the Protestant working class and did not favor predominantly nationalist areas such as Derry and South Armagh. O'Neill's economic policies alienated the nationalist community and provided strong support for the Northern Ireland Civil Rights Association (NICRA). Foreign investors accepted the existing hegemonic power bloc, not wishing to disrupt the status quo (MacLaughlin and Agnew 1986). Hence, O'Neill's new economic policies did not prove to be a major demarcation from the policies of Lord Brookborough's government (Arthur 1987; Guelke 1991; MacLaughlin and Agnew 1986).

O'Neill's frequent visits to Catholic schools and his historic meeting with the southern Irish prime minister Sean Lemass certainly suggested, at least symbolically, that O'Neill was trying to end sectarianism in Northern Ireland. However, to initiate substantial change within the province, O'Neill had to wait for the push from the radical People's Democracy (PD), elements within NICRA, and the reform demanded by the British prime minister, Harold Wilson (Arthur 1974, 1987). Patrick Buckland (1981) noted that the reforming zeal and change of direction in O'Neill's policies were a result of various internal and external pressures rather than a genuine desire for substantial change. O'Neill's empty rhetoric was evidenced by the location of the new university of Ulster in the small mainly Protestant town of Coleraine rather than the predominantly larger Catholic city of Derry.

O'Neillism was purely a political mechanism to reassert Unionist Party control over the Protestant working-class vote, deflecting it from the secular ideology of the NILP (Bew et al. 1979, 1995). The high rate of unemployment created a socialist-oriented Protestant working class who had become disenchanted with traditional Unionist Party economic policies (Bew et al. 1979, 1995). O'Neill's policies, therefore, were not concerned with a modernized industrial structure but were concentrated instead on the basic needs of the working class and in preventing true socialist policies from evolving in Northern Ireland (Bew et al. 1979, 1995; Boserup 1972).

O'Neill tried to placate the Protestant working class and ended up alienating the local officials and members of his party. In trying to appease Harold Wilson's Labor government by acceding to the demands of the civil rights movement, he estranged the Protestant working class, who joined forces with local disenchanted unionist politicians to remove O'Neill from office (Arthur 1974, 1987).

The lack of support for the IRA's crossborder military campaign of 1956–62 to "liberate" Northern Ireland insured that IRA activity was terminated because of insufficient support from the indigenous population, clearly demonstrating the passivity and noninterest of the minority Catholic population of Northern Ireland (Bowyer-Bell 1974; Kelley 1982). However, O'Neill's political actions did not indicate a policy of appeasement toward the nationalist community.

Why did O'Neill meet with the southern Irish prime minister, Sean Lemass, and make any conciliatory gestures towards the minority community if his primary motivation was only to placate the Protestant masses? Was antisectarianism an integral part of

O'Neill modernism and the image that was being postured of Northern Ireland's economic future? O'Neillism did little to dismantle sectarian structures within the Province, but rather was aimed at negating the need for reformist policies to end sectarianism, creating employment for all, and integrating the minority community into the political running of the government (Bew et al. 1979, 1995). O'Neill's symbolic gestures of reconciliation must be extended to include the outside influences of the world capitalist system, the Lemass government in the Irish Republic, the influence of liberation movements in Third World countries, and the British Labor government under Harold Wilson.

One could argue that O'Neill's policies were solely to appease British public opinion. The Northern Irish government had to respond to perceived changes in Whitehall's attitude to the situation in Northern Ireland (Arthur 1987; Bew et al. 1979, 1995). The Wilsonian Labor government that came to power in 1964 intended to carry out largescale reforms in Northern Ireland. Prime Minister Harold Wilson was probably influenced by world events at that time, such as the civil rights campaign in the United States, the decolonization process that had begun in Africa and Southeast Asia, the events in Hungary in 1956, and the popular 1968 uprisings in Czechoslovakia (Wright 1987). Prime Minister Wilson, perceiving that O'Neill's modernizing policies could transform the sectarian nature of the state, did not want international public opinion to focus on the Northern Ireland situation (Guelke 1988; Wilson 1989).

The Unionist Party saw the potential reforms of the Wilson regime as a threat to the dominance of the Unionist Party and the future of devolved government in Northern Ireland (Arthur 1974). Therefore O'Neill came to the fore in order to curb this threat by initiating cosmetic policies and gestures of reconciliation toward the minority Catholic community. Yet O'Neill experienced a sustained onslaught from the right of the Unionist Party because he tried to appease Prime Minister Wilson first and the Unionist Party second. O'Neillism was successful in reasserting Unionist hegemony over the Protestant working class and in curbing political conflicts in the unionist bloc as a whole right up until the emergence of the NICRA in 1968 (MacLaughlin and Agnew 1986). The fear of political change caused the Protestant community to countermobilize, and the archaic institutions that were set up to protect the majority in 1922, alienating the minority in the process, could not deal with the problem of domestic mobilization in the late 1960s (Crighton and MacIver 1991; Duffy and Frensley 1991).

Civil Rights, Extremists, and Violent Confrontation

O'Neill's empty rhetoric spawned the mobilization of the Northern Ireland Civil Rights Association (NICRA) founded in 1967 to fight the mistreatment of the minority community in Northern Ireland (Arthur 1974, 1987; Guelke 1991). A series of marches by NICRA led to a number of vicious attacks on the nonviolent protestors by both the RUC and Loyalist gangs, which attracted the attention of both the British and Irish governments and the international community (Arthur 1974, 1987; Irvin 1996a, 1996b). A crack had appeared in the sectarian system, therefore, when NICRA advocated the inclusion of Catholics within the Northern Irish political superstructure (Coakley 1985).

One could argue that O'Neill's false platitudes forced NICRA onto the streets in order to band the unionist alliance together by taking Protestant working-class support away from the NILP to unite in common cause against the traditional enemy: the Catholic (Wilson 1989). On the other hand, Rose's study of the events of 1968 found that a substantial majority of both communities supposed that O'Neill's policies had made significant changes in bicommunal relations (Moxon-Browne 1983). Indeed, 56 percent of Protestants and 65 percent of Catholics fell into the change-for-the-better category (Moxon-Browne 1983; Rose 1971).

It is important to point out that the six-point program of NICRA initially demanded the same rights as British subjects for Catholics but quickly escalated to the more radical demands of the recognition of the distinct ethnoreligious identity of Catholics in a consociational power-sharing governmental arrangement (Coakley 1985; Devlin 1968; Irvin 1996a, 1996b). O'Neill's government had agreed to some of the demands by November 1968 and eventually conceded the rest by 1969 (Darby 1976).

NICRA was a nonviolent organization that tried to demonstrate its nonsectarianism in spite of the direct confrontationalism of the People's Democracy (PD) group (Hewitt 1981). NICRA was formed by activists from the McCluskey Campaign for Social Justice, Wolfe Tone Society Republican Clubs, supporters of the constitutional Nationalist party (Social Democratic and Labor Party), PDs, and moderate Protestants, among others.

The mobilization of NICRA was, in part, a consequence of the growth of a much larger Catholic middle class that was unwilling to accept second-class status in Northern Ireland. The role of education in creating this new middle class that also rejected the Republicanism of the IRA and demanded a role within the state has been much cited (Irvin 1996a, 1996b). However, it was also argued that the important change in the Catholic population of Northern Ireland was not the growth of the middle class but the decline of the Catholic working class in relation to the Protestant working class over the forty-year period (Bew et al. 1979, 1995). This suggests that the immediate impact for reform in the mid to late 1960s was political and not purely economic, and it also explains why the movement would have a more enduring popular impact among the Catholic working class. The political triggers or indicators of the mobilization appear to be the return of the Labor Government in 1964, sympathetic to reform, and the response of the Catholic minority to O'Neillism (Hewitt 1981).

On the unionist side, hard-line Protestants, such as the Reverend Ian Paisley, were out to crush the liberal tendencies of O'Neillism, which they saw as threatening their political and economic position. The first split within NICRA began to emerge when PDs went ahead with the Belfast-Derry March in January 1969 despite misgivings by some civil rights leaders, reflecting a growing militancy within parts of the movement (McCann 1974). The march, which was aimed at intensifying the already great strain on O'Neill, showed a traditionalist contempt for the likely practical political consequences (Arthur 1974, 1987; Farrell 1980). This line of thought, which has been put forward by several writers, corresponds to a large extent with the perception of the problem by the British government. Under both Labor and Conservative administrations there was a sense that O'Neill could successfully bridge the sectarian divide (Arthur 1974, 1987).

Splits began to emerge within the ranks of the civil rights movement with leaders unsure about how to react to the intensifying violence. The left wing saw that the movement, instead of leading to working-class unity, was in fact heading towards a polarization of Protestants and Catholics (McCann 1974; Farrell 1980). By 1970, the street fighting in Derry and Belfast fragmented NICRA and overwhelmed the lately acquired marxism of the IRA (Darby 1976, 1983).

Britain, Direct Rule, and Polarized Sectarian Conflict

The British government was responsible for foreign affairs and security and literally left the Northern Irish parliament to its own devices between 1920 and 1969, condoning the discriminatory practices of the Unionist government by not doing anything about them (Arthur 1987). The British government was content to leave Northern Ireland on the periphery of the British political spectrum (Buckland 1979, 1981). The clashes between NICRA marchers and Loyalists and the sectarian rioting and mob violence in Belfast forced the British government in 1969 to deploy British troops in a peacekeeping role onto Northern Ireland's streets and in 1972 to impose direct rule from London (Arthur and Jeffrey 1988). After the rekindling of political violence in Belfast, people in Catholic ghettoes turned to the IRA to protect their neighborhoods (Bowyer-Bell 1974; Curtis 1984). The British troops and government were now perceived as the protagonists in the conflict, and it was deemed to be the British government's responsibility to do something about the deteriorating political situation (Kelley 1982).

British troops have tried to contain the violence perpetuated by paramilitary groups. However, relations among the security forces and the minority community have not remained cordial throughout the troubles. Catholics view the actions of the security forces with suspicion and disdain (Darby 1976, 1983). The various policies of the British government have been aimed at marginalizing the discontent and alienation of the Catholic population (Cunningham 1991, 1994).

For example, between 1969 and 1971 the British government introduced a policy of neutralization, which disbanded the auxillary B-Special police force and disarmed the RUC, and accommodation by reform of local government, which replaced local authorities with district councils with certain powers being transferred from local to central control (Bew and Patterson 1985). These policies failed to accommodate Catholics into the Northern Ireland political system because it failed to eradicate the structural causes of Catholic discontent such as unemployment and bad housing (Aunger 1975, 1983; Birrell and Murie 1980; Hepburn 1983; Miller 1983). The B-Specials were disbanded but reappeared as the Ulster Defence Regiment (UDR), and the RUC were rearmed. There was little comfort in these British policies to assuage Catholics or to increase their faith in the state or security apparatus (Boyle and Hadden 1985).

The internment and mass screening of Catholics in 1971 was an effort to deter and annihilate the PIRA and to build up intelligence records (O'Malley 1983; Rea 1982). However, when innocent members of their community were arrested and held, the Catholics saw the action as a political apparatus of discrimination and repression, which helped burgeon the recruitment drive of the PIRA (Beresford 1987). Internment was seen by the British government as a political response to a particular political situation (Bew and Patterson 1985). The Northern Ireland parliament, Stormont, was abolished by London in 1972. Although the British government was reluctant to increase its involvement in Northern Ireland, it had to do so when international media attention focused on its illicit political position (Guelke 1988). The British government found it difficult to implement direct rule because the PIRA had been working toward this end as a transitional goal (Guelke 1988). The British government perceived this policy as a temporary solution within Northern Ireland, which would eventually revert to a system of a devolved power-sharing government (O'Leary and McGarry 1993).

The British government had no intention of integrating Northern Ireland into a United Ireland which might provide an even stronger domino effect or catalyst for Scotland and Wales' nationalist movements to secede from the realm (Nairn 1977). The aims of British policy during this period were to eradicate the violence of the PIRA and to find a political solution pleasing to both the Protestants and the Catholics (Bew and Patterson 1985; O'Leary 1989). The British government made efforts to replace the Protestant-controlled local parliament with an executive body in which Catholics would be guaranteed places and their political and national aspirations towards Irish unity would receive institutional recognition (Arthur 1987; Coakley 1985; McGarry and O'Leary 1990).

The Sunningdale Conference of 1973 between the British government and representatives of the main political parties across the political spectrum in Northern Ireland set up a power-sharing executive in January 1975. This initiative collapsed, however, in May 1975 as a result of the crippling effects of the Ulster Workers Council (UWC) strike throughout the province. It was a notable victory for hard-line Loyalists and a major defeat for the British government (Nelson 1984; Wilson 1989). The British government was criticized both at home and abroad for not deploying troops in key sectors of the economy in Northern Ireland to prevent sabotage by the UWC (Bruce 1992). The government, however, saw no point in defending an executive that would have fallen because of SDLP insistence on an Irish dimension (O'Malley 1983). The Sunningdale executive is the nearest Northern Ireland has so far ever come toward the political accommodation of both traditions. This example of the British government's lack of enforcement of the Sunningdale Agreement, displayed in her failure to oppose the Loyalist strike, leads one to increasing skepticism about the chances of success of any power-sharing initiative for Northern Ireland.

The Secretary of State for Northern Ireland, Mervyn Rees, tried to introduce a constitutional convention in 1976. The SDLP refused, however, to take part in the executive without an Irish dimension. Secretary Rees found it impossible to progress to devolved government, a situation which led to a constitutional impasse between all parties to the convention (Arthur and Jeffrey 1988). Direct rule was not favored by the British government because it necessitated too much involvement by the British government. One-party majority rule was a nonstarter with the nationalist community because it would mean a return to a Stormont hegemonic style of Protestant politics (O'Leary and McGarry 1993). Power sharing proved totally unacceptable to the unionist community because it would include an Irish dimension. Northern Ireland was in a constitutional limbo in 1976, with the British government at a loss for a political solution (O'Malley 1983).

Internment without trial proved to be a disastrous exercise and prompted the introduction of the nonjury Diplock courts. After the Birmingham bombings of 1974, the Prevention Against Terrorism Act (PTA) was introduced as a temporary measure to curb the PIRA's indiscriminate bombing of commercial and civilian targets in Britain (Boyle and Hadden 1985). As a result of these security policies, Catholics in Northern Ireland became further alienated from the political institutions and processes in the province (Bew and Patterson 1985; O'Leary and McGarry 1993). By 1975 it was clear that the British government's security policy was not working, because violence had not decreased. The PIRA had begun to use car bombs on commercial centers to cripple the economy in Northern Ireland, and many innocent civilians were murdered (Darby 1976; Galliher and Degregory 1985; Kelley 1982).

By 1976 Britain's interpretation of the political situation began to change as the government redefined the problem in Northern Ireland as criminal acts carried out by criminals, rather than political acts carried out by a PIRA at war with the British government (Beresford 1987). A policy of "containment" and an "acceptable level of violence" was introduced with an emphasis on law and order (Darby 1983; Bew and Patterson 1985). The idea was to contain the conflict within the boundary of Northern Ireland in order to prevent a spillover of violence into either the Republic of Ireland or the United Kingdom. To that end, the British government accepted that there would be a number of civilians and security forces personnel killed from the violence each year.

Further, criminalization officially ended special-category status for political prisoners which had recognized the political nature of the conflict (Boyle and Hadden 1985; O'Leary and McGarry 1993). Those arrested for PIRA terrorist activities were now treated as ordinary criminals. However, Republican prisoners were not treated as other criminals as they were arrested under different legislation, tried in nonjury Diplock courts, and housed in H-blocks in Long Kesh prison. Angered at being characterized as criminals rather than political soldiers, PIRA prisoners initiated the "blanket" and "dirty" protests. They refused to wear their prison uniforms and instead wore blankets. After a short time, they escalated to the dirty protests and smeared the walls of their cells with excrement. These protests eventually culminated in the hunger strikes of 1981, in which ten Republicans starved themselves to death (Beresford 1987; Boyle and Hadden 1985). The hunger strikes increased the support of Sinn Fein, the political wing of the PIRA, and embarrassed Britain internationally, putting pressure on the British government to find a political solution (Guelke 1988).

Second, the policy of "Ulsterization" which, like Vietnamization, increased the use of the RUC and the UDR in maintaining law and order in the province, while using the British army as a second line of defense (Cunningham 1991; Gaffikin and Morrisey 1990). Ulsterization was perceived as part of government policy for the normalization of Northern Ireland, that is, trying to make Northern Ireland like any other region in Britain (Bew and Patterson 1985). How could one even contemplate comparing Northern Ireland to Yorkshire or Staffordshire, when it has political conflicts and divisions not apparent on the mainland? Ulsterization was part of a British strategy to extricate herself as much as possible from the Northern Irish problem by moving British troops away from the front line in order to prevent a public outcry in the metropolis over the deaths of British soldiers (Bew and Patterson 1985).

The main criticism of the security policy was that it led to the adoption of the "supergrass system" and the "shoot-to-kill policy" of an undercover RUC and the Special Air Service (SAS) group in the early 1980s (Boyle et al. 1980; Stalker 1988). The supergrass system ensured that members of the PIRA were given political immunity or amnesty if they gave evidence against their former comrades in court. The shoot-to-kill policy allowed the security forces to shoot suspected terrorists on sight. However, many innocent Catholics were killed in the process. The nationalist community perceived the RUC, the UDR, and the British army as immune from prosecution for sectarian assassinations (Boyle and Hadden 1985; Stalker 1988). Thus, these policies further increased Catholic alienation from the British political system, whose apparatus was seen as corrupt and its system of justice as one-sided (Rolston 1987; Stalker 1988). However, the RUC became more acceptable to the nationalist community after the 1985 Anglo-Irish Accord when the police force had to confront rioting Protestant mobs (Arthur and Jeffrey 1988).

In addition, economic policies have increased unemployment, have led to greater structural inequalities between Protestants and Catholics, and have helped sustain sectarianism (O'Leary and McGarry 1993; Rea 1982; Rolston 1987). Catholics in Northern Ireland are 2.5 times more likely than Protestants to be unemployed (Moxon-Browne 1983). This applies regardless of whether the areas are Protestant or Catholic. The aim of Secretary of State for Northern Ireland Roy Mason's economic policy in the late 1970s was to bring the Northern Irish economy into parity with the rest of the United Kingdom. Contradictions were apparent in British policy during the Mason period because the British government did not understand the nature of the conflict, nor did it attempt to (Bew et al. 1995; Watt 1981).

The Northern Ireland problem has not been high on Britain's political agenda, and the government's major priority has been to limit the cost of this involvement; thus the responses to economic inequality and unemployment can be described as superficial and palliative (Bew and Patterson 1985; Bew et al. 1995; O'Leary and McGarry 1993). The policy of trying to make Northern Ireland like any other region within the rest of the United Kingdom has resulted in massive cutbacks in public spending, especially in education, leading to increased unemployment, alienation and has intensified polarization (Bew et al. 1995; Cunningham 1991, 1994; Gaffikin and Morrisey 1990).

Also, constitutional initiatives resulted in the consultative document introduced in 1979 by Humphrey Atkins, Mason's successor as Secretary of State, which stated that direct rule was not a satisfactory basis for the government of Northern Ireland; but he ruled out the possibility of an Irish dimension, which would include the Irish government being included in any future political settlement (O'Malley 1983). This approach was doomed to failure and was eventually abandoned in November 1980. John Hume, M.P., leader of the SDLP, refused to participate in any discussions with the unionist parties if an Irish dimension was not included on the political agenda.

Humphrey Atkins was succeeded as Secretary of State for Northern Ireland by James Prior in 1981. Prior's "rolling devolution" was another attempt to introduce devolved government to the province. A Northern Ireland Assembly was set up which applied for devolved powers in certain areas provided there was widespread support for these powers by all of the major political actors in Northern Ireland (O'Leary et al. 1988). How could this assembly gain credibility as an adequate forum for government when the nationalist community was not represented? The SDLP boycotted the assembly and went south and set up a New Ireland Forum with the nationalist parties of the south (Mair 1987).

The New Ireland Forum was part of another development in the constitutional sphere that began in December 1980 with the start of the Anglo-Irish process, that is, recognition that the Irish Republic must be consulted in attempts to find a viable political solution to the crisis in Northern Ireland (Kenny 1986; Mair 1987; Schmitt 1988). The Anglo-Irish process was intended to involve biyearly meetings of both governments and the setting up of joint working committees. Success was minimal up until the signing of the Anglo-Irish Agreement in November 1985; the summit held at Chequers in 1984 rejected outright the forum report (Gaffikin and Morrisey 1990).

The new Secretary of State for Northern Ireland, Tom King, presided over the historic signing of the Hillsborough Accord in November 1985 between the then British prime minister, Margaret Thatcher and the Republic of Ireland's former *taoiseach*, Dr. Garrett FitzGerald. The British government had finally acknowledged, for the first time since 1922, that the Irish government had a role to play in the internal affairs of Northern Ireland (Aughey 1989; Cox 1987; Mair 1987; McGarry 1988; O'Leary 1986, 1987, 1989). The effectiveness of this international agreement, signed between two sovereign nations, the 1991 Brooke Initiative, and the 1995 Framework for Peace to move Protestants and Catholics toward an internal peaceful settlement, has proved to be an important departure in Anglo-Irish relations (Arthur 1986, 1987; Bew et al. 1995; Roberts 1986, 1987). While these constitutional initiatives may have benefitted the relationship between both governments in the short term, they have not yet helped both communities to resolve the conflict (Byrne 1995).

Children's Perceptions of Conflict in Northern Ireland

Over the years these historical standpoints have become more deeply ingrained in the minds of each successive generation, and the outbreaks of violence have merely served to reinforce them. My focus here is on some of the religious, political, economic, and psychocultural sources of intractability that socialize children into the fundamental nature of the bicommunal divide in Northern Ireland.

We have traced important historical junctures because history is handed down from one generation to the next and internalized in the youngest of minds (Akenson 1973; Coles 1986; Fields 1975; Whyte 1986). Now, it is necessary to identify some of the main sources of intractability of the ethnic conflict in Northern Ireland: conditional loyalty to the queen, enclaving, ethnic identity, double minority, the border, terrorism, communal deterrence, conflict over resources, and symbolism.

To many outside observers, the religious conflict between Christians in Northern Ireland appears anachronistic and illogical in modern era politics (Hickey 1984). However, religion and politics become fused in the dynamics of the conflict. An example of this is the role of "conditional loyalty." Northern Ireland Protestants' loyalty to the Protestant queen of Britain is conditional on the British government's keeping Northern Ireland part of the United Kingdom. Conditional loyalty is a political mechanism that becomes more pronounced in periods of political crisis, that is, when Protestants believe the British government is no longer fulfilling its side of the political bargain (Miller 1978). Such a crisis was the signing of the 1985 Anglo-Irish Agreement which was seen by Loyalists as giving the Republic of Ireland a political input into how Northern Ireland should be governed and a step toward a united Ireland.

Religious Factors of the Conflict

Religious Factors: Conditional Loyalty

To many observers of the bicommunal conflict, such a perception of the relationship between the government and populace in Northern Ireland appears anachronistic and illogical in the modern era of politics (Hickey 1984). Religion serves as a more important mobilization tool for Protestants than Catholics. For example, the conditional loyalty that evolved among Protestants in Northern Ireland most closely resembled the Scottish variant of contractarian thinking known as covenanting (Miller 1978). By its very nature conditional loyalty is a political mechanism that becomes more pronounced in periods of political crises. As long as the central authority is fulfilling its obligations, the loyalty of the ruled resembles that of loyalty based on noncontractarian models. The concept of the contract gains political importance only when the ruled believe that the central government is no longer fulfilling its side of the bargain. Ulster loyalism is not a smooth continuum but rather a history of long periods of calm, when the idea of conditional loyalty is barely noticeable, punctuated by political crises when the language of conditional loyalty is resurrected (Miller 1978).

There is no contradiction in Protestant opposition to the British parliament, since Protestants are ultimately loyal—not to Parliament or the Crown but to their religion (Bell 1976; Bruce 1986, 1992). Protestants will remain loyal to Britain only as long as Britain guarantees their political station in Northern Ireland (Miller 1978). The fact that Protestant loyalty to Britain is conditional illustrates that for all Loyalists, everything is subordinate to religion (Bruce 1986; Miller 1978). Only religion has unconditional loyalty, and this is applicable to both the unchurched as well as the active church goers (Wallis et al. 1986, 1987; Wright 1973). Protestant allegiance to Britain may be conditional, but it will take something more overtly repugnant to Protestantism than the 1995 Framework for Peace Document[4] to rouse the majority community into open rebellion. The communities see each other's religious beliefs as radically different. Protestants fear what they see as the superstitious mysticism and symbolic nationalism of the Catholic Church, whereas Catholics are afraid of the Protestant political outlook and not the religion (Heskin 1980; O'Brien 1972). Children are socialized into each particular side's religious nationalism (Coles, 1986). Religious beliefs and imagery divide children in the province.

Religious Factors: Enclaving

A strategy of either voluntary withdrawal or forcible territorial expulsionism divides Protestants and Catholics into homogeneous areas in Northern Ireland (Boal and Douglas 1982). Political violence by Republican and Loyalist paramilitaries is used to reinforce residential patterns and territorial group identification, resulting in the greater physical separation of the two communities (Whyte 1981, 1986).

As violence recurs in Northern Ireland, Protestants and Catholics seek the security of segregated living in enclaves occupied predominantly, and in most cases overwhelmingly, by fellow ethnic group members (Wright 1987). Both communities become more territorially defensible, thus facilitating tranquillity. Residential segregation or communal polarization is reflective of a long and continuing mistrust between Protestants and Catholics (Boal and Douglas 1982).

Sometimes the psychocultural barrier or ideological wall between Protestants and Catholics is breached for reasons of economic pragmatism. On occasions when the sectarian wall is ignored for such reasons, a policy of civility is adhered to (Harris 1972). Topics of controversy are avoided; notably, religion and politics become taboo and are not discussed. A series of norms develop which are self-perpetuating, and even extend, on occasion, into new areas of cooperation (Harris 1972).

Residential segregation, therefore, allows both communities to preserve their own way of life and minimizes the amount of contact that takes place among Protestant and Catholic children across the bicommunal divide. It is a potent reinforcing agent of other forms of sectarian segregation: children attend separate schools, play different sports, and patronize different candy stores (Whyte 1986, 1990).

Political Factors of the Conflict

Political Factors: Ethnic Identity

The fundamental nature of the conflict is the overwhelming Protestant and Catholic commitment to a British and Irish identity respectively (Trew 1983, 1986). Protestants are clearly seen by Catholics as a distinct ethnic group, and Catholics are perceived by Protestants as disloyal descendants of the native Gaels, posing a threat to the very existence of Northern Ireland and the Protestant population (Buchanan 1976; Kelley 1982). Spotting[5] members of the other community, surnames, and membership in cultural, religious, and sports organizations are cultural tools used by both children and adults to distinguish members of each community (O'Donnell 1977).

Nurtured over the years, these identities become deeply entrenched in the minds of young children. While Catholic children look "over the border" for their ethnic roots, Protestant children have always considered themselves to be in a "state of siege" in defense of their British ancestry. The Northern Ireland problem is a conflict of national identities coinciding with religious identities (Agnew 1989; Tovey 1975; Whyte 1990).

Political Factors: Double Minority

The Northern Ireland conflict can be seen as a conflict of identity and of double minorities (Jackson and McHardy 1984; Whyte 1978, 1990). In other words, Catholics are a minority in Northern Ireland and a majority in an all-Ireland context. Protestants are a majority in Northern Ireland but a minority in Ireland as a whole. Clearly, this double minority or minority/majority situation has implications for the way the different groups view the world about them and, indeed, the way the world views them (Whyte 1990). Both ethnic groups in Northern Ireland have viewed their opponents as intent on genocide at some time or another (Creighton and MacIver 1991). Each group is faced with belonging to a minority, depending on whether the population of the region or the island is considered (Whyte 1990).

Protestants in Northern Ireland have developed a kind of siege mentality with respect to their political predicament, and this seeming paranoia is a key aspect of the conflict (Stewart 1977). Protestants perceive the threat emanating from the Catholic community as real. The Republic of Ireland is viewed as an inherently hostile state, a real threat, and any move towards a conciliatory gesture or rapprochement with the Republic of Ireland and Catholics in Northern Ireland is determined as a step down the slippery slope to a united Ireland (Bew et al. 1995; Mair 1987; Roberts 1986; Whyte 1990).

With regard to the minority's relationship with the Northern Ireland region and the majority ethnic group, Catholics were alienated by the very nature and form the state adopted, and especially by the way in which the state came into existence via violence and bloodshed (Bew et al. 1979, 1995; Farrell 1980). This alienation, therefore, stems both from their own attitude toward the state and from their treatment within it (Coakley 1985; Farrell 1980; O'Dowd et al. 1980).

The fact that Protestants have different national loyalties from Catholics means that the Protestant position is uncompromising since the former are perceived as enemies of the Protestant people (Whyte 1990). There is great political polarization, and when a political threat or a perceived political threat is discerned, the middle ground disintegrates and polarization intensifies (Miller 1978; Rose 1971). The problem with this situation is that it upholds a Protestant belief that Catholics are not totally commited to being part of the United Kingdom, and that, therefore, they are not trustworthy or dependable enough to be treated as equal citizens to the majority (Coakley 1985; Nelson 1984). The double minorities' similarity is one which certainly opens up all sorts of political connotations for the conflict (Guelke 1988; Jackson and McHardy 1984; Whyte 1978, 1990).

These are the different schemata with which Protestants and Catholics understand their respective identities. Coles (1986) found that Protestant and Catholic children are socialized into two separate ways of thinking about identity and the social world. For example, Catholic children believe that partition should be ended whereas Protestant children believe that their allegiance is to the British sovereign and see themselves as British (Coles 1986).

Political Factors: The Border

The opposition Irish nationalists felt towards partition did not fade away once it became an accomplished fact (Coakley 1985). Protestants believe that they have been forced to maintain peace by building a tight security apparatus, and that real or perceived threats, such as terrorist attacks, have made special security arrangements necessary (Farrell 1983; Wright 1987). During the fifty years of unionist control of the political system in Northern Ireland, the Catholics of the province were clearly regarded as enemies of the state (Bew et al. 1979, 1995; Farrell 1980, 1983; McCann 1974). Stringent security measures gave almost unlimited powers to such Protestant forces as the B-Specials and the RUC and were used to control the nationalist community and protect the border between Northern Ireland and the Republic of Ireland (Farrell 1980, 1983).

One may be struck by the durability and strength of both ethno-religious identities in Northern Ireland over the question of partition (Tovey 1975). Children are socialized into adopting these understandings of partition. Protestant children are interested in maintaining the British link and are not going to be persuaded by either constitutional or unconstitutional measures to change their minds (Coles 1986; Trew 1983, 1986). On the other hand, Catholic children believe that the root of the conflict is the British presence

(Coles 1986; Trew 1983, 1986). Catholic children want to embrace their Irish heritage, which lies "over the border" in the South.

Political Factors: Terrorism

New symbolic issues or causes assist in perpetuating the conflict in Northern Ireland (Agnew 1989). The Enniskillen massacre of Protestants in 1987 and those murdered in Frizzell's fish shop on the Shankill road October 1993, and the random sectarian murders of Catholics by the UVF and the Ulster Freedom Fighters (UFF) instill a fear of outright genocide in the minds of both communities. The political authority in Northern Ireland, therefore, finds itself challenged by so-called political movements committed to terrorist activities who operate on behalf of an uncertain number of people, but who do not represent a majority of Northern Ireland's citizens. The paramilitary organizations operate illicit businesses in the manner of organized crime with extortion and racketeering being the most prominent and visible pursuits.

Terrorism is a reality in Northern Ireland, and reluctance to deal with terrorists or their spokespersons is a natural reaction. The recurrent pattern of terrorist activity in Northern Ireland suggests that one is dealing with a complex psychological and political problem, the self-sacrifice of the terrorist. A lust for self-destruction and psychological gratification is the most fulfilling act of the terrorist because it is the ultimate form of self-fulfillment (Rapoport 1971; Ziegler 1990). This nihilist threat arrayed against the very existence of the state polarizes both communities in Northern Ireland so that a political vacuum occupies the middle ground.

When terrorists attack members of the other community, the attacks are taken to be representative of the views of all those on the other side (Harris 1972). Whether or not this is true is unimportant, because it is the perception of the victims rather than the attackers that is vital in the development of intercommunal conflict (Harris 1972; Wright 1973, 1987).

Therefore, this psychological climate of violence embraces the personal and everyday activities of Northern Ireland's young people. Children may become pathologically obsessed by the atrocities carried out by the various terrorist groups (Fields 1977). The effects of ongoing violent behavior force children to cope psychologically with death and destruction, and many young people develop psychological problems (Cairns 1987; Coles 1986; Fields 1977; Fraser 1973; Straker 1992).

Political Factors: Communal Deterrence

Intercommunal violence usually is representative of a long-simmering, deep-seated hostility between social groups in a given population (Kriesberg 1982). These groups are defined by personal characteristics or highly significant criteria such as religion or ethnicity so that segments of the population stand in opposition to each other (Gurr 1993; Volkan 1984; Williams 1982). The antagonisms transmitted through the political socialization process are very strong. The two communities in Northern Ireland are habituated to politically opposing each other (Whyte 1990). Rokkan and Urwin (1982, 1983) have shown that certain cultural, economic, and other conditions increase the probability of ethnic unrest in a region.

There is a much greater likelihood that violence will be directed by the majority against the minority community because of the sudden flaring up of group hostility propelled by high levels of emotions (Enloe 1973; Esman 1977). Violence is used to reassert some pattern of subordination in the power relations between the strong and the weak. Violence is employed by both segments of paramilitary organizations for the purposes of communal deterrence (Wright 1987).

Paramilitary violence makes an enduring bicommunal conflict a virtual certainty. Children in Northern Ireland are alert and sensitive to sectarian murders and assassinations taking place around them (Cairns 1987; Coles 1986).

Economic Factors of the Conflict: Conflict over Resources

In Northern Ireland ethnic rivalry is used as a political mechanism or lever to distribute politico-economic resources in the society (Agnew 1989; Wallis et al. 1986). Populist governmental ministers in Northern Ireland designed measures to maintain economic inequality between Protestants and Catholics in the fields of housing, employment, and regional policy (Farrell 1980; O'Dowd et al. 1980; MacLaughlin and Agnew 1986). The divisions between Protestants and Catholics in Northern Ireland can be explained in terms of the economic privileges enjoyed by Protestants, and this explains in part the continued Protestant support for retaining the constitutional link with the United Kingdom (Farrell 1980; Munck 1985; Probert 1975).

The absence of opportunity for Catholics in Northern Ireland has related, above all, to power sharing at authority levels, but also to business opportunity; not because there would exist restrictions in business regarding Catholics, but simply because favors would be passed out among groups of kinship, however weak, and the Protestants, both through Loyalist and British power, had far more favors to pass out. Indeed, the growth of a Catholic upper-middle and true middle class is a relatively late development in terms of wealth accrued through business and industry (Bew et al. 1979, 1995; Farrell 1980; O'Dowd et al. 1980). Hence, children may be aware that Catholic areas have a higher rate of unemployment than Protestant areas. Catholic children may know that their chances of finding employment in Northern Ireland are rather low (Coles 1986).

Psycho-Cultural Factors of the Conflict: Symbolism

Protestants believe that their cultural symbols, flags, and holidays must be displayed in Northern Ireland (Agnew 1989; Wallis et al. 1986). Marches celebrating the triumph of William of Orange at the 1690 Battle of the Boyne on the twelfth of July serve the tradition every year of reconquering territory in nationalist areas and of displaying Protestant symbols, values, and symbolic folk rituals (Wallis et al. 1986; Wright 1973, 1988). Likewise, Northern Irish Catholics feel entitled to display nationalist traditions, values, and symbols to commemorate Irish nationalist events such as the Easter Rising of 1916 (Agnew 1989).

The conflict has involved many human sacrifices or martyrs for the cause, best exemplified by the hunger strikes of 1981. Bobby Sands, one of the ten Republican hunger strikers, tried to emulate Patrick Pearse by reconstructing the sacrifice of Jesus Christ on the cross (Feehan 1986). Irish Catholicism and Irish nationalism have been mutated and fused to form a syncretic mysticism (O'Brien 1986). A strong link exists between Republican violence and Catholicism centered on the redemptive nature of a blood sacrifice or sacralization (O'Brien 1986).

On the Loyalist side, paramilitary violence escalates during periods of political crises (Bruce 1986, 1992). The language of violence comes to the forefront when British policy initiatives, such as the 1995 Framework for Peace, are perceived as a threat to Northern Ireland's constitutional status within the United Kingdom and Britain's willingness to abandon Northern Ireland's Protestants to the dictates of Irish nationalism. The siege mentality is thus reinforced, and Northern Irish Catholics take on the mantle of disloyal citizens (Miller 1978).

Consequently, nationalist symbols tend to further exacerbate the bicommunal conflict by fostering the growth of sectarian stereotypes and prejudice (Agnew 1989). Children, through lack of physical day-to-day contact, live in complete ignorance of each other. Some Protestant children are led to believe that the conflict is a struggle between the evil Antichrist (Catholicism) and good (Protestantism) (Coles 1986). Symbols become the means through which identity is understood.

Political Authority

In a mid-1970s study, a substantial proportion of preadolescent children sampled in England perceived the queen as considerably more important than the prime minister (Greenstein 1975). Northern Irish Protestant children's loyalty to the British monarch is unquestionable and strongly celebrated through various rituals of the Crown, for example, Twelfth-of-July marches (Coles 1986). Catholic children, on the other hand, may not identify with the queen (Coles 1986).

Protests against the most recent political event in Northern Ireland's politics, the 1995 Framework for Peace, revealed Protestant opposition to the British prime minister. Poorer Protestants are distrustful of central government (Harris 1972). Northern Irish Loyalists believe that it is not disloyalty to the queen to refuse loyalty to the British government which demonstrates its disloyalty to Northern Ireland's Protestant community (Miller 1978). Coles (1986) found that some Northern Irish Catholic and Protestant children also did not like the British prime minister. Consequently, Protestant and Catholic children may have different orientations and images of the prime minister.

Conclusions and Summary

Beginning in the twelfth century, Northern Ireland's historical experience falls into a pattern of ethnoreligious divisions that constitute the core of today's intractable conflict there. The fact that this experience adheres to the historical and political cleavages addressed in this chapter is valuable confirmatory evidence. Several themes are obvious in this necessary historical review. First, since the Anglo-Norman invasion of Ireland in the twelfth century, there has been a recurrence of rebellion in the Catholic community against British rule (Lyons 1973). Second, political differences exist between the two communities in the province over the legacy and legitimacy of the border. Third, there is the continued presence and inactivity of the British government in Northern Ireland in the guise of honest broker (Stewart 1967).

Some scholars regard the nature of the conflict as essentially a religious struggle (Bruce 1986; Hickey 1984; Miller 1978); others define it in terms of intra-Protestant divisions (Bew et al. 1979, 1995; Harris 1972; Todd 1987; Whyte 1983; Wright 1973); still others perceive it as either a dispute over national identities and loyalties (Moxon-Browne 1983; Rose 1971) or as having primarily economic foundations (Bew et al. 1979; Bew and Patterson 1985; Morgan 1980; Munck 1985; Probert 1978).

Inability or unwillingness to concede any ground would seem to be the major characteristic of both traditions in Northern Ireland (Agnew 1989). Constitutional Nationalists, on the one hand, fear that if concessions are not forthcoming, then the physical force advocates (PIRA) can claim they hold the only solution. Nationalist leaders such as John Hume take center stage, and this is reflected by hard-line attitudes on the other side. Polarization results. The fact that there has been a tradition of physical force in Ireland also contributes to Republicans and Loyalists' willingness to use violence in certain circumstances. Protestants, on the other hand, feel betrayed by both the British government and their own political leaders.

While identification of uniformities in political behavior in Northern Ireland is an important contribution to general theory, a satisfactory political development theory which seeks to explain how children figure out the nature of their political world would enable the political scientist to perceive how children develop politically in such a flashpoint region (Dodge and Raundalen 1987, 1991; Straker 1992). Recent research has focused on the effects of cognitive learning on integrated schooling (Irwin 1991), which, of course, is an important new phenomenon in the Northern Ireland educational structure. It would, perhaps, be appropriate now to direct more academic efforts toward examining the political development of children within the unique historical, religious, and ethnic features of Northern Ireland's two communities. The texture of their community experiences and what their lives are really like provide a valuable contextual background for the reader.

The conflict in Northern Ireland reinforces the ethnic identities of both groups, constructing, to a large extent, the political orientations of both communities in the process. Consequently, the violence and sectarianism of "the troubles" have emotional and psychological effects on children living in Northern Ireland and ultimately affect their attitudes and perceptions of conflict and political authority. What are these attitudes? What do they mean?

3

Political Learning and Children

Introduction

ONE of the central concerns in international relations decision-making research to date has been how to identify the effects of cognitive development on individuals' perception of their political environment (Allison 1971; Hermann 1994; Janis 1972; Jervis 1976; Synder and Diesing 1978). The focus of the research presented here is similar, but rather than concentrating on the cognitive processes of adults, the focus is on children's images of conflict and political authority.

There are several reasons for this different approach. First, the Northern Ireland conflict is too complex to study whole, so we need to divide the problem into a number of significant areas in order to understand this complicated conflict zone. Second, I am interested in identifying possible effects of integrated education on Belfast children's perceptions of conflict in Northern Ireland. Third, the increase in ethnoregional conflicts in the post–Cold War period suggests that it is an opportune time, therefore, to focus on children's political attitudes toward a conflict that has proved very difficult to resolve.

Political Behavior: Individual and Small-Group Decision-Making

There has been considerable attention in the field of international relations to the realist assumption of the state as the principal unitary rational actor in the international arena (Morgenthau 1956). More recently, this theoretical premise has been challenged by foreign policy scholars for whom cognitive processes of individuals and small groups serve as their primary focus of analysis (Allison 1971; Hermann 1994; Hermann and Preston 1994; Janis 1972; Jervis 1976; Synder and Diesing, 1978). This foreign policy school emphasizes the ways in which cognitive distortions subvert the realist view of decision making as rational.

How have scholars looked at the political psychology of individuals and small groups? The work of Robert Jervis (1976), to take one example, discusses the significance of irrational consistency. Incoming information, shaped by particular dramatic events, that conflicts with the political images stored in a person's schemata is dismissed or ignored. These oversimplified analogies have a major impact on decisions made by a person who operates in an emotional fog. Jervis refers to what he thinks is a tendency to ignore the significance of political context in decision making.

Other scholars focus on how stress and psychological pressure affect rational calculations. Social pressure enforces conformity, and the hidden agendas of small groups lead to poor decisions as policy makers indulge in irrational thinking which ignores other courses of action. Bias and misperception creep into policy decisions as the group is encouraged to operate with the same kind of rationality (Janis 1972). Outgroups and independent critical thinkers are replaced by what Janis (1972) calls groupthink.

A three-tier model (rational actor, organizational, and bureaucratic) suggests an alternative image to the realist assumption of the state as the principal rational actor in international politics. Organizational routines and proceedings determine and influence decisions and outcomes as coalitions and countercoalitions form among competitive bureaucratic actors mustering their political power to make the final policy decision (Allison 1971). The best policy choice may not be made, therefore, because the interests of contending bureaucratic actors may become more important than the national interest.

A theory of international crisis behavior posits that the thin line between a rational and an irrational decision maker may depend on historical context because the same cognitive processes (images adversaries have of the political situation and of each other) that produce foresight in one situation can lead to blind rigidity in others (Synder and Diesing 1978). Hence, an individual's morality and behavior toward another person are restrained by individual group interests, historical context, and pressure to conform to group norms and values. New information which contradicts these images is likely ignored. Cognitive psychology may provide a partial explanation of how decision makers, children, or any persons formulate goals over time and perceive and classify states of their milieu as they do. Themes of trust or distrust and cynicism or acceptance of political authority are seen as some of the most important prerequisites for a stable political culture. An analysis of children's political images may shed new light on the reasons why the Northern Ireland conflict is so difficult to resolve as bitterness and stereotypes are handed down from one generation to the next (Coles 1986).

Psychophysiological Theory

Political development is an area of focus for an interdisciplinary group of scholars who elaborate and develop the theory of Jean Piaget (1969, 1972, 1976) on the nature and functioning of children's psychophysiological development. The political development perspective focuses on the political milieu affecting children's political learning. A major premise of political development theory is the idea that knowledge of children's political orientations and the differences or similarities between different age peers are crucial to understanding the functioning of a state's political system.

Jean Piaget (1976) and Lawrence Kohlberg (1981), for example, consider children as active participants and modifiers of political learning during the socialization process. Much of what children learn about space, time, and distance is a universal consequence of active exploration (Piaget 1976). The concepts of childrens' actions are actively reconstructed from their experience, so that doing and learning are indistinguishable since there is constant interaction between the object and the person.

A child's consciousness, therefore, progressively and reciprocally works inwardly to cognize its own actions and outwardly in the understanding of external objects. Any situation that interrupts the automaticity of the child's sensory-motor behaviors can ignite the formative process of awareness (Piaget 1976). A child becomes accurately aware of behavior on a certain task through its movement toward equilibrium, which is achieved through two axes of adaption or constructivity: assimilating the new task in terms of what has gone before and then accommodating it in the schemata (Piaget 1976). Consequently, a constant reequilibration is necessary as cognitive forms encounter obstacles, become unstable, and require restabilization.

Stages of cognitive development—motor-individual character, egocentric stage, incipient cooperation and codification of rules—are found in all cultures and result from the child's more general cognitive development, but they can be slowed or hastened (Piaget

1969, 1976). The move from one stage to the next is essentially due to the child's own cognitive constructions and reconstructions, and the sequence is irreversible as each stage is logically more complex than the rest (Piaget 1972). As the child's belief in external objects begins to solidify (Piaget 1972, 1976), so does his or her sense of self and ability to manipulate things realistically rather than magically. The child must pass through stages of increasing complexity and sophistication before he or she can become an adult, taking stock of sequences and consequences, remembering what has been experienced and used in various actions and what has been remembered (Flanagan 1991; Piaget 1976). In the context of Northern Ireland, Trew (1986) and Irwin (1991) found that most primary school children do not reach the final stage of cognitive development—that is, sophistication—until they are about ready to enter second-level schooling. The older children become, the greater the difference in their intellectual development and the movement toward an abstract stage of cognitive development (Greenstein 1965).

Directly induced experience, adult-mediated information, and the transmission of politics via the use of symbols combine in a complex manner in the development of cognitive structures of the politics of children (Connell 1971; Rosenau 1975). In other words, a child's political understanding involves the interaction of messages provided by the child's sociopolitical and cultural environment and his or her level of mental development. Symbols and signs identifying religious affiliation are understood by Northern Irish children by the age of eleven (Cairns 1982).

Similarly, Kohlberg (1981) stresses political socialization as molding a child to an a priori set of conventions. Kohlberg (1981) argues that as a child gets older, he or she passes through three stages of moral growth, with justice as the foundation principle upon which all stages are based:

Preconventional: reward and punishment
Conventional: normative concepts of good and morality
Postconventional: utilitarian

Kohlberg (1981) argues that appropriate moral education encourages students to move beyond lower, less adequate stages of moral reasoning as a person gets to a given stage only by passing through the earlier stages. The value of Piaget and Kohlberg's model is that it describes levels of cognitive and moral development as sequential, irreversible stages.

Political Development Theory

The ideas of Piaget have created a great debate in the political behavior literature over how the early political learning of children is maintained, reproduced, and deepened, and about the role of certain cultural and historical factors in this process. Critics caution against a total acceptance of Piaget's theory because he outlines these stages without uncovering the mechanisms of how one moves from one stage to the next. For example, Keil (1979) and Markman (1989) argue that Piaget's discussion of developmental phenomenon and categories does not distinguish between living and nonliving physical objects.

Several important pieces of research on various theoretical assumptions about the political socialization of children have addressed the issue of political development in children's behavior. Greenstein (1965) traces the origins of the work on political information and learning to as far back as Plato, then to Hobbes and Locke, and, more recently, to Piaget. Political socialization analysts emphasize the importance of studying the political orientations of children not only in determining disaffection with the political system, but in probing images of political authority, the ideas of homeland, and nationalism (Coles 1986; Straker 1992). Greenstein's (1965) work is particularly valuable in examining the various means of socializing children in different social classes in relation to studies of cognitive development and political cognition. Although children from different social classes grow up in very different worlds, the differences are more than purely physical phenomenon; they are also psychological, and they lead to different forms of socialization (Greenstein 1965).

Recently there has been a revival of interest in children's political development at the subnational or regional level (Bilu 1989; Cairns 1987; Coles 1986; Dawes 1990; Dodge and Raundalen 1987, 1991; Punamaki and Suleiman 1990; Straker 1992; Yogev and Ben-Yehoshua 1991). Within the global context, recent changes that have taken place have led to an upsurge in local regional nationalism and ethnoregional strife at the expense of state sovereignty (Vayrynen 1984).

There have been debates in the literature about whether the political development of children can be analyzed empirically in cross-cultural studies. Some claim that the findings point to the fact that open-ended stories can be harnessed to tap the diversity of children's images of political authority across nations (Greenstein and Tarrow 1970a, 1970b; Greenstein et al. 1974; Greenstein 1975). Others claim that analysis of qualitative interviews over time display evidence of a child's socialization process and colorful political expressions (Cairns 1987; Connell 1971; Coles 1986; Straker 1992). According to Connell (1971), based on work with young Australians, children begin to understand and develop political assumptions at an early age. Connell (1971) used direct extensive interviews to tap into children's belief structure, which gave the interviewer time to probe specific issues while allowing the child plenty of opportunity to muse and expand on political topics reflecting his or her thoughts and ideas.

Coles (1986), aside from relying solely on interviews with young children, lends further support to the argument for political development theory. He contends that it is possible to induce children's perceptions of their environment because themes of nationalism, religion, war, hostility, history, and political fantasies are reflected in the caricatures of their drawings and paintings. Similarly, Straker's (1992) case studies of black South African youths show the richness in texture of these young people's vivid accounts of their political environment.

In this study I seek to combine these approaches of political development theory in the study of children's perceptions of political conflict and political authority in Belfast, Northern Ireland. I will use political development theory in a different sense from that proposed by a number of political development and socialization theorists (Greenstein and Tarrow 1970a, 1970b; Greenstein et al. 1974; Greenstein 1975). They argue that political development occurred when children's images of political leaders were explored by using semiprojective short stories in Britain, France, and the United States. I will express this version of political development theory in terms of children's imagery of political figures and the causes of social conflict, exploring differences and similarities between age groups in an integrated and a nonintegrated school in war-weary Belfast.

The major drawback in the Greenstein and Tarrow (1970a, 1970b) multimethod approach is in setting up a category scheme once the field research is complete. It is a very time-consuming and tedious task involving a combination of both the manifest and the latent content of each communication (Babbie 1986). The advantage of such a method is that it permits adaptability in question design.

The Greenstein and Tarrow (1970a, 1970b) short stories work within the setting of controversial topics, permitting children or adults to feel comfortable about revealing their opinions on sensitive issues. Hanfmann and Getzels (1955), for example, described the personal interactions and the motives underlying them by presenting United States citizens and Soviet expatriates with a verbal description of an interpersonal situation and asking them to describe its probable development and outcome. The semiprojective technique was used by the authors because its realistic technique allowed each person to elaborate on his or her underlying political attitudes.

The main question is how children's political development can be empirically measured. Academicians have been critical of the significance given to fixed-choice questionnaires (Easton and Dennis 1969; Hess and Torney 1967; Tolley, 1973) in the study of children's political attitudes. For example, Sears (1969) suggests that interviews may be a more appropriate research instrument than fixed-choice questionnaire items, since children may not fully understand the meaning of particular words or phrases. Children in the early stages of cognitive development may not be fully aware of the political milieu surrounding them (Converse 1970; Piaget 1972).

Other researchers recognize a multiplicity of factors, such as exams, guessing, and response-set bias, which may affect how children respond to particular questions on the research instrument (Converse 1970; Greenstein 1975; Sears 1968). As children are continually taking tests in school, a questionnaire may be perceived as an exam that necessitates answering questions even if one doesn't fully understand the problem or the issue at hand (Sears 1968). Children may also guess an answer regardless of the content of the question (Greenstein 1975).

The claim by Converse (1970), Greenstein (1975), and Sears (1968) that children find it difficult to respond to fixed-choice questionnaires reveals the weakness of analyzing the political images of children based on this measure. Irwin (1991) noted that the exploration of children's friendship groups at Lagan College integrated school in Belfast, Northern Ireland, could be carried out by using a very basic paper-and-pencil questionnaire combined with participant observation and a content analysis of children's essays on various themes. A distinction can be made between single- and multimethod approaches. Other researchers have used a multiplicity of methods and tests such as semiprojective incomplete short stories (Greenstein and Tarrow 1970a, 1970b; Greenstein et al. 1974; Greenstein 1975), paper-and-pencil questionnaires and interviews (Greenstein 1965), interviews and participant observation (Connell 1971; Straker 1992), interviews, drawings, and paintings (Coles 1986), and participant observation, small essays, and paper-and-pencil questionnaires (Irwin 1991).

While one cannot deny the usefulness of many research methods in exploring children's worldviews, I adopt the parapolitical stories of Greenstein and Tarrow (1970a, 1970b). Storytelling, a part of both traditions and cultures in Northern Ireland, allows children to create their own stories. By its very form, storytelling also permits the researcher to probe sensitive issues in accounting for similarities and/or differences in the political orientations of Belfast schoolchildren.

Two major oversights in the political development and socialization literature regarding children are (1) the lack of in-depth and substantial comparative political development work focusing on children in conflict zones and (2) the scant attention devoted to the comparative study of the possible effects of integrated and nonintegrated education on children's political learning in strife-ridden regions. Political development theorists, for the most part, have chosen not to address empirically the political imagery of children living in conflict regions. Very few cross-cultural comparative studies of children in conflict zones have been used by researchers in the political development literature.

The only work on children in conflict regions has been on societal cleavages that connect with the political life children encounter (Coles 1986; Dawes 1990; Fields, 1975; Punamaki and Suleiman 1990; Straker 1992), comparative work by the Erickson Institute and other scholars on children in a wide variety of war experiences (Bilu 1989; Dodge and Raundalen, 1987, 1991; Garbarino et al. 1991; Yogev and Ben-Yehoshua 1991), and a comparison between integrated schoolchildren in Givat Goren, Israel, and Lagan College, Belfast (Irwin 1991). This lack of empirical research is problematic if we are to try and understand the early political learning of children growing up in areas of tension and violence. Because of the escalation in ethnic tensions worldwide in recent years, we need to expand our studies to formulate a more theoretically derived classification scheme for political attitudes that can be used to categorize children in conflict. This scheme needs to reflect theoretical assumptions that are manifested in children's perceptions of political institutions, authority, and conflict.

A recent study of 60 black South African activists from the Leandra township between 12 and 22 years old demonstrated the incredible psychological trauma that these young people suffered under the apartheid system (Straker 1992). Coming from poor, impoverished districts and broken homes, many of these uneducated young activists were involved in the political violence that embraced the townships—the necklacing of touts, the stoning of South African Defense Force (SADF) armored personnel carriers, the burning of houses belonging to black police officers, and the violence directed against them by the SADF. Straker's (1992) indepth interviews provide a fascinating psychological profile of these young activists, their leaders, and what motivated them to join the struggle against the SADF and the government.

Straker's (1992) 60 case studies provided a chilling yet excellent analysis of the personalities and lives of each of these young people and how they operated in an environment characterized by conflict. However, Straker's (1992) findings would be further strengthened if she had included other townships, and white, Asian, and colored youth in the analysis to provide an overall picture of the society by having a greater cross section of the community that was representative of all South African young people.

The earliest empirical global study which attempted to measure the political life of children in regions characterized by conflict was undertaken by Coles (1986). Coles, examining the political and psychological development of children's ideas, concluded that children have a high level of common sense, with some of his sample expressing a kind of political morality. Coles also found extravagant fantasies with regard to violence across the developmental strata of children that suggested a pattern of similarity between conflict regions, leading to the conclusion that even the youngest child supported the use of violence to achieve political objectives.

There were two main problems with Coles's analysis concerning the classification of countries and the classification of factors that children experience in their daily lives (Coles 1986). He decided a priori on focusing primarily on Northern Ireland and South Africa because it was in these conflict regions that he best came to understand how context influenced the politics of these children (Coles 1986). In classifying psychopolitical constructs, he used the general category of nationalism, omitting other categories that may be important explanations of conflict within these national settings. This study seeks to build on Coles' (1986) richly descriptive study through the use of more sociopolitical categories to explain political behavior.

Fields (1975) used a similar method to measure levels of political development through a different empirical analysis of three countries. She adopted the Piaget-Kohlberg cognitive development approach within a Northern Ireland context to compare children from Belfast, Dublin, Watts, and Detroit. Children in the age brackets six to ten years and eleven to fourteen years were compared over the 1971–72 and 1973–74 time periods. She found that both the younger and older children from the United States were morally at a lower level or stage than children from the other two sample groupings. She concluded that the authoritarian and conservative environment of Northern Irish society provided an atmosphere where children conform to the established norms and values and reject those who break the rules and regulations.

There were some methodological problems associated with this study, however. Fields's (1975) work examined only the development of morality between different-age peers and ignored some of the other important socialization categories (church, school, family, class) that may contribute to the conservative nature of Northern Irish society. The main problem with her method is the selection of countries for the analysis of children's psychological development. Northern Ireland's political reality differs from that of Watts, Detroit, or Dublin. The political dynamics and the levels of violence lead to completely different social and cultural contexts.

Other attempts have been made by scholars in Northern Ireland to research children's worldviews by studying tolerance (Salters 1970) between Catholic and Protestant grammar-and secondary-school children, intergroup attitudes and attribution among young Protestant and Catholic children (Stringer and Watson 1991), friendship levels among primary- and second-level schoolboys (Russell 1974), friendship groups among Protestant and Catholic boys and girls in an integrated school (Irwin 1991), and social distance among Protestant and Catholic further education students (Fairleigh 1974). Also, other academics have focused on the effects of "the troubles" on schoolchildren's political images (Cairns 1991; Darby 1977, 1987; Dunn 1989; McEwen 1990; Murray 1983, 1985; Smith 1990). Developmental research on children in Northern Ireland has been limited, however, as the result of the lack of a sophisticated methodological device to measure children's evaluative and connatative behavior regarding sensitive topics.

A more recent cross-cultural study comparing integrated schools in Israel and Northern Ireland indicated that integrated secondary education can improve relations between Protestants and Catholics in Northern Ireland, while stronger sociocultural factors made social integration between Ashkenazic, Sephardic, and Eastern Jews more difficult to achieve in Israel (Irwin 1991).[1] The main problem with Irwin's method was his selection of Givat Gonen, a school which tries to build cultural bridges only among Jewish children. A better choice may have been Neve Shalom, a school which promotes the integration of Jewish, Christian, Muslim, and Druze children.

The general findings of Irwin (1991), Moffat (1993), Wright (1991), and Stephenson (1991a, 1991b) indicate the importance of integrated education in promoting a better understanding and acceptance of each tradition and ethnic identity in Northern Ireland. The Irwin (1991) study also indicates that the friendship patterns formed at the integrated school are later translated, by past pupils, into lasting friendships across the intercommunal divide. We must compare integrated and nonintegrated schools if we are to discover the possible impact of integrated education on children's world views (Byrne 1994). Such a comparative study would enhance the debate concerning the possible influence of integrated schooling on breaking down sociocultural barriers and improving community relations.

Before testing to see whether there are similarities and differences between children in integrated and nonintegrated schools in Belfast, children's political attitudes must be classified according to the research question at hand. What is needed here is a dynamic classification of children's orientations that accounts for movement in the political orientation patterns over time. As the political climate in Northern Ireland is dynamic, important changes and developments are missed, because very often researchers do not use the same methods to replicate studies longitudinally. If political science is to contribute to political development theory, we need to take into consideration changes in the political system over time in any attempt at studying children's political attitudes. We need a dynamic classification of children's worldviews.

Part of the difficulty in classification stems from the diversity of focus of previous writings. Connell (1971) and Greenstein (1965, 1974, 1975) at various times in their political writings have attempted to classify the political orientations of children toward political authority. Coles (1986) and Straker (1992) elaborated on the problem of nationalism, while Fields (1975) examined the development of morality among children and Irwin (1991) measured friendship-group patterns. A concerted effort by scholars to derive a classification of children's world views to analyze the political life of children in conflict zones and to identify the variables which can be rigorously tested in empirical studies would note important changes over time in the political development of children. I will use the classification schema of Whyte (1990) and Greenstein and

Tarrow (1970a, 1970b) to explore Belfast schoolchildren's orientations to conflict and political authority.

From political psychological research to date, we can conclude that few empirical studies on the Northern Ireland conflict attempt to explore the possible links between integrated schooling and children's political orientations. Since Colin Irwin's (1991) work, there has been no comprehensive attempt to study and compare the possible effects of integrated schooling on young adults in Northern Ireland with children in other divided societies. Irwin's study needs to be reevaluated in light of theoretical writings by Murray (1985), Rose (1971), and Trew (1986) all of which suggest that integrated education may have little impact on intergroup relations.

We need to compare the political orientations of children in divided societies who go to integrated and nonintegrated schools to search for differences in children's political learning and political behavior due to these differential educational experiences. The mechanism of political attitudes requires a basic understanding of the stages children experience in their understanding of political reality. Children residing in democratic societies, which combine consensual politics with liberty and freedom, perceive their political environment differently from children living in conflict regions. The latter combine low levels of trust and belief in political institutions with violence and anarchy (Fields 1976; Straker 1992).

The school systems in these societies combine a different mix of civic processes, depending on the society in question. For example, Northern Ireland functions differently in the United Kingdom from England, Wales, or Scotland because of the different cultural, historical, and political processes at work within the region that affect children's respective experiences. Hence, the political issues involved in children's political development in Northern Ireland have constantly shifted over time, but the structure of the political system based on a bipolar society has remained fairly rigid and stable. Because the historical and cultural roots of division takes considerable time to heal, we can expect minimal changes in what is an intractable conflict for the moment. Conflict resolution programs are an ongoing endeavor, and educational and political innovations, which transform relations between the communities, occur only gradually (Byrne 1994; Whyte 1990). It takes time for these innovations to diffuse existing cultural stereotypes and prejudices and for the development of new values that can be incorporated into the existing cognitive and sociopolitical structures of Northern Irish society (Byrne 1993).

To summarize, we can expect distinctive political orientations for children in different regions of the United Kingdom. Children in England are expected to exalt political authority and have different attitudes toward conflict. Children in Northern Ireland, Scotland, and Wales are theorized as having more intense and mixed orientations to conflict and political authority. While one cannot deny the existence of many factors in maintaining cognitive structural similarities in Northern Irish children's development, I simply argue for the possible significance of age and school differences and/ or similarities in accounting for children's images of conflict and political authority.

We need answers to such questions as: (1) How do children in different schools in conflict zones respond to crises in their political development? (2) Do they respond in the same way? (3) Are some children more successful than others in adopting and moderating political images? In discussing the political orientations of schoolchildren in Belfast, I will address these questions and attempt to extend political development theory by incorporating in the concluding chapter a brief understanding of educational and political policy possibilities in the discussion.

Children's Political Images

Some scholars have analyzed the political development of children (Coles 1986; Connell 1971; Easton and Dennis 1965; Hess and Torney 1967; Garbarino et al. 1991; Greenstein and Tarrow 1971a, 1971b). They demonstrate that it is necessary to research the fundamental processes of early socialization to explain how political attitudes are acquired, changed, and stabilized over time.

The socialization process prepares children for patterns of cooperation and conflict in their society (Cancian and Gibson 1990). Children in their formative years can be taught to hate and accept violence and terrorism as the normal state of affairs. Childhood recognition and acceptance of conflict and bloodshed create a vicious cycle of violence, one that is difficult to break in adulthood. Antisocial behavior can become the norm for children, since each side is taught to be suspicious of the other (Rosenblatt 1982; Volkan 1984). In focusing on the political attitudes of Belfast children we may find their perceptions of the conflict reflect their direct experiences and more general perceptions shared by their respective communities.

Obviously, not all elements of children's political developmental theory are directly relevant to this study of children's political images in Northern Ireland, but I will investigate some of the important theoretical notions, such as affective over cognitive learning, attitudes toward authority, the relationship between age and school type, choice of role models, and attitudes toward political institutions and the Northern Ireland problem. In Chapters 5 and 6, I discuss the empirical research findings of schoolchildren's political imagery in Belfast, Northern Ireland.

The Classification of Children's Interpretations of Conflict in Northern Ireland

The classification that I employ to organize the political images of schoolchildren toward conflict in Belfast, Northern Ireland, is based on a classification by Whyte (1990). He uses a dynamic model to divide previous research according to elements of the Northern Ireland conflict scholars stressed. I selected the Whyte classification for a number of reasons. This most vivid and accurate account of "the troubles" is one of the most important scholarly contributions to the literature about the conflict. Second, the study represents the most comprehensive attempt in the Northern Ireland literature to date to carefully classify alternative interpretations of the conflict. Third, this comprehensive study corresponded to the political attitudes of the sample in this study. Fourth, the academic clarity and illustrative content about interpretations of the conflict represented an important contribution to theoretical and empirical work on Northern Ireland. The categories selected for the theoretical framework were based on an earlier study by Whyte (1978).

From the Whyte's (1990) study three aspects of the Northern Ireland conflict were identified: causes, interpretations, and solutions. Whyte (1990) further subdivided causes of the nature of the community divide into religious, political, economic, and psychological dimensions. The premise is that each of these factors contributes to the segregation of both communities in Northern Ireland. Responses to or interpretations of the conflict were similarly divided into four groups, representing nationalist, unionist, marxist, and internal-conflict interpretations. The guiding principle here was to survey the principal interpretations of the Northern Ireland conflict. However, this work will focus on schoolchildren's interpretations (philosophical and environmental responses to violence) of the conflict, excluding Whyte's categories. Finally, Whyte discusses various constitutional proposals or solutions to the conflict.

The sample of schoolchildren in this study will be measured against some of these mechanisms of change.

In this study, I retained Whyte's (1990) classification with some minor adjustments aforementioned. The only drawback to employing this scheme was that other classification headings were not used (Darby 1976; Lijphart 1975; Rea 1982). It would have been preferable if these other simplifications could have been classified, but this was impracticable because such a schema would have made matters very complicated.

Therefore I will assess the extent to which Whyte's (1990) classification matches children's responses. By comparing Whyte's (1990) classification to children's political orientations, I will shed light on the connections between children's political development and the conflict in Northern Ireland. My purpose is to demonstrate the importance of studying the impacts of maturation and, to a lesser degree, integrated education on explaining children's attitudes to conflict in Northern Ireland.

The most important contribution that international relations and political psychology has to offer to the study of children's political development is the accurate identification and outlining of regional ethnic conflicts. The regional subsystems' links with the other regional subsystems are likely to differ by historical, political, psychocultural, and socioeconomic aspects. This represents a preliminary step toward analyzing, documenting, and describing the possible effects of integrated schooling on children's political development in ethnoterritorial conflicts.

The Classification of Children's Images of Political Authority

An empirical and theoretical debate concerning the nature, direction, composition, and effects of children's orientations toward political authority has occupied an important place in the study of children's political development and socialization. Classical and contemporary theorists argue that the early political learning of children plays a critical role in the acceptance of a country's political regime and institutions. My research follows in this tradition.

While Greenstein and Tarrow (1970a, 1970b) have elaborated in a general sense on the expected behavior of children from each of three countries—France, the United States, and Britain—with respect to images of political authority, there have been few attempts to test these notions among different age peers within conflict areas. A significant lack of empirical research on these children's orientations toward political authority is evident.

The classification that I will apply to children's images of political authority is based on a comparative study of children in three countries (Greenstein and Tarrow 1970a, 1970b). This study examined cognitive, evaluative, and connotative attitudes of children toward political authority. A multimethod analysis of political images in the children's environment was used to determine the development of children's political information about political figures (the queen and the prime minister) and whether affective was more positive than cognitive learning. Greenstein and Tarrow (1970a, 1970b) identified more than forty images that had a high similarity for all three countries.

They collapsed these images into three theoretically relevant categories—(1) the cognitive content of political imagery, (2) evaluative aspects of political imagery, and (3) evaluations of both the head of state and head of government. They interpreted these images of political authority along axes of categories that the children's political development literature has held to be theoretically important.

Greenstein and Tarrow (1970a, 1970b) took the classic New Haven study of Greenstein (1965) into account, where Greenstein argued that children's political behavior learning is continuous longitudinally when one chooses political role models. Greenstein and Tarrow tried to build on Greenstein's research by selecting the same categories to test the political imagery and learning of children in a crosscultural study.

There are a number of reasons why I based the classification of children's images of political authority in this study on the Greenstein and Tarrow study. The advantage of this theory over other theories of children's political development is that it provides a historical and cultural context within a methodological format, which allows children to explore their own political orientations. Greenstein and Tarrow (1970a, 1970b) isolate about forty images common to all three sets of children in their study of American, British, and French children. It is obviously impossible to examine the many political images that are apparent in the child's environment. I was interested in only the most representative images from each of three categories: cognitive, evaluative, and connotative. These three categories also correspond to theoretically relevant categories in the children's political development literature.

Political development theorists (Coles 1986; Connell 1971; Greenstein and Tarrow 1970a, 1970b; Greenstein 1965, 1975; Irwin

1991; Kohlberg 1981; Piaget 1969, 1972) have argued for a long time that children's learning patterns about their milieu allow for the precedence of affective over cognitive learning. Children in ethnoregional conflict zones are expected to develop their political information about political institutions by moving from concrete images when young to more abstract knowledge as they become older (Coles 1986; Dodge and Raundalen 1987, 1991; Irwin 1991; Straker 1992). The upsurge in political violence in Northern Ireland in the fall of 1991, when the field research was carried out, stimulated the schematas of children in the sample. The empirical study represents an important step in understanding schoolchildren's images of political authority in conflict zones where cultural differences between separate ethnoreligious groups simultaneously provoke supportive or positive and hostile or negative attitudes among children to political authority, thereby exacerbating and providing a continuation of the conflict.

In the discussion chapter, I retain the same classification of categories as delineated by Greenstein and Tarrow without any changes. I use the same three theoretically relevant categories but add to their original number of images of political authority.

Political Socialization

Many factors contribute to children's political attitudes. Researchers find strong correlations between geographical location; social class and education; race, gender, and age; and peer-group pressure and parental influence. Political socialization scholars study political behavior and development among children to explain such phenomena. How have scholars classified political socialization? Political socialization, according to Dawson and Prewitt (1969), must be understood as the process by which a group transmits its culture and a person learns about that culture. In the first perspective, political socialization molds the political culture of a group. In the latter perspective, political socialization allows a person to obtain political information, permitting that person to understand how his or her political environment operates.

Other scholars, however, contend that political socialization is a process through which individuals acquire both behavior and attitudes that are pertinent to politics. For example, Fred Greenstein (1965) argues that political learning occurs not only in childhood but throughout the lifespan of an individual. Easton and Dennis (1969) simply interpret political socialization as a developmental process whereby persons comprehend and acquire their patterns of political behavior. Hess and Torney (1967), on the other hand, note that political socialization is a process through which young persons acquire the political norms, values, and attitudes of their group. Political socialization is a process in developmental and evolutionary terms in which the political learning of children is internalized and constantly adapted and modified as the young child biologically and physically progresses towards adulthood. Children are affected by political events that surround them and are able to perceive and comprehend such political phenomena that take place in their environments (Coles 1986). Research is needed to examine the extent to which political themes are most salient for children as an indicator of how they are likely to behave as adults.

In an interesting paper Evenson (1994) suggests that the opportunity now exists to pull the work of cognitive development together with political socialization to form a crossroads for finding a mechanism for the beginning of abstract thinking. A person takes in and processes information at the same time as he or she absorbs the norms, values, and behaviors of the community. Evenson (1994) argues that Greenstein (1965) saw difficulties in developing ideological orientations in children's inability to think abstractly. Such an approach could use sentences using political vocabulary to determine whether the political thought process is as rapid for all children, and occurs in the same order, or whether children have particular concepts for political phenomena (Evenson 1994; Senehi 1994). We may see that class and education determine cognitive development, which in turn impacts on political attitude formation. We now trace what scholars have written on political socialization in general and in particular what they have written about the socialization process in Northern Ireland.

One could argue that living in a society where violence is an everyday occurrence is bound to have an effect on the political orientations and behavior of children (Cairns 1987; Coles 1986; Straker 1992), especially those children who may or may not recognize the legitimacy of the security forces and who provide the cannon fodder to burgeon the ranks of paramilitary organizations. "The troubles" politicize the young people of Northern Ireland into being aware of either accepting or rejecting the other culture and the political authority in the state.

The political socialization process in Northern Ireland has failed to create common attitudes because the deeply divided culture has ensured that the socialization process has worked to preserve each separate cultural identity and tradition. Consequently, there has been no substantial break in the socialization and behavioral patterns of children, that is, the intergenerational shift has remained static. Thus, childhood learning may be an important factor in the behavior of adults (Dawson and Prewitt 1969), which in turn has important implications for the political system in Northern Ireland.

Political Socialization in Northern Ireland

How does the political socialization process operate in Northern Ireland? Harris (1972) places emphasis on how both Catholics and Protestants perceive the social situation in determining the nature of their interrelations in Northern Ireland. The more Catholics perceive society to be dichotomized, the more they will feel themselves to be targets of sectarian discrimination. This ingrained feeling tends to lead towards mirror imaging in which discernment of the other as enemy-belligerent propagates a self-fulfilling prophecy (Cancian and Gibson 1990; Volkan 1984). It serves to influence how they interpret events at the local level, which in turn helps to reinforce the view of society as being dichotomized. This awareness of major political differences at the national level is crucial in maintaining local divisions (Harris 1972). Harris (1972) emphasizes, then, the objective basis to divisions in society by outlining the religious, ideological, and economic interests of the Protestant community. Harris (1972) stresses that these divisions have determined the nature of relationships within society. Pure economic type arguments alone are not sufficient.

Frank Wright (1973) likewise seeks to explore the nature of the relationship between Protestants and Catholics by concentrating on the perceptions both communities have for each other. This deep division ensures that each community has very little direct contact with one another, and relies totally on what it learns from its own community about the other communal group (Wright 1973). As a corollary, the ideologies of each community are autonomous (Wright 1973). This results in ideology structuring experience rather than vice versa. The result is that the ideology of one community determines its views on the condition and aspirations of the other community and, hence, decides on the desirability or otherwise of cooperating with them. This is fundamental in the economic sphere, especially in rural areas of Northern Ireland where farmers depend on one another at harvest time (Byrne and Carter 1994).

Segregated schools are also important instruments of political socialization in Northern Ireland. In a comparative study of a Catholic school in a Catholic working-class area and a Protestant school in a Protestant middle-class neighborhood, Murray (1985) stresses that ethnic identity and religious symbols were more important psychocultural mechanisms than class structure in creating prejudice and tension and that these cues had an influence on the attitudes of pupils and in promoting ignorance and intolerance. Murray (1986) and Whyte (1978, 1986, 1990) are of the opinion that segregated schooling is one of the most important agents in promoting sectarian conflict. Future research needs to compare the integrated and nonintegrated educational sectors as well as include other agents of political socialization in the analysis of children's political imagery of their immediate environment.

Conclusions and Summary

Most researchers accept that education, socialization, political psychology, and international politics are inextricably intertwined in political behavior. However, theories of political behavior tend to lack fully explored notions of these links. One of the main objectives of this study is to chart some of the many connections between political psychology, political socialization, and education from children's political behavior perspective.

There is a great deal of speculation in the literature concerning the effects of integrated education on the political orientations of schoolchildren in Northern Ireland. Many of these notions are based on speculation or observations of particular schools. There have been few detailed empirical studies undertaken between the integrated and nonintegrated school sectors in Northern Ireland to ascertain the accuracy and significance of these developments. Little comparative research has been undertaken on the importance of integrated schooling as a conflict resolution mechanism in intractable conflicts. My research represents a step in that direction. In this study, I attempt to understand children's political orientations toward conflict and political authority through an empirical investigation of the political behavior of schoolchildren in Belfast, Northern Ireland.

The theoretical framework that I apply throughout this study is children's political behavior theory (Greenstein and Tarrow 1970a, 1970b). There are some advantages to this perspective. It attempts to understand processes at work in the development of children's political orientations and the reality of their environments. Children's political behavior theory incorporates an understanding of the integration of different levels in children's developmental psychology, such as, for example, affective over cognitive learning. In this study, I will evaluate the accuracy of children's political behavior theory in explaining children's political attitudes in Belfast, Northern Ireland. I also attempt to add to children's political behavior theory by exploring the possible significance of integrated schooling in explaining patterns of children's political orientations.

4

Children in a Troubled City

Introduction

In this study the perspectives of thirty-five Belfast schoolchildren are presented. The research design involved both quantitative analysis as well as qualitative analysis through semiprojective interviews, content analysis, and participant observation.[1] The empirical questions addressed are (1) Why do children consider this particular conflict so difficult to resolve, and what are their solutions? and (2) What are children's images of political authority? These questions explore children's assumptions about causes and possible solutions to the Northern Ireland conflict, whether political authorities are benign or malign, and whether political relationships are hierarchical or polyarchical.

This research builds on Irwin's (1991) study of integrated schooling in Belfast, Northern Ireland, which used paper-and-pencil exercises and participant observation techniques to focus on the attitudes of primary schoolchildren. My approach is different because I extend the research agenda on Northern Ireland, using Greenstein and Tarrow's (1970a, 1970b) storytelling techniques, to include a comparison of the world views of children in both the integrated and nonintegrated schools.

Semiprojective storytelling techniques are a widely accepted qualitative research strategy (Hanfmann and Getzels 1955; Jahoda et al. 1959; Greenstein and Tarrow 1970a, 1970b). This technique provides the investigator with a wide assortment of information, permitting deeper insights into children's responses and their meanings. The subjects tend to express their own feelings through the behavior of a central character in the story (Jahoda et al. 1959).

Historical and cultural analyses have already been applied in the literature and historical discussion sections highlighting the salient issues that drive the two communities apart in Northern Ireland. Because storytelling is an integral part of the cultural traditions of both communities in Northern Ireland (Coles 1986), this semi-projective method allows respondents to build a story around a central character or characters. This method allows each child to tell his or her own story through the behavior and actions of these real authority figures. This is especially important in a society where suspicions and paranoia run deep and where people are wary of those who ask direct and pointed questions of a political or religious nature (Harris 1972).

The conflict and its development in the cultural environment have been outlined; the origin of its intractability has been described and its historical development in Northern Ireland's political culture traced. Historical examples, such as home rule, the 1920 partition of Ireland and the outbreak of "the troubles" in 1969, have been cited to illustrate different viewpoints. Various assumptions concerning educational and general political policymaking will be critically evaluated in a concluding chapter. I now turn to the respondents and schools who participated in this study.

Subjects and Demography

Characteristics of the Population

Following Irwin's (1991) work, this study will focus on secondary rather than primary schools in the Belfast area.[2] Irwin's analysis of friendship groups at Lagan College, Belfast, found that only children in the 11–12 age bracket tended to have internalized complex characteristics of group identity. In this study, the 11–12 age bracket is compared with an older, 15–16 age bracket in both an integrated and nonintegrated school. A number of very useful studies have been carried out over the years comparing Catholic and/or Protestant nonintegrated schools (Darby et al. 1977; Darby and Dunn 1987; Dunn and Smith 1989; Greer and Long 1989; Murray 1985; Farleigh 1974; McEwen 1990; Russell 1974; Smith and Dunn 1991; Smith and Robinson 1992) or focusing on a single nonintegrated school (Canavan 1989; Salters 1970) or focusing on integrated schools (Dunn 1989; Hughes 1995; Irwin 1991, 1995; McEwen et al. 1993; Morgan et al. 1992; Moffat 1993; NICIE 1991a, 1991b, 1991c, 1991d, 1991e, 1991f; Wilson and Dunn 1989). In this study, we seek to explore both sectors.

Research Location

The area chosen for the project was Belfast, the capital and largest city of Northern Ireland. Belfast is a seaport and commercial and industrial center at the mouth of the Lagan River. The city was an important industrial center during the late nineteenth century. The population, including suburbs outside the city boundary, in 1982, was under one million; it was approximately 70 percent Protestant and 30 percent Catholic (Boal and Douglas 1982).

Belfast is also important because it was the seat of the government of Northern Ireland from 1920 until 1972, when direct rule was imposed by Westminster because of an escalation of violence. Belfast has experienced recent "troubles" that include a considerable number of sectarian assassinations, bombings of commercial targets, and shooting incidents involving members of the security forces and paramilitary organizations such as the PIRA and the UVF. As a result of the violence, the physical and emotional polarization in Belfast can be compared to Luanda, Zagreb, Kigali, Dili, Muqdisho, and Colombo, where ethnic divisions have also created bipolar societies.

The Schools

It is impossible to classify schools in Northern Ireland as either Protestant or Catholic because all controlled or state schools are officially nonsectarian (Murray 1985). It is even more complicated when a school might have 20 percent of its pupils Catholic and 50 percent of its staff Protestant and still be perceived as a Protestant school. The managerial structure of a school may not be indicative of a school's religious designation, because it may have transferred into the maintained or private status category (Darby and Dunn 1987; DENI 1989a, 1989b, 1989c, 1989d).

For the purposes of this study, a school that has been able to maintain a 47/50 percent Catholic/Protestant and 3 percent other pupil and staff ratio, and whose religious choice is Christian, is defined as "integrated." On the other hand, schools whose pupil intake, teaching, and managerial staff and religious and cultural ethos are either predominantly 90 percent Protestant or Catholic are defined as nonintegrated. It is hypothesized that differences may exist among schoolchildren's political attitudes toward conflict and political authority. Also, younger children, in comparison to the older age groups, may not have very coherent views about the differences between the political roles of the queen and the prime minister, and causes of the bicommunal divide in Northern Ireland.

Before examining the similarities and/or differences between schools and age peers, I had to find schools willing to take part in this study. I considered that the best policy within both the integrated and nonintegrated schools was to make my intentions clear to the school principals at the outset. They were concerned that no sensitive or uncomfortable questions be asked of their pupils. A formal letter was sent in March 1991 to twelve schools in the greater Belfast area, outlining my research interest.

Two out of twelve schools responded positively to follow-up phone calls requesting the principal of each school to participate in the project. These two secondary schools are an all-ability coeducational integrated school and a nonintegrated coeducational grammar school.[3] Both schools have similar cachement areas but have had very different experiences and fortunes in their formation and establishment. They also represent interesting studies because one is integrated and the other is nonintegrated. Permission to enter the schools was granted by the school authorities.

I arrived in Belfast toward the end of September and spent about five weeks in each school. To help create a favorable climate, I brought Syracuse University pens for children in both schools. The integrated school, located in a staunch Loyalist area, is about seven miles from the city center. The atmosphere in the integrated school was electric. As I stood in the hallway watching these children run, laugh, and play, I began to comprehend what the school was all about. That same buzz of excitement was also to be found in both mixed-staff rooms (by gender and religion) where teachers were quite willing to chat about their experiences of working in the school and supply me with a never-ending flow of tea and biscuits.[4] I enjoyed these frank and open discussions very much and learned a lot of information about the school, teachers, pupils, and parents. Teachers asked me to talk in their history, geography, and religion classes. This proved to be a very enjoyable experience, especially because the younger children tried to determine whether I was a Catholic or a Protestant by inquiring whether I was a Rangers or a Celtic soccer supporter.[5] Also, the principal and vice principal of the school were very helpful and cooperative, ensuring that I had all the essentials—interview room, tape recorder, and a supply of students—to meet my needs.

The nonintegrated school is also located in the southeast of the city in a more affluent neighborhood. My experiences at the nonintegrated school were very different. Gone were the openness and

DEMOGRAPHIC TABLE
Distribution of Subjects According to Religion, Sex, and Type of School

Sex	Type of School	Protestant	Hindu	Catholic	Total
		Age 11 to 16	Age 11 to 16	Age 11 to 16	
FEMALE	Nonintegrated School	8	0	0	8
	Integrated School	4	0	5	9
MALE	Nonintegrated School	7	1	0	8
	Integrated School	5	0	5	10
TOTAL		24	1	10	35
Note: N = 35					

dynamic atmosphere that I had experienced in the integrated school. Pupils were cordial and polite, whereas when I walked into the male staff common room, disturbing a game of billiards in the process, no one spoke to me. As the examination period and Christmas recess beckoned, I would have no casual conversations with teachers here. However, the headmaster was a charismatic and hospitable man who, with one of his senior staff members and the senior librarian, offered me every courtesy and assistance possible under the circumstances.

I was afraid that my research would be vetoed right up until the moment I completed my surveys: Belfast was in turmoil at the time and anything could have happened. The escalation of bombings and sectarian killings by both the Republican and Loyalist paramilitaries in the fall of 1991 prevented any possible cooperation from other schools and also placed the researcher's life at risk. Catholic taxi drivers were being assassinated at an unprecedented level by Loyalist paramilitaries. Also, the PIRA began its escalation of selective bombings of departmental stores and security stores.

In fact, a teacher at the integrated school reported to me that a member of a paramilitary organization had been asking about my research. This may or may not have been the case, but it was decided that I should change my residence several times during the course of the research. There was a bomb threat at the integrated school during my stay there. Again, this may or may not have been related to my work there, but it was a reminder of how politics and education are related, and of how the political conflict intruded on these children's daily lives.

Field Work

All of the children in this study were interviewed during the late fall and early winter of 1991. The subjects in the study were ten Catholic and nine Protestant pupils from the integrated school, one Hindu male and fifteen Protestant male and female students from the nonintegrated school, representing two different age groups, 11–12 years old and 15–16 years old (See Figure 1). One pupil from the integrated school refused to be interviewed on the day.[6] In total, 35 subjects were included in the final sample.

The 35 children who were interviewed were selected to ensure a representative spread for sex, age, and school type. In these interviews, children were asked to respond to a series of questions seeking their perceptions toward political authority, conflict and its resolution. The only consideration in the selection of children was to ensure representation from both schools.[7] This enabled closer comparisons to be made between children's political orientations in an integrated vis-à-vis a nonintegrated school. Permission to carry out the research was granted by parents as well as school authorities.

Both secondary schools are located in southeast Belfast, and two school populations were chosen in geographic proximity for comparison. The integrated school's principal requested the first- and fifth-year teachers to organize a random sample of male/female and Protestant/Catholic pupils, representing a reasonable spread of academic ability in both age groups. A random sample was selected by the teachers of the nonintegrated school.

Apparatus

Preparing the Research Materials

The preparation and organization of the field research stage was devised carefully. All the necessary equipment, facilities, and formal contacts were arranged well in advance. A classroom in the integrated school and the library and ladies' staff room in the nonintegrated school were chosen as interview sites in the belief that familiar settings would reduce stress and anxiety during the interviews. The interviewer and each participant had face-to-face contact at all times, the tape recorder being placed to one side.

I was not restricted totally to the semiprojective storytelling guide; probing comments of respondents led to a line of questions about conflict and political authority that furnished valuable and paramount information. Children described pictures of violence, pain, terror, and love connecting to contemporary and historical images, revealing how "the troubles" have permeated the emotional behavior of Northern Ireland's young people.

Research Instrument

A carefully selected number of the semiprojective incomplete political stories of Greenstein and Tarrow (1970a, 1970b) were administered to all subjects. This research instrument consists of twenty-eight stories; however, only five stories were chosen because I was permitted approximately 80 minutes to speak to each student. I decided that, for this exploratory study, it was better to concentrate on a select number of stories, gathering as much information as possible rather than overloading the interview schedule with all twenty-eight stories. This strategy also had the advantage of giving the students time to build up and expand their stories. (See Appendix 3).

Following each story was a series of probes, indicating how the subject believed the central character(s) in each story should have acted or responded to the political dilemma posed. The subjects were permitted to elaborate on political issues triggered by the story. At the conclusion of the storytelling, subjects were asked their age for classification purposes. Children were also asked about their parents and why they had choosen to go to that particular school. Preselection by academic ability was the criteria that determined why children attended the nonintegrated school. Children attended the integrated school for a variety of reasons, including a decision by the parents, grandparents, or child, the desire of the child to try something different, and because a friend was attending.

Procedure

At the completion of the interviewing stages, the principals procured a list compiled from school records containing the father's and mother's occupations and the religion and name of each pupil. Both school principals requested fictitious names and no surnames be mentioned in the analysis.

Items

The Greenstein and Tarrow (1970a, 1970b) methodology that had proved successful in a comparative study of children in three countries was used in this study to desensitize controversial topics and to permit access to the children.

First came a sequence of open-ended incomplete stories set in a child's immediate environment. The format of such questions included the respondents explaining the outcome of a scenario, in which a window is broken and the dilemma posed of whether to obey one's parents or the policeman when crossing a road. Second, the children were asked to explain the roles of the queen and the prime minister to a foreign child (fixed-choice items) and to establish which leader is more important for Northern Ireland. Last, an incomplete story (the queen's car speeding), located in the adult political environment, called on children to imagine the outcome of an interactive episode between two authority figures.

The Greenstein and Tarrow (1970a, 1970b) research instrument links the individual stories used in the interview stage with the empirical findings on images of political authority. The open-ended stories in the one-on-one interviews allowed participants to construct replies in any of several areas. For example, some of the schoolchildren in this sample chose to discuss the conflict directly in the stories they created. I addressed the issue of the Northern Ireland conflict and the importance of children's political development by focusing on the following questions: (1) How do children explain the conflict in Northern Ireland? (2) How do children fit into the conflict? and (3) What do these children say can be done to resolve the nature of the conflict?

Administration Procedure

The interview schedule was administered on a one-to-one basis to both first- and fifth-year pupils attending an integrated and a nonintegrated school. During the presentation of instructions to each pupil, I stressed that "this is not a test" and emphasized that "nobody inside or outside the school will hear the tapes." They were assured that the tapes would be destroyed after transcribing and that different names would be used in published research to ensure confidentiality—both of which have been done. Respondents were asked if they fully understood the storytelling interviewing procedure before we commenced.

The Interviews

The format was based on face-to-face interviews which took place within the schools. The standardized storytelling interview schedule used in both schools was very flexible. A significant proportion of the time allocated to each individual interview was given to attempting to build up rapport and to put each pupil at ease. After the introduction, all respondents took the opportunity to "open up" and express their ideas and feelings towards each of the items posed to them. Complete anonymity was guaranteed to every pupil. Because of the prevailing climate of violence in Northern Ireland, this trust had to be assured even more emphatically than would normally be the case.

My multicultural experience and exposure of living in other countries plus my knowledge and experience of Northern Ireland made me sensitive to the need to build in safeguards for the emotional and cultural protection of each pupil. Both Protestant and Catholic pupils were told that they were being interviewed as part of a research project. The interviews were carried out over a ten-week period in which the researcher averaged 2–3 interviews per day. On average, the thirty-five interviews lasted approximately sixty to eighty minutes each. Teachers at the integrated school made sure that pupils came to their interviews on time, ensuring that everything went smoothly. The procedure at the nonintegrated school differed in that each pupil had to report to the head librarian at a prearranged time. Respondents were told not to disclose any information to other project participants about the questions asked. In general, the cooperation received was remarkable; collection of the data took approximately ten weeks.

Study Design

Empirical Findings

The study findings were analyzed by the researcher controlling for age and school type. It was important to break down the data by school type because I explored differences and similarities between age groups in both schools. Reporting by homogeneous age groups will allow future comparisons with similar age groups in both schools with peers in other schools in Northern Ireland, and in different conflict-ridden zones in other areas of the world. For analysis the children were classified into two categories of age and school type.

Concepts and Variables

What is meant by "Protestant" and "Catholic" requires further clarification. Harris (1972) and Rose (1971) provided the Protestant/Catholic classification which has been used by many scholars writing on the Northern Ireland conflict (Bruce 1986; Hickey 1984). A Protestant or Catholic child will be identified as any child reared in the Protestant or Catholic religious faith and community tradition. This entails a child's parents identifying themselves as either Protestant or Catholic who attend church or chapel at least once a month and who consciously impart Protestant or Catholic doctrine to their children (Wright 1973).

Independent Variables

The independent variables used to explore schoolchildren's political orientations are age and school type. Age is an interval measure variable, whose attributes 11, 12, 15, 16 are standard intervals. The nominal variable, type of school, is measured by the attributes integrated and nonintegrated school.

Dependent Variables

To analyze children's political attitudes to the Northern Ireland "troubles," I based an additive index of what children perceive as causes of the conflict on the simple cumulation of the following dependent variables: religious aspects, political aspects (violence, national identity), economic aspects, and psychocultural aspects.

An index of children's responses to the conflict was constructed through accumulation of two dependent variables: philosophical violence and environmental violence.

Finally, children's solutions to the conflict are based on an index including three dependent variables: law and order, integrated education, and belief structures. Similarly, children's perceptions of major political roles in Northern Ireland were elicited by the following dependent variables: cognitive explanations of political authority, evaluative awareness of political authority, and conative feeling toward political authority.

The attributes composing each of the above dependent variables "yes" with a value of one and "no" with a value of zero are distinct and mutually exclusive from one another.

Operational Definition of the Variables

The totality of children's perceptions represents their images of conflict and political authority. Children living in Belfast, Northern Ireland, have direct experience of the conflict that in turn shapes their political orientations. A given child could have disparate views on conflict and political authority that enable the researcher to analyze his or her attitudes.

Fifteen key concepts and children's quotes will be presented in the next two chapters. The data were also submitted to quantitative content analysis; its numerical part was tested with the SAS statistical package for the social sciences, and is presented in the appendix. The statistical information illustrates the richness of detail and nuance in the respondents interviews to be presented in chapters five and six.

1. Age
The sample was divided into two age categories: 11–12 and 15–16. Political learning develops gradually with older children at more advanced stages of cognitive development. As the child matures intellectually, cognitive development influences political learning.

2. School Type
The second independent variable selected, type of school, may reinforce cultural and political differences, making the integration of children in schools difficult. The sample used in this study came from both integrated and nonintegrated school environments.

3. Religious Aspects
Northern Ireland is segregated by religion into two communities—Protestant and Catholic. Protestant is normally used to represent members of all the various Protestant denominations and Catholic is normally used as a term for Roman Catholics. My purpose is to examine the respondents' stories to discern how often and in what way children refer to religious aspects of the bicommunal conflict.

4. Political Violence
Protestants and Catholics are psychologically marked by political violence in many ways. I investigated whether the children's stories

indicate a reaction to paramilitary terrorism and political violence in negative rather than in positive ways.

5. National Identity
Choice of national identity indicates that political differences exist between the two communities. I determined, from these children's stories, whether Irish identity remained much more popular among Catholics, and British identity among Protestants.

6. Economic Aspects
The economic gap between Protestants and Catholics contributes to a sectarian society. References to an economic differential between the two communities, leading to intercommunal violence and poverty, were determined by a close scrutiny of each child's stories.

7. Psychocultural Aspects
Psychological forces intensify the depth of feeling within each community. An analysis of each child's stories determined whether stereotyping and prejudice display the sensitivities and anxieties of the "in-group" toward the "out-group."

8. Philosophical Violence
Between 1969 and 1995, more than 3,150 people died as a result of political violence in Northern Ireland. The conflict is perceived by many Northern Irish citizens as intractable and unsolvable. The children's stories reflected whether violence is accepted as a way of life.

9. Environmental Violence
Force is recognized as justifiable and as the only effective political instrument by the terrorists. It was interesting to learn whether children's stories reflect that the political environment in Northern Ireland spawns death and destruction, impacting on the dismal worldview of both communities.

10. Law and Order
Protestants and Catholics dislike the violence and terror used by paramilitary groups. The stories of school children in this sample may reflect that both communities are willing to approve of stronger measures by the security forces to combat terrorism.

11. Integrated Education
The parapolitical stories of Protestant and Catholic schoolchildren may suggest that they are well-disposed to the idea of integrated education as an important stepping-stone to peace and reconciliation in the amelioration of the Northern Ireland conflict.

12. Belief Structures
The schoolchildren's stories may indicate that there is an optimistic consensus on the part of young people with regard to possible solutions to the Northern Ireland problem.

13. Cognitive Explanation of Political Authority
When schoolchildren are explaining and describing their political lead-

ers, the differences in levels of information among them may be greater among older age peers than among younger age groups.

14. Affective Awareness of Political Authority

In the evaluative content of political imagery, differences may exist between younger and older schoolchildren in their awareness and attitudes toward the differences between the head of state and the head of government.

15. Conative Feelings Toward Political Authority

In asking the schoolchildren to express dispositions about the behavior of a policeman to take action against the queen, differences may exist between the age groups' reaction to the breaking of a public law by an authority figure. This may also, perhaps, reflect religious differences between Catholics and Protestants.

Coding

The Greenstein and Tarrow (1970a, 1970b) data were coded by (1) defining the situation, such as, a child composing a story taking the innocence or guilt of the character into consideration; (2) categorizing the outcome of the episode, such as, a respondent accepting the framework of the given story or challenging its frame of reference; and (3) coding for specific themes, so that a reflective reading of each person's story provides theoretically interesting themes in the story completions.

I determined applicable coding categories for the Belfast study from intensive examination of the open-ended story completion data, and from the Whyte (1990) and Greenstein and Tarrow (1970a, 1970b) works. A coding instrument was drawn up that provides specifically for all the different kinds of items found. Both the coding procedures and data were submitted to the Montgomery and Crittenden (1977) test in order to offer a reliable record of events relating to children's perception of authority figures and the conflict.[8] Each statement then is coded in terms of

1. the image of the character(s)
2. the definition of the situation
3. the outcome of the episode
4. the evaluation of the character
5. the action, and
6. the number of times a particular theme is mentioned by each respondent

(Greenstein and Tarrow, 1970a, 1970b).

The coding applied to each statement was dichotomous. For example, if the theme of "violence" was present in a particular statement (that is, present in a child's ending of a story), then that statement was coded "1" on the variable "violence" as it pertains to outcome.

The Pretest Stage

In the pretest stage the research instrument was administered to a random sample of secondary students in a medium-sized town in County Tipperary in the Irish Republic, to probe for respondents' understanding of the stories. I pretested the data collection instrument to uncover defects. The research instrument was tested in June 1991 by interviewing three male and three female pupils between the ages of thirteen and seventeen attending the local male Christian Brothers and females' convent schools in Cashel, County Tipperary, Republic of Ireland. The pretest yielded valuable information, and, as a result, the questionnaire was amended.

I decided to place the nonpolitical question *("Two children are playing in their room. Their parents are out. When the parents return, they notice that there is a window broken in the kitchen.")* first on the interview schedule for the Belfast sample, rather than commence with a political question. This strategy allowed children to use their imagination, relax, and get over their shyness and nervousness. The pretest also suggested that it was more appropriate to change the country, on the original Greenstein and Tarrow (1970a, 1970b) interview schedule, from England to Northern Ireland for question three *("There are some things about England that I don't understand.");* the pretest subjects could not identify with England.

The Belfast Study

We need new research methods to understand the political lives of conflict environments (Cairns 1987; Coles 1986; Garbarino et al. 1991; Punamaki and Suleiman 1990; Straker 1992). Researchers should examine empirically children's political development in conflict regions (Dawes 1990; Irwin 1991; Yogev and Ben-Yehoshua 1991). This data set represents one of the first comprehensive attempts at examining children's political development within a conflict area with multimethod lenses.

The present study is a cross-sectional preliminary attempt to formulate hypotheses for a future follow-up in-depth study of children in Northern Ireland, Israel, and South Africa. It is a psychopolitical analysis of children's mind-sets that may be intellectually insightful about the perceptions of children to the "troubles" in Northern Ireland.

The Belfast data set stands out as an example for future empirical analysis of children's political development in strife-ridden regions. The data set is rich and complete. Each of the individual narratives provides detailed information on the psychopolitical orientations of schoolchildren from both schools, which can be used to study children's attitudes to political conflict and political authority.

5

How Children Think and Feel about Conflict and Its Resolution

Introduction

IMAGES of political conflict are important in determining the political attitudes of Protestants and Catholics in Northern Ireland. During the course of the field research, key political events such as the 1991 Brooke Talk roundtable discussions on the future of Northern Ireland's position within the United Kingdom and the 1991 sectarian murders and bombings by Republican and Loyalist paramilitaries were significant political transformations that affected and altered the political behavior of both adults and children residing in the city of Belfast.[1]

The purpose of this chapter is to try to move toward some kind of understanding of how children perceive intercommunal conflict and its possible resolution within Northern Ireland. Young children are influenced by their particular cultures, values, and norms. It is important to gain insights into how they will adapt to peace despite their exposure to political violence. The worldviews and political perceptions of Belfast children, largely shaped during childhood and adolescence, will impact on the future. When they are adults they will lead and constitute the societies of the coming decades within Northern Ireland. It is important to recognize their political imagery as it specifically relates to conflict and peacebuilding.

The respondents presented below express recurrent themes to explain why the Northern Ireland conflict appears to be so intractable. It must be remembered that not all 35 respondents volunteered to discuss the current situation in Northern Ireland.[2] The themes presented here evolved from a sequence of questions based on these children's understanding of government and politics in their everyday lives (Greenstein and Tarrow 1970a, 1970b).

Results and Discussion

Religion as a Cause of the Conflict

It is interesting to note that when the political images of children from both schools are compared clear similarities emerge. Protestants at both schools and Catholics at the nonintegrated school frequently identify religion as a primary cause of the intercommunal conflict in Northern Ireland.

IMAGES: PROTESTANT CHILDREN AT THE NONINTEGRATED SCHOOL

Stan is a 16-year-old Protestant who lives in Craigavon, a suburb of Belfast. He is asked the question about who is more important for Northern Ireland, the queen or the prime minister. Stan views the conflict in terms of Protestant efforts to maintain the union, uphold religious freedom, and oppose Irish unification.

> STAN: A lot of people in Northern Ireland want to stay within Great Britain instead of joining the South, because they believe they're British and they prefer the way British people live, and the government is not the Irish government. Plus, it's a religious thing. Most of the people in the South are Catholics, and most of the people up in the North are Protestants. After certain wars and things they want to stay separate from the people in the South. *[16-year-old Protestant male]*

Stan's description of specific elements of attachment to a British identity and the religious separateness of Northern Ireland from the Irish Republic suggests an incipient awareness of one aspect of the nature of the community divide: society has one major division around which all other divisions cluster—religion.

Jessica, a 15-year-old Protestant female student at the nonintegrated school, lives in a residentially middle-class area in the suburbs of south Belfast. She also explains the importance of the religious division in Northern Ireland:

> JESSICA: I'm a Methodist and I know a lot of people who go to this college, and it is sort of integrated if you like. But the Catholics do have their own schools and they separate themselves from the rest of us. You're not really aware of Catholics at the school. It's something you don't really talk about. I'm sure things like H-Test and telling

people going by their names goes on, but it's never happened to me and it's never happened in this school. Those people who go to this school are from quite well-off families. Maybe it's the poor or less-educated kids that go to secondary schools; that's the way they've been brought up, to think about the other side.[3] *[15-year-old Protestant female]*

Jessica falls into the category of children who recognize religious divisions in society but explain these divisions in terms of class. These inferences are based on the impression that violence occurs in working-class rather than middle-class neighborhoods and are more the consequence of working-class Catholics in controlled or private schools and working-class Protestants in state schools.

Northern Irish society has two groups of people molded in their own religious and cultural traditions and encapsulated in a political structure which has forced them to continue living together. Both pupils at the nonintegrated school suggest that Protestants seek to preserve their distinctiveness, since if that separateness were to evaporate there would exist no political basis to remain separate from the Republic of Ireland. The importance of the queen as symbolic head of the Protestant Church is recognized by both Protestant children as leading inevitably to sectarianism, since the queen preserves the link with Britain and secures the politico-religious identity of Northern Irish Protestants.

Not all students, however, believe that religion leads to a bipolar society. Jennifer is an 11-year-old pupil at the nonintegrated school who responds to the stories with creative scenarios and full-blown accounts of "the troubles." Jennifer lives on the Malone Road with her parents. The episode of the queen and the policeman triggered the interviewer to pose a question on integrated education:

JENNIFER: I think it's brilliant. I don't mind that at all. I think it's brilliant because there are Catholics and Protestants here but no one cares, they're all the same. It's not as if everyone who has a different religion has a red cross on their head or something 'cause it doesn't matter. I think that's brilliant, there's nothing wrong with it at all. *[11-year-old Protestant female]*

Jennifer's descriptions of the inconsequence of religious divisions in the nonintegrated school reinforces the fact that the nonintegrated school is a middle-class grammar school. She simply may not be aware of the religious diversity that constitutes the working-class Protestant position in relation to their working-class Catholic neighbors.

IMAGES OF RELIGION AS A CAUSE OF THE CONFLICT: CATHOLIC
CHILDREN AT THE INTEGRATED SCHOOL

Now hear a working class pupil at the integrated school. James
is a 16-year-old Catholic male. He is from the Falls Road in West
Belfast, a strong Republican area, where the intercommunal conflict affects the everyday lives of its residents. James is asked how
he would describe the queen to a foreign child:

> INTERVIEWER: *What does the queen mean to both communities in
> Northern Ireland?*
>
> JAMES: You would have to say that the queen is the head of the
> Protestant church and explain what she means to the Protestant com-
> munity. That's being a bit bland and putting it a bit bluntly. There's
> more to it than that. Then you'd need to say that there are people who
> resent that fact. But you really can't see why they find it. That would
> be my opinion. The queen is a figurehead for the Protestant community.
> So a Catholic would identify the Protestants with the queen and go
> "Oh, the queen." *[16-year-old Catholic male]*

In his story James describes the religious attachment of Protestants
to the British queen, but he also points out that Catholics resent
this relationship. While James's political images of the queen are
perceived as cementing partition, Joanie is explicit in relating religious differences to themes of death.

Joanie is a 12-year-old Catholic female attending the same integrated school, who lives with her family in the Ballymurphy district of Belfast. She makes statements such as the following when
explaining the role of the queen to a foreign child:

> JOANIE: Then he says he doesn't understand about the rioting. The
> petrol bombers. Well, it's just about the religion, Catholics and Protes-
> tants. A boy got stabbed the other day in Carryduff, did you hear? Two
> boys were chopping up meat and they had an argument over which
> way to chop, chop. And they had a fight and the 17-year-old [Catholic]
> boy got stabbed to death because of it [religion] and then he says I
> don't understand because it's so stupid. *[12-year-old Catholic female]*

Clearly James is intolerant of those who espouse a religious attachment to the British queen, believing that they are anti-Catholic and
antinationalist. Joanie views the whole conflict in terms of one
community killing the other over religious differences.

Here is an example of Anne, a 16-year-old Catholic female who
believes that the integrated school has influenced the relationships

between both religious groups in the school, bringing both communities together. Anne is from a mixed parentage—one Catholic and one Protestant. Her Protestant father drives a taxi and her mother is a housewife. Anne has been brought up to be tolerant and to respect diversity:

> ANNE: You come in and you hear stories about how Catholic eyes are closer together, and Catholics walk on one side of the road and Protestants on the other, and you hear all the different wee stories about their friends; and "my Dad did this and." You sort of just realize, What does it matter? If you get on with somebody you get on with them, if you don't, you don't. Religion just doesn't come into it. *[16-year-old Catholic female]*

Anne believes that prejudice and sectarianism stems from ignorance because "all people are the same."

In the opinion of some of the above respondents, religious differences are at the heart of the bicommunal divide in Northern Ireland. This item is more important for children in the integrated, as opposed to the nonintegrated school (appendix 2, table 1). Also, the older age peers, as opposed to the younger age peers in both schools, do not see the conflict as religious nationalism. This may, in part, be explained by the fact that older children see other causes of the conflict as their political knowledge develops.

Catholic pupils are also more likely than Protestant pupils to mention that religion is a cause of the conflict (appendix 2, table 2). Catholics may be suggesting that religious differences dichotomize society, thereby exacerbating the conflict.

Political Causes of the Conflict

VIOLENCE

The political authority in Northern Ireland finds itself challenged by movements that some deem to be liberation movements and others describe as terrorist action. In Northern Ireland, the PIRA is committed to socialist culminations, but then virtually all so-called liberation organizations are so committed. The IRA separated into two paramilitary outfits, the Irish National Liberation Army (INLA) and the Irish People's Liberation Organization (IPLO). The 1991 upsurge in shootings by Loyalist paramilitaries demonstrated that civilians were not completely unaffected by political violence.

Are the Republican and Loyalist (UDA, UVF, UFF) paramilitaries nationalist organizations? Probably, only insofar as both have nations in mind, but so do all other such groups. Some would contend that Republican and Loyalist paramilitary organizations appear to operate on behalf of an uncertain number who do not represent a majority of those who would belong to the nation so desired, and, to that extent, are not popular. It is, of course, difficult to substantiate such a statement, in that such clandestine forces do not state open support very often.

While some pupils attempt to define the conflict in terms of religious differences, others highlight the role of paramilitaries in polarizing both communities and in creating a heightened sense of alienation within the Protestant community.

IMAGES: PROTESTANT CHILDREN AT THE INTEGRATED AND NONINTEGRATED SCHOOLS

Some Unionists ardently believe that public authority in Northern Ireland is not doing enough to counteract PIRA terrorism or keep Northern Ireland British. Since the 1985 Anglo-Irish Agreement, Protestants who have become alienated from the British government are prepared to support the mobilization of an illegal paramilitary Protestant Action Force (PAF). This in turn has exacerbated the British prime minister's problem of getting Unionist politicians to participate in the current Framework for Peace talks to formulate a political framework for new cross-border institutions and powersharing structures in Northern Ireland.

In the story about the queen and the prime minister, there is little ambiguity about the knowledge of the following fifth-year pupil from the nonintegrated school about the prime minister's political role against terrorism within Northern Ireland. Russell is from Newtownards. He is from a predominantly middle-class neighborhood. His father is English and is an officer in the British security forces. Here are Russell's remarks on this issue:

INTERVIEWER: *What does the queen do?*

RUSSELL: People in the country actually believe that it's their country and it's no one else's. The Loyalists look up to her. I don't particularly think they do, I think it's just because they don't want the South invading. They don't want Catholic rulership. Then maybe the Republicans look down on her. But even some of them wouldn't look down on her as much as the prime minister because the prime minister is the one that enforces things, because the queen doesn't say, for example, "Oh, I'm sending 500 new troops into Northern Ireland." She doesn't order internment, it would be the prime minister. *[15-year-old male]*

The realism of this fifth-year pupil's account contrasts vividly with other schoolchildren's perceptions of how citizens are affected by the political violence.

Here are some examples of responses by Jennifer, Cynthia, and Hazel, Protestant children attending the nonintegrated school, to the question about how people can promote peace in which the notion of paramilitary terror against the public is exhibited.

JENNIFER: 'Cause a lot of people, say someone like Gerry Adams, and he's the leader of the IRA, but no one can give proof of this because they're scared of being killed. I think it's sad because people would actually give evidence, but it's awful that they would get killed if they did. *[11-year-old Protestant female]*

CYNTHIA: They [the IRA] seem to think everything they do is right and if somebody else believes differently, they are wrong, totally, and they go and kill them, and they don't like the security forces who try and stop them, so they target them as well. *[12-year-old Protestant female]*

HAZEL: I think it's important for people all over the world to understand that there are people here who are good as well, rather than people who just blow up places. The IRA, for example, are very cunning, they can do all sorts of things. But it's up to us to keep our chin up and keep going and finally try and stop them. *[12-year-old Protestant female]*

These Protestant pupils believe that PIRA violence seeks to break the spirit of the Unionist community and drive Protestants into a United Ireland. They interpreted the violence as a need to fight even harder to maintain the union with Britain.

IMAGES: CATHOLIC CHILDREN AT THE INTEGRATED SCHOOL

The comments of James, a Catholic student from the integrated school, reflect an incipient awareness that small bands of paramilitaries perpetuate the conflict:

JAMES: There is an awful lot that needs change. You have to start with education for a start. The amount of people that would be involved with the paramilitaries on either side, if that stopped, that would be it. Everybody else doesn't seem to be like that. The amount of people who work for the Civil Service here and that represents the government. Most people don't think the way the paramilitaries do, it's just a very small number. If you look at other countries that are having trouble, like Italy, they have people like the Mafia and they kill more people in one year than we do here, it's just that it's publicized differently. It's publicized as a war here. It's like two wee gangs and that's the bit that needs to be stopped, the two wee gangs. *[15-year-old Catholic male]*

James believes that the various paramilitary organizations are to blame for exacerbating sectarian tensions in Northern Ireland, and for keeping the Protestant and Catholic communities polarized and segregated.

James's vivid account of Provisional IRA violence contrasts with a Catholic girl's description of the futility and fear people experience from the impact of the violence. Anne is from the integrated school and describes the impact of paramilitary terror and violence by explaining what it means for a married woman to lose her beloved husband to the gunman's bullet:

ANNE: I think that people nowadays aren't being as bad as they used to be even though "the troubles" are worse now, that's because of certain people or like certain gangs or whatever. A lot of people are just afraid, and if you're watching the news you see a Protestant woman's husband has been shot dead by an IRA man and she says "Please no retaliation." And you see the same happening to a Catholic and she's asking for no retaliation, but they can't really come out and speak their minds because they're so afraid. *[16-year-old Catholic female]*

These perceptions by all age groups in both schools about political violence being directed by a minority against the majority is supported by statistics which indicate that Republican paramilitaries have accounted for approximately 58 percent of fatalities and 26 percent by Loyalist paramilitaries (O'Leary and McGarry 1993). Loyalist paramilitary sectarian killings dramatically increased between 1986 and 1994. The political violence of the paramilitaries has instilled fear in both communities. Punishment shootings and kneecappings are carried out regularly by kangaroo courts against convicted offenders and touts for the security forces.

Against the current background of political activity and efforts to find some sort of mutual peaceful settlement to "the troubles," gun and bomb attacks may have temporarily ceased but Loyalist and Republican paramilitaries continue to instill their own particular type of law and order within their neighborhoods.

There have been over 3,100 fatalities since the outbreak of violence in 1969, and these deaths and the fears they have engendered have marked both children and adults in many different ways. Violence in its various shapes and forms is an intricate part of the problem because it is a constant reminder of the hostility and political tension that exudes itself throughout Northern Ireland.

More fifth-year pupils at the integrated school, when compared to the other age groups, suggest that terrorists should be punished. There appears to be a small, but significant minority (25 percent) of first-year pupils at the integrated school, compared to the same age group (50 percent) at the nonintegrated school, willing to suggest that terrorists should be punished (appendix 2, table 3).

Specifically, based on this sample data, nearly half of the Protestant student body mention that terrorists should be punished (appendix 2, table 4).[4] Protestants generally feel that they are under attack from the PIRA and hence have a siege mentality, due to the fear and anger that becomes prevalent after terrorist attacks.

National Identity

The internal conflict for those who live in Northern Ireland consists of a continuous struggle of attachment to three separate identities—British, Irish, and Northern Irish. However, Protestants' choice of national identity is more complex than that of Catholics. Both communities predominantly aspire to a British or Irish identity, and this is manifested in symbolic celebrations of folklore and the past that combine to reinforce the intractability of the conflict in Northern Ireland. Some pupils attempt to fit the conflict into an important frame of reference; a close allegiance to the British Crown that reinforces a sense of British tradition and heritage for Northern Irish Protestants. Not surprisingly, some of the Protestant children from the nonintegrated school evoke a striking conception of the symbolic significance of the queen.

Images: Protestant Children at the Nonintegrated School

Tracey is from a fairly well-to-do Protestant neighborhood in South Belfast. She emphasizes the importance of a Protestant-British group solidarity:

TRACEY: So I think it's good the queen sends members of the royal family to see what the same variation is in both countries and see what our needs are and England's needs are. I think that's good because sometimes you feel a little bit left out. If there's a bomb in Ireland it's on the news for one day, but if it's in England it's on for weeks and weeks. *[12-year-old Protestant female]*

Tracey is frustrated and angry that the media ignores Northern Ireland. She feels that the media is biased. In the following case, Stan articulates the influence of the queen in preventing the government from "selling-out" Protestants' Britishness.

INTERVIEWER: *What kind of powers does the prime minister have that the queen might not have?*

STAN: Seeing that the queen is the head of Great Britain, or if it's not up to the government, whether they can't give Northern Ireland away, really she has the final word on what happens to the country. The prime minister may advise her about what she should do, but if it comes down to it whether the queen wants to give the country up or give it its independence, she'd usually take the prime minister's advice, but if she thought it was wrong she might not agree with him. I think she has the power to stop him but I'm not clear on it. *[16-year-old Protestant male]*

Implicit in their stories is the view that the British media and the British government are insensitive and unsympathetic to Northern Ireland's Protestant community. For a clear understanding of any aspect of Loyalism and the formation of terrorist groups, it is imperative to accept the central role the Crown plays in Northern Irish politics. It is not disloyalty to the queen to refuse loyalty to the queen's government, especially if that government is threatening to end partition and break the link with the union.

The salience of national identity also coincides with partition. Nationalists see the Northern Ireland state as an alliance forged between the Unionists and the British government, who remained in Northern Ireland for economic and political reasons, keeping both national identities divided. The majority of Catholics, therefore, identify with the Republic of Ireland and Protestants with the United Kingdom.

On the other hand, Protestants in Northern Ireland fear incorporation within a Catholic-dominated United Ireland. There appears to be a conflicting identity crisis among Protestants, although British identity is more salient. Britain's apparent willingness to abandon Northern Irish Protestants to the dictates of Irish nationalism has highlighted the siege mentality aspect of Northern Irish Protestantism.

In these examples of Protestant children's responses to aspects of national identity, the notion of the uncertainty of Northern Ireland's constitutional position plays heavily on the minds of Russell and Stan who attend the nonintegrated school. Russell argues that the British government wants to end the union and betray Protestants into a united Ireland. He believes that the government should be committed to integrating Northern Ireland fully into the United Kingdom:

> RUSSELL: The prime minister changes his ways depending on who says "right." So they can clinch a business deal by selling Northern Ireland to the South. If they could do that then they'd do it. It would be better for England because first and foremost the prime minister's loyalty is to England and then Northern Ireland. I think the queen believes Northern Ireland should be kept because there's a majority there and it is meant to be a democracy. So the majority of the people over here wanted to be kept English, so I think it should. So that's why I think the queen is better. *[15-year-old Protestant male]*

Although Stan is intolerant of Irish unification, he believes that the queen will protect Protestants and prevent the government from unravelling the union.

> STAN: The people in Ulster are patriotic, and the queen is the head of the state for them. A lot of people in Northern Ireland want to stay separate from the South, and it would come down to the queen whether they'd stay with Great Britain, or go back to Ireland again. Northern Ireland is part of Great Britain and the people in the South of Ireland think that Northern Ireland should become part of Ireland itself, that it should be one whole country. *[16-year-old Protestant male]*

These children highlight the importance of a British national identity and illustrate the centrality of Unionism as a central issue in the intergroup conflict.

IMAGES: CATHOLIC AND PROTESTANT CHILDREN AT THE INTEGRATED SCHOOL

In contrast, the British monarch is perceived as a symbol of Britishness by members of the Nationalist community in Northern Ireland, which, in turn, serves to delineate group identity and membership. This is quite evident in the descriptions of the head of state by three Catholic fifth-year boys at the integrated school.

In his story Seamus expresses a vivid historical understanding of the role of the British government in creating partition and in allowing Protestants to practice discrimination against Catholics:

INTERVIEWER: *Who do you like best, the queen or the prime minister?*

SEAMUS: It's strange, because the queen, I feel it's the queen's fault for this conflict that we have at the moment. It was originally their fault. They self-proclaimed, defeated, and planted this place.[5] It's the prime minister that makes all of the important decisions on how Northern Ireland turned out. They decided partition, home rule, and Stormont. They did what they felt was best for the people concerned, but they did more for the Protestants in Ulster than for Catholics for a very long time. But they were the match for the kindling. They set it. It would be the government is more to blame than the queen, but the queen is the figurehead of England. It's the government's fault, but it's the queen's to blame for me. *[16-year-old Catholic male]*

In contrast, James assumes that Protestants espouse a British identity because of their attachment to the queen.

INTERVIEWER: *Would the Catholics resent the queen because she's head of state and the Protestant Church?*

JAMES: The head of state would come into it because she personifies it and people would sort of see England and the queen. There is a lot of resentment within certain factions of the community between Protestant and Catholic which doesn't really stem from anything. I would say the resentment goes back a long way and it's always been happening. It started with Protestants coming into Ireland and things like that and the people coming into Ireland and things like that and the people coming into Ireland were identified purely as Protestants. That's where it all started. It's just sort of Protestants against Catholics and that the queen is the head of the Protestants. *[15-year-old Protestant male]*

Also, Dermott, who is from the Republican stronghold of Andersonstown, suggests that the queen is to blame for the Northern Ireland conflict. He is offended by the cultural symbols and trappings of the monarchy.

INTERVIEWER: *Why is the queen important to the people of Northern Ireland?*

DERMOTT: It's just 'cause she's the figurehead of England, she symbolizes England. When I think of England, I think of the queen. I think of royalty, that would be England to me, not Westminster. It's just Buckingham Palace and the queen. I don't think it's very well founded, but it's how I grew up, it's how I felt about it. It was the queen's fault 'cause governments come and go, and the people that are in power fade from your mind but everybody remembers the queen *[16-year-old Catholic male]*

In contrast, Lora who is from a totally polarized, Protestant neighborhood in east Belfast argues that national identity issues have segregated her area from neighboring Catholic areas. She recognizes the salience of national identities in fomenting the intercommunal conflict.

LORA: I can see how this is research now. I think I'd show him the physical borders and everything. And this wee red line here is supposed to be part of Britain, and so technically if you think about it by law and by this physical wee red line, the queen is the ruler of this country and of Great Britain because we're a part of the U.K. and all that. And then I'd go, but these people don't think that this is quite a good idea; and these people do and they're fighting about it; and they're some people who don't really care; and then there's people who've left and there's people who've come back and people who've come around and don't know about it and so I'd start off with the physical border line and move on. *[16-year-old Protestant female]*

Lora understands the role of national identities in keeping both communities divided in Northern Ireland.

In summary, Tracey and Stan are enthusiastic supporters of royalty, whereas the three Catholic boys recognize but do not identify with the symbolism and longevity of the monarchy. It is not difficult to believe that these differences on national identity anticipate similar differences among Northern Ireland's two traditions. These respondents have acquired a familiarity about some political aspects of the community divide: (1) uncertainty of Northern Ireland's constitutional position leads to tension among the Protestant community; (2) the queen and prime minister are perceived as both prevention agents and causes of terrorism; and (3) terrorism perpetuates the conflict. Relevant political attitudes come to the fore as the realism of these children's accounts of politics captures a broad spectrum of ideas, fears, and responses particular to the Belfast area.

The importance of attitudes and views toward ethnic identity as an important instrument of causation in the Northern Ireland conflict is obvious to any person familiar with the current contemporary strife. This is especially so for the Protestant community. Here, however, Protestant children at the two schools have different views regarding the British monarch. Protestant children from the integrated school are much less likely to see the queen as a symbol of Protestant identity (appendix 2, table 5).

Younger children from both schools are unlikely to mention partition as a cause of conflict (appendix 2, table 6). However, the older children in the nonintegrated school are very likely (much more so than fifth-year pupils at the integrated school) to mention partition. These findings suggest that Protestant fifth-year pupils at the nonintegrated school are fully aware of the ramifications of a United Ireland for Protestant people. They fear that the British government may try to engineer Protestants into a Catholic-dominated Ireland. In previous political crises, Protestants have reacted against any attempt or perceived attempt by the British government to change Northern Ireland's constitutional position within the United Kingdom.

Also, more Protestant than Catholic pupils in this sample mention partition as a cause of conflict in Northern Ireland (appendix 2, table 7). There is a moderate relationship between religion and perceptions of the "border" as a source of conflict. Protestant pupils in both schools are more likely to see the conflict as a result of partition. These differences between Protestant and Catholic children leave little room for doubt with regard to the perceived connection between partition and the Northern Ireland conflict.

Economic Causes of the Conflict

There is considerable evidence to suggest that between 1920 and 1972 the government in Northern Ireland introduced policies to produce economic inequality between Protestants and Catholics. Instances of discrimination in housing, employment, and regional policy have been clearly identified as leading to sectarian divisions in a bipolar society.

IMAGES: HINDU AND PROTESTANT CHILDREN AT THE NONINTEGRATED SCHOOL

Middle-class schoolchildren from the nonintegrated school have already absorbed solidly held middle-class premises about the levels of relative deprivation and political violence within both working-class communities. Nabeel, who is from India, believes that poor, segregated, working-class communities are the recruiting grounds for the urban terrorist:

NABEEL: A lot of people, especially in this school, say that they wouldn't see "the troubles" in Belfast 'cause there's areas of Belfast people just wouldn't go into at all, they hardly know they exist. For example, if you go down the Falls Road, it's a completely different Belfast than down the Malone Road. When you go down there, you can see why there are "troubles," why people join terrorist organizations like, because they don't stay in school like us. *[16-year-old Hindu male]*

Also, implicit in Jessica's interview is the view that working-class people are ignorant, sectarian, and prejudiced. She assumes that middle-class people would not associate with people from the ghettoes.

JESSICA: Those people that go to this school are from quite well-off families. Maybe it's the poor or less educated kids that go to secondary schools that's the way they've been brought up to think about the other side. The other people, you don't associate with them. *[15-year-old Protestant female]*

Nabeel and Jessica quite accurately point out that poverty-stricken neighborhoods spawn prototype terrorists who turn to violence to alleviate their feelings of despair and heighten their sense of pride and fulfillment.

This perception of class differences holds true for the majority of nonintegrated schoolchildren. It is interesting, therefore, to consider illustrative fragments of my interviews with younger middle-class children from the nonintegrated school. The theme of upper-class supremacy is simply a reflection of how these children perceive relationships in Northern Ireland.

William, who lives in a wealthy suburb of southwest Belfast, responds to the unfinished story in which the queen's car is speeding and is stopped by a traffic policeman as follows:

WILLIAM: The police stops the car and they just think it's a very rich person, and they'd have to go reasonably easy on her 'cause they realize that person has a lot of power. *[12-year-old Protestant male]*

Similarly, Cynthia points out that the queen is a very powerful person.

CYNTHIA: They wouldn't want to put her nose out of joint. They would have to be really careful because she could have them arrested if she wanted to. I think she could do that because she has so much power, and anybody who roughly annoys her is dead meat. *[12-year-old Protestant female]*

The fact that these two children see the personage of the queen being above the law illustrates the salience of class in their lives.

But other responses elicit a sense of "fair play," reflecting a belief that everybody is equal before the law. Even though these children are aware that class differences exist in the society, Hazel, Jennifer, and Colin feel that the middle class should not receive preferential treatment.

Hazel believes that all people should be treated the same.

HAZEL: Oh, no, I don't think the world is a very fair place, depending on whether you're upper class or lower class or whatever. People who are more well-off than other people should be treated the same. They should let people with not as much money off rather than letting people who have more money off. *[12-year-old Protestant female]*

Similarly, Jennifer argues that the queen is not above the law.

JENNIFER: She should pay the fine because she's really just the same as us, only a little bit higher in power. She's got more power. But she should pay the fine, and the same with the prime minister. *[11-year-old Protestant female]*

Colin believes that anybody who breaks the law should be punished by the police.

COLIN: The queen sort of says, "I'm very annoyed that the police sort of ignore every law I break. I've as much right to be punished as anyone else in the country. So I'm going to say to the police, or something that they're not dealing with my bad behavior." *[15-year-old Protestant male]*

The fact that these children do not see the queen's behavior as an exception to the rules may help to explain how they extol the virtues of a conservative yet plural democratic society over the actions of any one individual.

IMAGES: CATHOLIC CHILDREN AT THE INTEGRATED SCHOOL

In contrast, the levels of violence, alienation, and poverty in Belfast are caused by class divisions, according to twelve pupils from the integrated school and nine students from the noninte-grated school. Here are some examples of responses by Gerry, Seamus, and Niall, Catholic working-class and middle-class chil-dren attending the integrated school who perceive structural in-equalities in society in general.

Gerry is from the town of Bangor on the Antrim coast. His story implies that poverty and unemployment affects the political situation in Northern Ireland:

GERRY: I don't know if I'd like the queen better, I don't know if this is true or not, but maybe the prime minister is not doing very much about the economy and the way people have to live here. The poor people only get so much to live on every week and they are not coping too well and their stomachs empty and they don't have enough for a house and there are ones out on the streets and he is not doing too much to try to stop all the jobs and all. *[12-year-old Catholic male]*

While Gerry expresses empathy with the homeless, Seamus, who is from Ballyclare, suggests that a wealthy queen ignores the plight of the homeless in the city of Belfast.

SEAMUS: The queen could give some of that money back to the gov-ernment to help with building and give a lot more to charities. Nobody knows how much she gives to charities if she does give any. She should do more for charities and more for the homeless here. *[16-year-old Catholic male]*

Niall is from a large Catholic middle-class family and lives in Ballycastle. Implicit in his story is the knowledge that, within poor housing estates, it is normal practice for young people to be in-volved in violent activities.

NIALL: I know it has a lot to do with class, like in an upper-class area you could still get very rebellious children because they were not allowed to do anything when they were children or when they were teenagers, so the children might rebel over that. But then you can get people the same living in an estate where all the houses are terraced and everything is the same and it can be very rough. *[16-year-old Catholic male]*

These children suggest that there are other structural economic issues, such as poor neighborhoods, unemployment, poverty, and hunger, going on in the society that certainly do not help the politi-cal situation. These assumptions about poverty and alienation are most probably the result of the economic mix of working-class and middle-class children at the integrated school. Such opinions are also more the consequence of the absorption of impressions created from other agents of socialization in the child's own immediate environment, since Catholic males find it more difficult to obtain employment in Belfast.

IMAGES: PROTESTANT AND CATHOLIC CHILDREN AT THE INTEGRATED SCHOOL

The perception of separate treatment for different classes, as in the following responses to the queen and the policeman story, is revealed by George, Joanie, and Patricia, who are first-year Protestant and Catholic pupils at the integrated school. These children suggest that the queen, by virtue of her social position, would be afforded preferential treatment by commoners. George is from the Protestant enclave of the Shankhill Road. He believes that the queen is different from ordinary people.

GEORGE: She wouldn't go out like us shopping and things. She would get her food taken to her by her servants and all. She wouldn't go downstairs and make her tea in the morning. The servants would bring it up to her. She would have bodyguards with her and behind her. *[12-year-old Protestant male]*

Joanie, who is from the working class Ballymurphy neighborhood, believes that the policeman would not punish the queen who is a powerful social elite.

JOANIE: But just say it was the queen that was going fast, then the police would do nothing. Then they're not going to be fair and stick to their own job and say, "Excuse me, can I see your license?" *[12-year-old Catholic female]*

Patricia argues that the policeman will not punish the queen because she is part of the royal family. Patricia lives on the Ormeau Road.

PATRICIA: The police stopped the queen and said that she is going above the speeding limit and the queen will think just because she is higher and that she is royalty that he won't say anything. *[12-year-old Catholic female]*

These young children are of the opinion that the queen or those from a higher social standing would be treated differently from those of a lower social background. We can usefully anchor the foregoing examples of distinct class differences shown by these children to the perception of society being dichotomized by class. This in turn influences how working-class Catholics and Protestants interpret events at the local grassroots level.

These Catholic and Protestant students from the integrated school perceive differences between middle-class and working-class people without incorporating the religious dimension into their analysis of poverty in the province. In effect, they are suggesting that there are other political cleavages at work in the society besides religious differences.

In general, these children suggest that underlying structural inequalities exist in Northern Ireland. As their stories indicate, class differences transcend religious differences. It is clear that children are more aware of, and are sensitive to, unemployment, poverty, and privileges for the wealthy in the society.

Psycho-Cultural Aspects of the Conflict

Protestants and Catholics are mistrustful of one another, do not really communicate at all, and use stereotypes to ensure that both communities live largely in ignorance of each other. It is important to note, however, that this stereotyping is most probably based on ignorance of the other group and lack of social contact. Where various other dimensions combine to lead to a segregated society, a deeply held intolerance and suspicion can readily exacerbate the conflict when a political crisis intensifies fear and punctures the fragile harmony that exists. The actions of any person who is perceived to be a member of the out-group are understood to represent the values of that community. Fear and suspicion determine the nature of relationships and contact in the overall society.

IMAGES: PROTESTANT CHILDREN AT THE NONINTEGRATED SCHOOL

In the story about the queen and the policeman, the interviewer asked a nonintegrated school student to conceive of the main stumbling blocks that prevent people getting together to try and make peace with each other. This is what Jessica had to say:

JESSICA: It's been going on for a long time. It's very prejudiced and very difficult for all the people. I think the government could do a heck of a lot more to try and counteract terrorism because they're just absolutely crazy. *[15-year-old Protestant female]*

Jessica seems to understand that cultural differences are emphasized by both communities, while sectarian violence by rival paramilitary gangs maintain a divided and polarized Northern Ireland.

IMAGES: CATHOLIC AND PROTESTANT CHILDREN AT THE INTEGRATED SCHOOL

Here are three young people—Anne, Trevor, and Donna—from the integrated school and how they relate to psychocultural aspects of the Northern Ireland conflict. Anne is an interesting example of a young woman whose parents are Protestant and Catholic. Mixed marriages are indeed a rare phenomenon in Northern Ireland, partly as a result of Loyalist paramilitary death threats and a refusal to recognize kin across the bicommunal divide.

> ANNE: First-year students come to this school from the Donegall Pass and the Falls Road and they said, "I never realized that Catholics are nice and they didn't beat me up. I always thought their eyes were closer together." These are the wee stories that you hear. I come from a mixed background, so I never really noticed any difference. It's funny listening to some first years and then the way they change their views. After the first year, people don't really care less, it doesn't matter. Religion doesn't really come into it now. *[16-year-old Catholic female]*

Trevor believes that English people are not fully aware of political matters within Northern Ireland.

> TREVOR: A lot of people in Great Britain as a whole don't understand that Northern Ireland and Eire (Republic of Ireland) are two separate entities, which is a bit weird. Therefore, everything has to be changed and people have to understand that. If you're over in England and a bomb comes on the news, people don't understand and they go, "A bomb, Ireland." They don't say Northern Ireland or Eire, they can't comprehend the difference. First of all, you have to understand why things are happening and why things started, and how are you going to stop everything and then get back to the talks again. *[15-year-old Protestant male]*

Trevor believes that we have to understand the nature of the conflict if we are to make a viable intervention to bring about peace. Donna who is from the staunchly Loyalist Belfast neighborhood of Tigers Bay pleads with her friends not to support the violence of the paramilitary groups. She expresses positive social norms about Catholics at her school.

> INTERVIEWER: *When you talk to people in your community, do you think you're having an effect on the way they perceive the world around them?*
>
> DONNA: Sometimes I do. It depends on what that person is like. If they're really, really Protestant and hate Catholics, then it's hard. If you ask them why do they hate them, then they just go, "Well, they go around blowing up people." We're doing that as well, why do you hate them? They say," But that's different," and she says "No, it's not different, it's just the same." It's wild funny, you know, when you get stuck into it. Some people think that because they support the IRA and that they support the UVF and the UDA, but nobody really does. You talk about it but you don't, it depends. *[15-year-old Protestant female]*

Trevor and Donna are agents of social change—Trevor desires a new Northern Ireland, while Donna strives to convince Protestant extremists to think differently about Catholics.

It is interesting to note that the imagery of prejudice as a cause of the conflict was expressed by more fifth- than first-year pupils (appendix 2, table 8). The understanding of such complex factors that underlie group behavior had not yet developed within the individual schemata of the first-year pupils in this sample.

An interesting finding of the study is that a significantly higher percentage of Protestant children in the integrated school mentioned prejudice as a cause of the conflict, than did Protestants in the nonintegrated school (appendix 2, table 9). This may suggest that contact with Catholics in the integrated school is affecting how these Protestant children view the conflict and the Catholic community.

Consequently, the psychocultural orientations of the integrated school's Protestant children appear to be the result of absorption of what the children may have learned from their teachers and peers in the school about how Protestants and Catholics are alike and about how children can make a positive contribution to a more peaceful society.

Responses to/Interpretations of the Conflict

Philosophical Violence

A precipitous increase in the level of violence up to the cease-fires, called by the Provisional IRA and the Combined Loyalist

Military Command during the fall of 1994, leads one to conclude that there is an acceptable level of violence in Northern Ireland. Violence by the paramilitaries continues in neighborhoods as they punish antisocial offenders. In other words, the conflict is perceived as a way of life because these children are growing up and experiencing firsthand what warfare is all about. Some people believe that the conflict is so intractable that it cannot be solved and will continue into the next century. I have selected some interviews that clearly illustrate that violence is a way of life for these young people living in Belfast.

IMAGES: PROTESTANT CHILDREN AT THE NONINTEGRATED SCHOOL

Images of hopelessness or futility are evident in the following interview with Jennifer, a young girl from the nonintegrated school:

INTERVIEWER: *What kind of policies would you like to see the prime minister introduce to combat terrorism in Northern Ireland?*

JENNIFER: They send troops and they sit and discuss it and argue about it, but they really don't do anything. And it's been going on for ages and ages and ages. And just sort it out and get the IRA out because they are just causing nonstop trouble. *[11-year-old Protestant female]*

Jennifer believes that the Provisional IRA are to blame for the continuation of violence, death, and the destruction of property in Northern Ireland.

IMAGES: CATHOLIC AND PROTESTANT CHILDREN AT THE INTEGRATED SCHOOL

Anne and Lora are two fifth-year students in the integrated school. They explore why violence is inevitable in Belfast. Anne is very scared because her father, a Belfast taxi driver, was physically threatened by paramilitary groups in the past. On a number of occassions they put a gun to his head and took his car to "go on a job":

ANNE: I just think it's so stupid the way the fighting is going on. I don't know what's going to stop it. There are only a few schools that are mixed. It just keeps going on, so many people are afraid. They're afraid to do anything, they don't know what to do. It's sick. You don't know why people do it and then come out and say I'm sorry. People mustn't have much conscience if they can just go out and kill somebody and then go home to their family and say "That's OK, good day's work." *[16-year-old Catholic female]*

Lora believes that it is a "no-win" political situation; violence breeds violence, and it will not stop.

LORA: I think the queen, the Loyalists, and the prime minister are hilarious, their ranting and raving about this and this, and there are people getting shot. If they take the troops out, the Loyalists will go haywire, and if they send more troops in, the IRA will go haywire. I said this to my mother, and she said the IRA are haywire anyway. *[16-year-old Protestant female]*

Anne and Lora, in their descriptions of political violence, suggest that the conflict will never end. These stories are told with an incipient awareness of what is going on in everyday life in Belfast. They manage to combine a clear knowledge that violence continues in a milieu that favors its continuation with the fatalistic assumption that it will never cease. Younger-age peers in both schools differ from the older-age groups marginally in their interpretation of the conflict (appendix 2, table 10). The older children in the noninte-grated school do not see the conflict as inevitable. However, the majority of students in both schools do in fact report that political violence is inevitable in Northern Ireland.

On the surface, this awareness of political violence indicates that children from both schools hold a pessimistic view of life in North-ern Ireland, supporting the predominant view in the literature (Coles 1986; Fields 1977; Heskin 1980). The children, especially the younger ones in this study, suggest that the conflict exists in and engenders an environment that perpetuates its continuation.

It might be expected, therefore, that some children in the inte-grated school may actively advocate social change while others hold the passive or apathetic viewpoint that violence is a way of life. Coles (1986) has argued that children become politicized by "the troubles" at an early age but that some are burnt out and apolitical by the time they reach their teens. If this argument about the active early political interests of children leading to a with-drawal from political life by young people is correct, we should find a significantly stronger philosophical viewpoint among the older children that violence is a way of life.

As predicted, fifth-year pupils from the integrated school mentioned that political violence was inevitable in Northern Ireland rather than their counterparts in the nonintegrated school (appendix 2, table 10). Compared to the more optimistic perceptions of fifth-year pupils at the nonintegrated school, the children in the integrated school seemed very aware of the inevitability of political violence in Northern Ireland. It might be speculated that these orientations may have something to do with the demographic balance of the integrated school. The structure of the student population at the school reflects the social structure of the wider society. Many students at the integrated school, from both sides of the communal divide, hail from working-class "hard-line" areas.

Since socioeconomic differences between classes are reinforced and affected by religious segregation, working-class pupils at the integrated school may see the social structure as operating to their disadvantage. Conflict and violence become a way of life for them. As Northern Ireland is one of the most economically disadvantaged regions within the European Union (EU), with a higher-than-average rate of unemployment, many working-class children may not possess a positive orientation toward future political change within Northern Ireland. The possibility, therefore, exists for these trends to continue and even accelerate, if government policies do not tackle the structural causes of unemployment in the province.

Environmental Violence

Catholic and Protestant children from working-class areas hold an apathetic world view, believing society is against them and that they have no way out. They can be "lifted" and beaten by the security forces or receive punishment shootings, or beatings from paramilitaries to "keep them in line" or end up being murdered. Some of these children are obsessed by death, destruction, and a sense of hopelessness. Life is very cheap since the paramilitaries operate successfully within their own communities through intimidation and punishment. Ordinary citizens are afraid to inform the security forces of paramilitary activity; thus violence can be carried out by these groups within their own neighborhoods without fear of any retaliation by the RUC or the security forces. Death and the fear of violence are psychological phenomena which affect one's very daily existence in the province.

Images: Catholic Children at the Integrated School

Even though the interview schedule bore only indirectly on emotional issues and more on behavior relating to the political system in Northern Ireland, the frequency with which Joanie's stories turned to themes of death and violence were too ubiquitous to be accidental. Joanie is from a working-class background in the nationalist Ballymurphy area of the city. She is a pupil at the integrated school. Her apathetic and dismal view of her political world is reflected in her ending to the broken window story:

JOANIE: The police try to find her, and they find her in the British state. Mummy and Daddy didn't hear about this and they went to the fridge where all the bodies are and they had to identify and find out it was the fifth one down. And they find her and they start crying and the funeral is two days after that. The boy that died, Freddie was it we called him, came back to his sister Maria and Maria just sat there in shock. Then he told his mother the truth and she says, "As long as I know I didn't kill you." [12-year-old Catholic female]

In contrast, Anne is a 16-year-old Catholic student at the integrated school. She comes from a mixed family background. Her reference to assassinations and fear of violence have a contextual basis in the 1991 sectarian murders of taxi drivers in Belfast. She seems to imply a prevalent fear of her father, a Protestant, being murdered by either Republican or Loyalist paramilitaries by refracting this feeling through an emotional outburst:

ANNE: People are afraid. There's just so many people being killed. My Dad is a taxi man and he works with a mixed taxi firm. My Dad has been attacked twice by them, once by Catholics and once by Protestants, and neither one knew what religion he was. Once they tried to take his car. My Dad isn't the type who would hand it over to them. He wouldn't give it to them. They pulled out a gun and he went into the house and they pushed their way in the front door and they put a gun to his head, so he had to give them the keys and they took the car and that was that. [16-year-old Catholic female]

Both girls from working-class families have absorbed the perception that Northern Ireland is a very violent place in which to live.

Older children appear less likely to mention violence than the younger children in this study (appendix 2, table 11). A prevalent fear of everyday violence reflects the fundamental differences in the perceptions of children in the two schools. Pupils at the integrated school were more likely to mention that Northern Ireland is a violent place in which to live than were children in the nonintegrated school. One possible explanation that might explain these differences is that those outside the kin group in Northern Ireland are considered strangers and outsiders, no matter how close their contacts might be with one another in some respects. The result is that both Catholics and Protestants live in segregated neighborhoods and remain in complete isolation from the other community's way of life. The fear of those outside one's family and neighborhood is projected onto the larger society. Some of the integrated schoolchildren live in violent neighborhoods compared to the nonintegrated schoolchildren who reside in middle-class cosmopolitan areas.

Solutions/Mechanisms of Change

Since the outbreak of "the troubles" in 1968, many possible solutions to the Northern Ireland conflict have been put forward by politicians, scholars, policy makers, and grassroots activists. What all of these approaches have in common is that trying to find a solution that both communities can live with is like trying to find water in the desert. In this section, however, I discuss issues that various children in the sample found appropriate as possible structural and psycho-cultural mechanisms to reduce community tensions and prevent the outbreak of further violence.

Law and Order As a Solution/Mechanism of Change

Law and order issues were given priority by a number of students as a means to curb terrorist activities in the province. Six pupils from the integrated school and five students from the nonintegrated school proposed that the queen is in a strong political position to uphold democracy in Northern Ireland.

IMAGES: PROTESTANT CHILDREN AT THE NONINTEGRATED SCHOOL

More pupils from the nonintegrated school are of the opinion that the prime minister is in much more of a strategic and vital position to prevent terrorism than the queen. The viewpoints of

Michael and Hazel clarify the notion of the prime minister's actual political powers.

Michael is from the Malone Road, a residentially mixed, affluent area, near the Queen's University. He articulates the influence of the prime minister in preventing terrorism within Northern Ireland:

> MICHAEL: The prime minister and the government send over soldiers to govern Northern Ireland and keep it in order. That's important because without British soldiers over here there would be quite a lot of chaos. Terrorists totally destroy families and communities and stuff and recently there's been a lot of bombs. And if there was no law there would be more bombing and fear, I suppose, in Northern Ireland. *[15-year-old Protestant male]*

Hazel views the political role of the prime minister as strategically important in the war against terrorism.

> HAZEL: The queen doesn't have an awful lot to do with what happens, and the government and the prime minister are trying to do a lot to help because of the IRA. They're trying to change things, as it were, so the prime minister is probably more important in my view. *[12-year-old Protestant female]*

These assumptions about public authorities' reaction to terrorism exhibit a degree of awareness of the imagined importance of both the queen's and the prime minister's actual political roles. These children are also aware of the significance of the democratic plural process in any strident movement toward peace and stability in the province.

It is interesting to note that most support for the security forces emanates predominantly from Protestant students at the nonintegrated school. In the story about crossing a dangerous road, the interviewer found that the children carry out the policeman's wishes out of obedience, trust, and respect. This may be in part due to the conservative nature of Northern Irish society or to the fact that the security forces are invariably made up of Protestants who protect the wider society against Republican and Loyalist terrorism. Here are one student's comments which illustrate differences in opinion regarding the security forces. Jessica is a fifth-year pupil from the nonintegrated school:

> INTERVIEWER: *What are the main stumbling blocks that prevent people getting together and trying to make peace with each other?*

JESSICA: It's been going on for a long, long time. It's very prejudiced and very difficult for all people. I think the government and the army could do a heck of a lot more to try and counteract terrorism because they're just absolutely crazy. *[15-year-old Protestant female]*

Jessica would like to see more British troops on the streets of Belfast to combat the terrorist activities of the Provisional IRA.

Images: Catholic and Protestant Children at the Integrated School

Here are some examples of Gerry's and Trevor's responses about how one would expect the queen to act against terrorists in Northern Ireland. They are both students at the integrated school.

Although Gerry believes that the queen should do more to prevent violence, he appears to be intolerant of Protestants. He believes that the queen should banish Protestants to the mainland because "Ireland is for the Irish":

GERRY: The queen would be trying to stop "the troubles" and sort something out between them, and maybe this would stop the fighting and make everyone live happily ever after, and if anyone was caught they would be put in jail for life or something like that there, it would stop it. Or she could take all the Protestants and force them all to go back to England and maybe because in Ireland most of it is Catholic and that it should be Catholic, or something like that there. *[12-year-old Catholic male]*

Trevor who comes from the seaside town of Larne suggests that the queen should not remain politically neutral. This view, and his argument that "the queen should stop the terrorists," informs his preference for political intervention from the head of state.

TREVOR: If the queen did make a commitment and come out against terrorism it would work well, but I don't think she would because I feel that the queen would like to stay in between everything and sort of instruct the government on what she would like to happen, but she does come out and condemn the bombings, but she can't be seen to go strongly for one side or the other. She doesn't agree with either of the sides conducting the bombings, so she condemns them both, and she's right. *[15-year-old Protestant male]*

These descriptions demonstrate a specific understanding of the queen's importance as a political actor in dealing with terrorists in

Northern Ireland. Both of these young men seem confused between the political roles of the head of state and the head of government, believing that the queen is actually in a stronger political
position to prevent violence.

An integrated school fifth-year pupil, Seamus, believes that the
police are doing a good job, reflecting a strong approval of police
action against the paramilitaries:

> INTERVIEWER: *Would that resentment of the police be for both
> communities?*
>
> SEAMUS: It is now, yes. It never used be. It used to be just the
> Catholics, but now that the police are doing a more efficient job, so
> that they're stopping Protestants and Catholics from murdering people.
> They're trying to protect everyone now. But I don't resent the police
> because it's really only them protecting me. It's only them protecting
> me from all the other types of people around here. *[16-year-old Catho-
> lic male]*

In the wake of past security measures directed mainly against the
minority community, it is interesting to note that this Catholic student supports police efforts to curb terrorist crime. If there is any
lingering ambiguity about whether Seamus's feelings toward the
security forces are positive, there is no doubt when he continues
to support police actions in his story. Here are his further remarks
on this point of view:

> SEAMUS: There's been a lot of times I've been very happy to see the
> police around here. I think everybody resents them a bit because you
> could get lifted and get a kicking. That's the police, they're only doing
> their job right. But I think they're doing their job better than they ever
> have been.

The possibility of tougher law and order measures leading toward
a lasting solution to the Northern Ireland conflict is an important
and interesting discovery. The measures proposed by pupils suggested support for public authorities in Northern Ireland. The two
communities' experience of violence has been dramatic, and the
upsurge in terrorist atrocities during the course of the field research certainly impacted the lives of these children.[6] Attitudes
toward both paramilitary organizations and security forces are
quite hardened as everyday violent actions intensify polarization.

The British government has reacted to terrorist organizations in
a number of ways. A policy of criminalization ended internment
and special category status for political prisoners, resulting in the

Republican Hunger Strikes of 1981; Ulsterization increased the use of both the RUC and UDR in the maintenance of law and order in Northern Ireland, while the application of a shoot-to-kill policy and a supergrass system alienated the minority community from the political institutions and democratic processes in Northern Ireland.

Catholic students are more skeptical than Protestant students about the ability of the government (police, army, etc.) to control the conflict (appendix 2, table 12).[7] The security forces in Northern Ireland are perceived by the minority community as being immune from prosecution and as being biased against Catholics. It does not hold, however, that the security forces per se are invariably popular among both communities. In the wake of the Anglo-Irish Accord of 1985 and the 1995 Framework for Peace, members of the RUC were attacked as (former Irish prime minister) "Haughey's police" and "Lundy's" (traitors) by Protestant extremists for upholding the law. The overuse of plastic bullets and political assassinations has also created mistrust and suspicion among some members of the Catholic community toward the security forces.[8]

Integrated Education As a Solution/Mechanism of Change

Apart from the small but growing integrated education structure, there is total segregation in the Northern Ireland education system, since Protestant and Catholic children go to separate schools (appendix 1). The establishment of integrated schooling may help to break the vicious circle that encourages prejudice and sectarianism to thrive and to allow an atmosphere of true community spirit to flourish instead. The cultural and historical cues from which children learn their ethnic discrimination and differences could be transformed as they learn from one other. The integrated sector could assist in lessening community tensions because the experience of parents, teachers, and pupils would spread to the broader society. However, cultural hostility and historical bitterness may be structurally too deep for integrated schooling to make any significant difference.

IMAGES: PROTESTANT AND CATHOLIC CHILDREN AT THE INTEGRATED SCHOOL

The fifth-year students at the integrated school tend to feel, however, that their experiences have had a positive impact on their way of thinking and behaving. Here are some examples of Ronnie, Anne, Niall, and Seamus's responses on the importance of integrated schooling in changing perceptions and behavior:

Ronnie suggests that integrated education is an important building block in creating a democratic and peaceful society in Northern Ireland.

INTERVIEWER: *How important is integrated education?*

RONNIE: It's extremely important because it's the future of everything that's happening here because it's going to be the next step towards peace and it's very important as the building blocks for a United Ireland. I like the social scene. There's integration in more ways than just the Protestant and Catholics getting together. It's like everybody getting together in social groups. *[16-year-old Protestant male]*

Anne sees integration as complex, involving people getting together across, not only the religious, but other divides as well.

INTERVIEWER: *What is it about this integrated school that makes it so unique?*

ANNE: You're not only getting Catholics and Protestants together, you're getting different classes together, like middle-class, working-class and upper-class [people], and then you can see that even different classes don't get on. I just think it's the atmosphere here. You come in and you think that Catholics will stay on this side and Protestants will stay on that side. This is what they expect, but if you throw all of them in together, you can't tell by looking at someone whether they're Catholic or Protestant. *[16-year-old Catholic female]*

According to Niall, the experience of integrated schooling has changed a number of children's attitudes about conflict and cross-community relationships.

INTERVIEWER: *How do you see change happening within society? What things do you think are important, and what role if any has integrated education got to play?*

NIALL: It has a big part to play. If every school in this country was integrated, it would change a hell of a lot of people's attitudes. Like when you came here first in first year now you're getting, "Oh, like you're a Protestant and you're a Catholic" and a lot of apprehension, but now there's none of that there now, like our whole fifth year know each other and we get on fine. There are never any arguments and there are never any fights. Like there are fights in first and second year, but probably over girlfriends or something, but there hasn't been a fight now in three years. *[16-year-old Catholic male]*

Seamus argues that for both Catholic and Protestant children, it is the experience of integrated education, not explanation or argument, that can alter what would most likely become lifelong prejudices about the other group.

INTERVIEWER: *Is it the parents that are reinforcing the conflict?*

SEAMUS: A lot of people can't learn because it's what they've known since they were kids. If they come to a school like this, they'll get along, but when they go home they'll have friends and they'll say you're going to a Catholic school or you're going to a Protestant school. It's too hard for the kids to explain that it is a mixed school. He'll just be doing what his friends are telling him to do. *[16-year-old Catholic male]*

These opinions about the role of integrated schooling may be the direct result of this school's integrative ethos and prosocial atmosphere. It appears that the process has had a profound influence on the way these youngsters perceive one another and the surrounding society. The issue of the role of integrated education as one possible means for the change of the Northern Ireland conflict from a zero-sum situation to a win-win outcome is raised predominantly by the integrated school's Catholic pupils. Among the most noteworthy findings is the fact that there is some variation between the opinions of Catholics and Protestants (appendix 2, table 13).

This item is quite important as a difference between the political attitudes of Protestants and Catholics in both schools. Catholic pupils at the integrated school are markedly more committed to the idea of integrated education leading to a more plural society. Therefore the integrated environment does not appear to have much of an effect on Protestant children in this sample. However, some Protestants in the integrated school do support and advocate more integrated schooling. The difference revealed in the variables could be interpreted as the belief of Catholic respondents in the integrative educational structure as a positive mechanism and contributor to change in Northern Ireland's society and they have much to gain from such social change. Further research is needed to test this preliminary finding in a more in-depth and broader study of integrated schools in Northern Ireland.

It would appear that the experience of the integrated school has been a major determinant in the attitudes of Catholic rather than Protestant children in this sample. These Catholic students seem to suggest that integrated education may assist in transforming psychocultural perceptions of the "other" in Northern Ireland. It can be concluded that integrated education may be an important step to the personal growth and moral development of some of the older pupils attending the integrated school.

Perceptions of Possible Social Change

The Northern Ireland "troubles" have been perpetuated for so many generations because the conflict is embedded in a complex intermeshing of forces that drives a solid wall of ideological steel between the two ethnoreligious groups. The seeming intractability of this ethnoreligious conflict appears not to hold out much hope for a peaceful settlement, but a lasting solution may be reached by a peacebuilding process from the grassroots up which proceeds gradually in intermediate stages (Byrne 1995; Moxon-Browne 1983).

Are the children interviewed in this study optimistic about the future of Northern Ireland and their role within it? Half of our total sample believe that change is possible. Ten children from the integrated school and seven students from the nonintegrated school tend to think of the conflict as having some positive outcome. However, one could contend that their reasons differ.

IMAGES: PROTESTANT AND HINDU CHILDREN AT THE NONINTEGRATED SCHOOL

It is important to list examples of the nonintegrated school's perceptions of possible social change. It is to this task that we now turn as we outline Russell's, Melissa's and Nabeel's opinions about possible social change.

Russell epitomizes Protestant feelings of insecurity, siege, and fear of the unknown. He highlights Protestant suspicions of future change and what it will bring to the people of Northern Ireland:

INTERVIEWER: *Do you see any possibility for peace and reconciliation between both traditions?*

RUSSELL: Yeah, I do, actually, because the Protestants and the Catholics, even though they hated each other for years, it's never been the majority hating each other, it's always the minority who want to stir things up and change things. Whereas the majority would like to keep it sane and maybe change democratically. But at the moment, they can't really stop it going back to the South. It will eventually because the balance will change. Everything will change. But there will be reconciliation at one stage, whether that'll be going back to the South or if it stays and the IRA just give up the struggle and the Loyalist groups just wise up. *[15-year-old Protestant male]*

Melissa believes that the prime minister will find it very difficult to accommodate Protestants who feel that their Britishness has been put in jeopardy by the pandering of the British government to the Catholic community. This is what she had to say about the issue:

INTERVIEWER: *What would you perceive as being the major difference or powers between the queen and prime minister and how is that important for Northern Ireland?*

MELISSA: I think the prime minister has more importance to Northern Ireland because of "the troubles" trying to solve it. I think he plays a more important role in Northern Ireland. He has to sort out Northern Ireland and try to come to a solution of how to try to stop "the troubles." It's a big problem. *[15-year-old Protestant female]*

Nabeel is of the opinion that if one resides in an affluent neighborhood then Northern Ireland is a typically normal society. It is in the impoverished working-class areas where violence impinges the daily lives of people that are not normal places to live in. This is what he had to say:

INTERVIEWER: *Is there anything else you wish to add?*

NABEEL: When my Dad first came to Northern Ireland I was eight or nine at the time, I had visions of wearing a bullet-proof jacket and dodging these bullets and bombs and grenades coming at me. It was ridiculous that idea. It is quite normal here, but then again there are some parts that are not normal places. That's one of the things about Northern Ireland. *[16-year-old Hindu male]*

Nabeel suggests that Northern Ireland is a typically normal society except for the terrorist attrocities that are committed by the unemployed and working-class members of paramilitary organizations.

IMAGES: CATHOLIC CHILDREN AT THE INTEGRATED SCHOOL

The following are examples of responses by Anne, Niall, and James, fifth-year Catholic children from the integrated school, those with, perhaps, the most to gain from any kind of peaceful rapprochement with the Protestant community.

Anne is tolerant in her perceptions of the Protestant community drawing on her upbringing in a mixed family environment, where religiously diverse values are practiced:

INTERVIEWER: *What is it about the school that makes the first years change?*

ANNE: Two boys come from within the same area, Finaghy; one was Catholic and one was Protestant and they knew each other vaguely. They both came from separate gangs. They came in and they were best friends, it was no in-betweens. It wasn't that they were best pals, because one was different from the other, but because they wanted to be friends, they realized there isn't any difference really. My Mum is Catholic and my Dad is Protestant. When they got married it was such a big thing, and they got married very young. They're now married 24 years through all their differences. If you want to make it work you can make it work. It depends just whether you're narrow-minded. *[16-year-old Catholic female]*

Niall is from the village of Ballycastle, situated among the rolling hills of County Antrim. He believes that a peaceful solution to the conflict is possible.

INTERVIEWER: *Is that the one you liked best?*

NIALL: Peter Brooke, now he's been over having meetings with John Major and all, trying to sort something out about this country, and he has called cease-fires. There was a cease-fire called last Christmas, but even though it lasted just for a week it was still his doing and it was up to him that it happened and he has helped a bit and he's still trying. He hasn't given up; he still tries because he cares. Peter Brooke realizes that this is a beautiful country and there are nice people in it and he just wants to help us. It's not our fault, and if he can change people's attitudes, the religion now would be a big one. *[16-year-old Catholic male]*

In the following story James articulates that the building of a "common ground" between Northern Ireland's politicians is possible at the federal European level.

INTERVIEWER: *What would you see as an idyllic solution?*

JAMES: The European thing that could work, there are quite a few M.E.P.s [Members of the European Parliament], and if they could get together in Europe, it could be common ground. There would be no way that anybody could condemn them, whereas there has been trouble with the Brooke Talks about whether to have the talks in Europe; there would be common ground and it might work. But it's all going to have to start from education because how do politicians start thinking the way they do. *[15-year-old Catholic male]*

These assumptions about social change are the result of the children's experience in the school, buttressed by other agents of socialization, such as the family. Older children in an integrated environment may become more tolerant over time in their behavior and political attitudes and their orientations toward members of the other community.

I have deliberately selected these interviews to provide clear illustrations of parts one and two of a thesis: (1) that middle-class Protestant children from the nonintegrated school perceive Northern Ireland to be a "normal" society because they are insulated from the conflict by being isolated from contentious and troubled areas in the city of Belfast and (2) that reconciliation between Catholics and Protestants necessitates a change of the status quo for middle-class Protestants that would also be to the benefit of Northern Ireland's working-class Protestants and Catholics.

Summary and Conclusions

One of the most striking findings is the greater optimism found only among fifth-year children in the nonintegrated school. These differences may arise because these children are aware that they will have the opportunity to leave Northern Ireland some day to work or to attend university in Britain. Also, this sample of Protestant pupils appear to be politically more aware than the other three age groups in the study, suggesting a different learning pattern. It would appear that first-year pupils in the nonintegrated school are socialized into thinking that conflict is inevitable in Northern Ireland. In contrast, 60 percent of the sample in the integrated school live in "hard-line" areas, where violence is an everyday occurrence. Their geographic location may explain their negative attitudes toward the conflict, violence, and paramilitarism.

Certain political causes of the Northern Ireland conflict, such as religion and partition, are more likely to be discussed by fifth-year Protestant pupils in the nonintegrated school because of the identity significance these issues hold for Protestants in general. Of Protestant children in the nonintegrated school, 73 percent hold benign views of the queen, whom they regard as a symbol of their national identity. It seems that these pupils also support law and order issues and actively oppose PIRA terrorism.[9] It must be pointed out that Protestant and Catholic children in the integrated school also oppose terrorists. The most important difference between Protestant children in both schools was the greater sensitivity of the integrated children to the possibility that prejudicial behavior might be a cause of the conflict.

On the whole, childhood learning patterns regarding conflict in Northern Ireland differ for both age groups in the integrated school. Knowledge about the different roles of religious, political, economical, and psychocultural factors in their political environment developed gradually in the sample of children studied here. It was interesting to note that only the fifth-year children from the integrated school advocated more integration as a possible solution to the conflict. None of the pupils in the nonintegrated school did so. Close friendship ties and the openness of the integrated school may be influencing the way these older children perceive the "other."

There appears to be no major fundamental difference in the political attitudes of Protestant children in this sample.[10] The uniformity in this group's political orientations may be explained within the context of majority/minority dynamics. Traditionally, majorities tend to be less sensitive to minority opinion. However, the distribution of opinions was not random regarding all aspects of the bicommunal divide. More Protestant children in the nonintegrated school mentioned the queen as a symbol of their identity. Protestants in the integrated school, on the other hand, mentioned prejudicial behavior as a cause of the conflict, and some made cynical remarks about the queen, which I was quite surprised to hear. The attitude in the latter case may be the result of Protestants mingling with Catholic children within the context of an integrated setting. Catholic support for integrated education as a possible solution to the conflict, rather than PIRA violence, is also a positive finding.

While there may have been some age and school variations, such differences may not be manifested at the macro level, thus raising a level of analysis problem for children's political development theory. At the micro level, integrated school researchers have found important differences (Hughes 1995; Irwin 1991, 1995; Moffatt 1993; Stephenson 1991; Wright 1990), but at the macro level, further studies are necessary to build on this research to include other schools and variables, since other agents of socialization may affect the behavior of children in the integrated and nonintegrated educational structures. Further research is needed to build on this exploratory study to include more schools from the integrated and nonintegrated environments to contrast the possible effects of the schools and other agents of socialization on children's developing perceptions of politics within Northern Ireland.

My results indicate that if we want to understand ethnoregional and international conflicts, we must understand children's perceptions of their own political reality. These findings suggest that children's political development theory needs to incorporate an understanding of children in conflict regions into its theoretical framework. To date, the theory has a very narrow notion of children in conflict zones (Cairns 1987; Coles 1986; Garbarino et al. 1990; Fields 1976; Straker 1992). The study of children can also be important and sometimes more important than any other mechanisms of researching ethnoreligious conflicts in order to seek a peaceful settlement and movement toward peaceful change and coexistence. Cooperative contact to create equal status among both groups in the integrated school appears to be working. However, further studies are necessary to include more schools to test some of the interesting findings in this comparative case study of Protestant and Catholic children in two schools in Belfast, Northern Ireland.

6
How Children Think and Feel about Political Authority Figures

Introduction

In this chapter, I discuss schoolchildren's orientations toward political authority, examining their ideas concerning the queen and prime minister with empirical evidence. In a previous study, Greenstein and Tarrow (1970a, 1970b) have noted the symbolic significance of both political roles in the political learning of English children. They allude to young English children's more benign views of the queen and older children's more balanced interpretations of the prime minister, especially the detail they use in describing the separation of powers and the political significance of the two political roles.

The political symbolism of the queen and prime minister also plays an important role in the socialization of Protestant and Catholic children in Northern Ireland. The queen and the royal family are forever in public view as a symbol of British historical values and traditions, evoking a sense of loyalty and duty from the public. The queen, as head of state and of the Reformed Church of England, is an important political and religious symbol of the Britishness of Northern Ireland's Protestants and of their Protestantism (Miller 1978). The queen having no partisan political affiliation generates popular support and loyalty from Northern Irish Protestants, who fear betrayal by Her Majesty's government, and who live in a state of constant siege. Protestants are fearful and suspicious of political change and are alienated from the British government and the prime minister (Dunn and Morgan 1994). The queen and the prime minister do not hold the same political or religious significance for Northern Ireland's Catholic community (Whyte 1990).

Consequently, the open-ended storytelling method is used to

133

elicit evidence of how the Belfast schoolchildren in this study imagine the political behavior of such important components of British political culture and socialization processes: the queen and the prime minister. The central questions that I will examine in this chapter are (1) What are children's perceptions of both leaders? and (2) Are there similarities or differences between age groups and between schools?

This empirical analysis of schoolchildren's images of political authority in Belfast, Northern Ireland, builds new databases to understand children's political life in regional ethnic conflicts. The data used in this chapter and the empirical work undertaken are a preliminary step in this direction. This chapter adds to our understanding of political development, political behavior, and conflict resolution from a politico-psychological perspective.

Explanation of the Role of the Queen to a Foreign Child

The political role about which Belfast schoolchildren had a comprehensive degree of knowledge, especially at the younger age levels studied, is that of the head of state. In this study, specific differences emerge in the cognition of first-year children's descriptions of the queen. All of the integrated school children tended to think of the monarch as the effective head of state, whereas half of the nonintegrated grammar school first-year children suggested an awareness of the queen's status as a political figurehead, yet an important personage.

IMAGES: YOUNGER CHILDREN AT THE NONINTEGRATED SCHOOL

We now turn to the responses of first-year children from the nonintegrated school, who exhibit a similar pattern of loyalty to the monarch firmly enthroned as the actual ruler of Britain. Doug is a young Protestant child from the Malone area of the city close to the Queen's University. The queen is described in a benign fashion by Doug, who has not yet fully comprehended the effective role of the head of state:

INTERVIEWER: *Suppose he says, "Tell me what the queen is?" What would you say?*

DOUG: The queen is a member of the royal family. There's been a king and queen for years. When she's married she tells the prime minister if he can do things or if he can't do things. When she dies her son or daughter takes over from her and carries on the job.

INTERVIEWER: *What if he said to you, "What does she do?"*

DOUG: Well, I don't really know what she does. She tells the government what they can do. I don't know what else she does. *[12-year-old Protestant male]*

Tracey, comparing the British prime minister to the president of the United States, has not really absorbed the real differences between head of state and head of government. Like Doug, she holds an idealistic image of how important politically the queen is to the people of Northern Ireland. Tracey is from an affluent Protestant neighborhood in south Belfast and believes that everybody should respect the queen:

INTERVIEWER: *Suppose he says, "Tell me what the queen is?" What would you say?*

TRACEY: I would say that America has a president and we have a prime minister, but the queen, she's the leader of Great Britain. She's the one that's in charge. I don't think that there's anyone higher than her. She's a member of the royal family. They're very important and they have Buckingham Palace; that's over in England. They go to different countries and they're sort of in with prime ministers of other countries. The queen goes to different places and stuff and she tries to go to different places and enjoy herself. But she's still very important and has loads of bodyguards; you may sometimes see her on the news. If he was ever in England he should go to Buckingham Palace and then he would know. But if he ever goes to an important castle, like Windsor, and if he sees a flag flying outside, he know's she's in there. All the people are expected to respect her as their queen.

INTERVIEWER: *What if he said to you, "What does she do?"*

TRACEY: She makes decisions like whereabouts do you intend to hold important meetings. She sort of bosses about the government and stuff. *[12-year-old Protestant female]*

The imagery of symbolism, benevolence, and positive affect in Tracey's description of the queen is common in all of these children's references to the monarch. Their imaginative and colorful stories have striking similarities and exhibit a clear pattern of cognitive development; both Tracey and Doug have yet to separate the political roles of the queen and the prime minister.

However, the following examples from the nonintegrated school exhibit a quite different set of assumptions about the notion of the crown as the actual leader and powerhouse of the British polity. Hazel and Teddy demonstrate in a solid and clearminded way the royal lineage system by which monarchs come to the throne in Britain. Here is how they describe the crown's role to a strange child from a faraway country.

Hazel is from a wealthy, predominantly Protestant suburb of south Belfast, where political violence does not really affect the everyday lives of its residents compared to other residential areas within Belfast:

INTERVIEWER: *Suppose he says, "Tell me what the queen is?" What would you say?*

HAZEL: The queen is the monarch. They used to be in charge of the country, but now the government are in charge. She is an important person, a bit like the president. She travels on royal occasions. It's usually the one family that the monarchs come from. When the queen dies or decides to give up the throne, her eldest son or daughter would become the king or queen. The queen is sort of the ruler of the land, but she doesn't actually have a lot to do with the government and what happens in the country.

INTERVIEWER: *What if he said to you, "What does she do?"*

HAZEL: An awful lot of the royal family and the queen especially are in charge of charities. They being in charge can often help people giving money to charities because they think it's good. If she wasn't there people would probably rebel. She sort of keeps the peace or whatever and she works with foreign relations and stuff like that. *[12-year-old Protestant female]*

Teddy has been brought up in the residentially mixed, middle-class Malone Road neighborhood of Belfast. His father is a civil servant. He depicts the figurehead role of the queen in his story:

INTERVIEWER: *Suppose he says, "Tell me what the queen is?" What would you say?*

TEDDY: Well, I'd probably say that the queen is instead of a president; she isn't exactly elected, it's just the family of the person that ruled the country, and the oldest child would be the king or the queen, or whatever. But she doesn't really rule the country because the political parties do most of it.

INTERVIEWER: *What if he said to you, "What does she do?"*

TEDDY: If people do particularly courageous things, she gives them medals, knighthoods, and she visits hospitals and opens places. *[12-year-old Protestant male]*

Hazel and Teddy's assumptions about the specific functions and role of the monarch demonstrate a vivid understanding of the head of state's status as a figurehead and the queen's subservient relationship to the prime minister. This may in part be explained by the fact that middle-class grammar school children are more exposed to politics in the home and by the media and have moved toward a more sophisticated and concrete stage of cognitive development than their first-year working-class counterparts in the integrated school.

IMAGES: YOUNGER CHILDREN AT THE INTEGRATED SCHOOL

In answer to the open-ended question regarding the queen, children in this study were asked to portray themselves explaining the role of the monarch to an imaginary foreign child. Here is how some Protestant and Catholic first-year boys at the integrated school responded to this episode.

Richard, for example, a 12-year-old Protestant boy from the Village very close to Queen's University, makes statements such as the following in depicting what he imagines to be a powerful political role for the queen:

INTERVIEWER: *For example, suppose he says. "Tell me what the queen is?" What would you say?*

RICHARD: The queen is a person that rules the land. If she says jump, you jump. She's a member of the royal family and is very important for the people in this country. She's a nice lady and she's very friendly.

INTERVIEWER: *What if he said to you, "What does she do?"*

RICHARD: She looks after her dogs in the countryside. She goes to Parliament and makes speeches and meets the prime minister at her palace and gives him her laws to carry out. But she doesn't get to choose how long people get to go to prison. She visits foreign countries and she makes decisions just like at the minute of joining Europe and having ambassadors. Things like that, telling the governments to do this and do that.

The fact that the prime minister attends Buckingham Palace to have a private and secret audience with the queen once a week suggests that Richard may perceive that the head of state is actually the head of government, with the prime minister being summoned to receive his or her orders for the week. For Richard, this omnipotent and powerful lady is very important for the people of "this country," Northern Ireland, because he believes she can delegate her laws to the prime minister and he or she must obey the queen. However, the British monarch, contrary to the portrayal in Richard's description, can advise and influence the prime minister but has no real power over the head of government. Richard may understand, respect, and admire the queen, but it is the prime minister and his or her cabinet who makes the rules and regulations that he has to live by.

Patrick is a young Catholic boy who comes from the nationalist Anderstown district of Belfast. Patrick loves to play soccer with his friends and he likes to watch soccer matches on the television. Patrick confuses the queen's husband, Prince Philip, with Queen Victoria's husband, Prince Albert, and demonstrates nationalist feelings by identifying with the Irish Republic:

INTERVIEWER: *For example, suppose he says, "Tell me what the queen is?" What would you say?*

PATRICK: The queen is a person who is higher than any other in the United Kingdom. She is wealthy and you should always speak highly of her. I'd tell her about the family and who is the heir of the throne and that her mammy was a queen once and Charles would be the next king. That there were kings and queens in the United Kingdom for hundreds of years. They always ruled the land. She is in charge of England, Scotland, Wales, Northern Ireland, but not the Republic of Ireland. The southern Irish have their own government, and they don't believe that someone from another country could come in and take over and so they have their own government. Our national anthem is about her. She usually goes to all the big sporting contests, the FA Cup Final, Ascot, and I'd tell them all about that. She's been to a lot of countries. She's married to Prince Albert, I think, I don't really know. It's very confusing the way she is a queen but he's only a prince. Some people think that if she is queen, he should be a king.

In describing the head of state to the foreign child, Patrick provides an animated and lively description of the queen's public role—visiting the sick in hospitals, attending national sporting venues, looking after the needs of her subjects, and wearing the magical attire that befits her role as absolute sovereign of the United Kingdom:

INTERVIEWER: *What does she do?*

PATRICK: She goes to other countries and meets kings and queens; sometimes Princess Diana comes along and they go to hospitals.

They're usually good with children or say if you were sick or had cancer or something. They have some sort of ceremony, I don't know what it is, where they have their crowns and their cloaks on and they all go up to the queen as she's sitting and sometimes she goes to the House of Parliament. She listens to what the Labour and Conservative Parties have to say and what they can do to make the U.K. a better place to live in. *[12-year-old Catholic male]*

Patrick's imagery of both the government and the shadow cabinet gathering in the House of Lords at the opening of Parliament to hear the queen's speech from the throne, which in fact is written by the prime minister, is provided with very clear understanding and accuracy.

The prime minister is the real political ruler of the United Kingdom, sheltering behind the queen who appears as omnipotent political power. The prime minister appears to take a back seat as the ceremonial trappings of the monarchy are projected by the media to a receptive British public (Sampson 1973). The historical continuity and cultural tradition the monarchy brings to Northern Ireland and Britain is evoked in Patrick's description of the queen. However, even though Patrick is well informed of the symbolism and benevolence of the monarchy, he does not appear to be aware of the queen's limitation of power. His perception of the leadership aspect of British politics reflects his own sense of positive affect rather than the reality of what the constitutional monarchy actually stands for.

Diana, an 11-year-old Protestant female, lives in a Protestant working-class neighborhood off the Shankhill Road in West Belfast. She thinks that the queen is a beautiful lady who looks after the interests of her subjects. She believes that the queen rules over the prime minister:

INTERVIEWER: *What does she do?*

DIANA: She is someone of authority, and if she thinks you are doing good she can make you very high. She goes and visits other countries. She has a crown she wears on special occasions and she can rule over the prime minister and if he does something wrong she can tell him what to do. *[11-year-old Protestant female]*

Diana appears to believe that the queen is the most powerful political figure in the United Kingdom and that the monarch's power supersedes those of the head of government, the ministers, and members of Parliament.

The underlying political assumptions that a first-year child, Joanie, from the integrated school has already absorbed are fully expressed in the following description of royalty and the individual political imagery of the monarch. Joanie comes from the Ballymurphy district of Belfast. This is what she had to say:

INTERVIEWER: *What does she do?*

JOANIE: Och, aye. The queen is a very important person, she has a lot of money. She's the richest person in the world, isn't she? Royalty, she goes a lot of places. She's got lots of sons and daughters, they have a big family, and she lives in England, in London in a lovely big castle. *[12-year-old Catholic female]*

Joanie's portrayal of the monarch focuses on the wealth accrued by the royal family, suggesting that a 12-year-old girl from a working-class background has already begun to notice the salience of class differences in society. As we noticed in the last chapter, children in the integrated school are tuned into the role that economics, poverty, and unemployment play in Northern Ireland.

The British public celebrate their country's historical past and cultural heritage by taking pride in the political symbolism of the monarchy. This pride in turn leads to political stability and the public's loyalty to the British system of stable government and liberal democracy. Northern Irish Protestants are loyal to the institution embodied in the personage of the queen because she protects their ethnoreligious identity. The monarch is both head of state and head of the Anglican Church. Her Majesty's government takes an oath of allegiance to the queen. Northern Irish Protestants are respectful of the queen but are not deferential or loyal to the queen's government. In general, these children's stories combine images of royalty, benevolence, and positive affect with the effective power of the crown that places the monarch at the center of a hierarchical power structure dominating Parliament, its members, and the prime minister.

IMAGES: OLDER CHILDREN AT THE NONINTEGRATED SCHOOL

Realistic political imagery of the effective power of the queen is depicted in the following explanations of the queen's importance by Nabeel and Jessica, fifth-year pupils from the nonintegrated school whose overall level of political information fits within the final concrete stage of Piaget's cognitive sophistication model.

Nabeel lives with his parents and brothers in a mixed upper-middle-class area in Craigavon. He presents an informative description of the symbolic and traditional significance of the queen in preserving the status quo within the United Kingdom:

INTERVIEWER: *Suppose he says, "Tell me what the queen is?" What would you say?*

NABEEL: Like, say, the queen is supposed to be the ruler of the country, is titled as the ruler of the country, and it is something that people in Britain have kept for a long time, having this queen, having royal family, and things. It's a pretty archaic system. I know everyone agrees with it, but there's a lot of tradition behind it. It could be quite difficult to remove it. A lot of people would feel you were destroying something, like destroying an old monument, if you took away the monarchy. Then some people see it as a symbol of the British government. Different people have different views about the queen; when they see it as a symbol some people don't like it, because of Northern Ireland, especially because in Northern Ireland they feel they shouldn't be ruled by Britain. Other people see it as a threat if it was taken away. Then again the royal family is quite symbolic; again a lot of people respect them, and makes a lot of money and things and a lot of ceremony involving things like crowns, which are very precious and things.

INTERVIEWER: *What if he said to you, "What does she do?"*

NABEEL: Her function is a symbol, really, she doesn't really have any purpose. Theoretically, she is supposed to hold the constitution together and things like that and dissolve Parliament, she's there as a figurehead for the government, and sees that the government has its traditions and things. *[16-year-old Hindu male]*

The accurate and colorful description presented by Nabeel contrasts vividly with historical narrative presented by Jessica who also distinguishes between the separation of roles. Jessica, who lives in a middle-class neighborhood in the suburbs of south Belfast, recognizes that the queen is in a weak position in the British polity:

INTERVIEWER: *Suppose he says, "Tell me what the queen is?" What would you say?*

JESSICA: The queen doesn't do much. She's sort of a figurehead for the country. She does have some power but not very much, but she doesn't actually lead the government. The prime minister and the cabinet do actually make a law. She's actually a figurehead but has some power, but not very much. She's just a figurehead for the country.

INTERVIEWER: *What if he said to you, "What does she do?"*

142   GROWING UP IN A DIVIDED SOCIETY

JESSICA: She does things for charities and so do other members of the royal family and they go and visit other countries and a lot of people and they don't actually work or anything. *[15-year-old female]*

Stan is from an upper middle-class family and resides in Craigavon just outside the city of Belfast. He feels that the queen will not allow the prime minister to abandon Northern Ireland from the union. He recognizes that the monarch is a constitutional bulwark against a united Ireland and a defender of the Protestant religion. This is what Stan had to say about the queen:

INTERVIEWER: *So is the prime minister the one you like best?*

STAN: I think the prime minister is probably better to run this country, that's what he is there for. The queen is just there as part of her family thing, and it's our heritage and things. It's nice to have a heritage and things. And the Protestants in Northern Ireland want no part of the Catholic dominated South. Personally I would rather the queen to rule our country because the queen always stays the same, but the prime minister can change, and some of them are good and some of them are bad. *[16-year-old Protestant male]*

We can assume from these statements by Nabeel, Jessica, and Stan that the queen reigns in a benevolent manner, whereas the prime minister rules the country. These older children realize that the queen is an apolitical figure, with real power residing in the hands of the prime minister and his or her cabinet. Nabeel, Jessica, and Stan recognize the ceremonial activities of the monarch as symbolic representative of the British nation.

The findings of previous research (Miller 1978; Moxon-Browne 1983; Rose 1971) also indicate that Northern Irish Protestants held the queen in high esteem because she protects their ethnoreligious identities. Perhaps Jessica is more aware that it is the queen's government that makes laws for Northern Ireland and not the queen. In fact, she goes on to add that the prime minister "governs most of the place, and he decides things and makes important decisions."

IMAGES: OLDER CHILDREN AT THE INTEGRATED SCHOOL

In contrast, fifth-year pupils at the integrated school are highly politicized, with some Protestants and Catholics surprisingly exhibiting political cynicism in their descriptions of the crown. These children are drawn to a political side of life that cuts across the ethnoreligious divide in the school, reflecting the mixed-class, gender, and religious structure of the student population, and stands in contrast to the more middle-class orientations of pupils at the nonintegrated school.

Liam depicts political cynicism in his political world view. He comes from a small village community thirty miles outside the city of Belfast. He has to bus sixty miles to school every day. He thinks that the royal family should be abolished because it wastes resources and is not needed by the people:

INTERVIEWER: *What does the queen do?*

LIAM: She's one of the richest people in the British Isles, but in my eyes she doesn't do anything. She attends royal variety performances, she pulls back curtains of flats and things, she doesn't seem to be very important, she does not seem to help people. They just waste money on themselves, like look at Prince Edward what's he's done. He's dropped out of the Marines or something like that there, just wasting the money he got, you know, like as my dad said you know she's gone on holiday and we are paying for it, like she's having a good time. *[16-year-old Catholic male]*

Liam's political images of the monarch are related to an economic interpretation of the institution as wasteful. We turn now to two middle-class fifth-year children at the integrated school whose responses also reflect shrewd, forceful, and objective images of political realism in their depictions of the queen as actual ruler. Here is what Tiffany and Seamus had to say about the political role and significance of the monarch.

Tiffany lives off of the Ormeau Road in Belfast city. In her story she portrays the queen as a magical figure in a fairy tale. Tiffany is a tolerant individual who does not support political violence or sectarianism from any quarter:

INTERVIEWER: *What if he said to you, "What does she do?"*

TIFFANY: I really don't know what she does myself. See, I'm not on either side, I've never been involved. The queen is just the queen, like in a fairy tale, like the good queen in the fairy poem. The queen has always been that sort of person. I think I'd have to show the person and maybe give them some articles to read.

INTERVIEWER: *But if this was a young kid and he said, "Well, what kind of things does she do?"*

TIFFANY: I don't know, she seems to get in the paper. She opens hospitals and things, and goes to the state and Parliament and she's the head of the Commonwealth. She's like a general, and every place she goes, people go, "Oh, the queen!" She's like royalty, she's setting a new fashion trend. *[16-year-old Protestant female]*

Implicit in Tiffany's story is the view that the queen is more like a fashion figure than a powerful political leader. Also, Seamus, who is from the village of Ballyclare outside of Belfast, tells the boy from another country about the political role of the monarch. He stresses that he would not tell the boy that he does not identify politically with the queen:

INTERVIEWER: *Suppose he says, "Tell me what the queen is?" What would you say?*

SEAMUS: I believe there is little conflict in the school. There's no fights at this school, where at other schools there's always fighting. Considering there are Catholics and Protestants together, I would help them as best I could. The queen is the monarch of Britain and the self-proclaimed monarch of Ireland. I don't think she is my monarch. I don't believe the queen rules over the north of Ireland. I know she does officially, but I don't recognize her as my monarch. But I would tell him that the queen is the monarch of the United Kingdom. But what I think she is, is my own personal belief. I wouldn't tell him that; he can make his own decision for himself.

INTERVIEWER: *What if he said to you, "What does she do?"*

SEAMUS: It's hard to tell what she does. She tries to brighten people's lives through visits. She opens hospitals. She's a figurehead more than anything else. If you think of England you think of the queen; that's one of the English things, having a queen. You think of the queen, you think of the English bulldog. She's a figurehead and she tries to help people through charities and visits. *[16-year-old Catholic male]*

Tiffany and Seamus fall into the category of children who recognize that the head of state is a figurehead. They explain the queen to the foreign boy in an objective fashion emphasizing the symbolic and benevolent significance of the monarch but stressing a personal nonpolitical attachment. The queen does not represent Seamus's political identity because he sees himself as Irish and the queen as British. The imagery of benevolence and symbolism are also exhibited in two working-class children's description of the queen to the foreign child.

Ronnie is from the working-class Protestant enclave of the Shan-kill Road in Belfast. He is a cynic, at least in regard to the effective powers of and allegiance to the queen. Here is his colorful account of what the queen does:

INTERVIEWER: *Suppose he says, "Tell me what the queen is?" What would you say?*

RONNIE: The queen is the figurehead of our nation, like a monarch. The person who is meant to be in charge of it all.

INTERVIEWER: *What if he said to you, "What does she do?"*

RONNIE: She has a bit of a busy job, opening supermarkets and Parliament and other places like that. She waves at people a lot. She is very good at waving at people and socializing and stuff. She visits other monarchs who wave at people, and go and open supermarkets and have a sociable time with them. She doesn't really do much. She is really for show, part of the trappings, just like everyone says, "Oh, there is the queen of England." She doesn't do anything at all really, except open supermarkets and goes on ski trips. *[16-year-old Protestant male]*

Anne, on the other hand, explains why some people in Northern Ireland may not like the monarch:

INTERVIEWER: *Suppose he says, "Tell me what the queen is?" What would you say?*

ANNE: The queen is the queen of England and she really doesn't have much to do. Mostly Irish people and people here that consider themselves Irish wouldn't have anything to do with her and wouldn't really like her. There might be one or two Catholics that might think she is okay. She's popular in England.

INTERVIEWER: *What if he said to you, "What does she do?"*

ANNE: I don't know either. She's in charge of England. She makes sure the country is running well. But some members of the royal family have been in Northern Ireland. I really don't know a lot of what she would do. I suppose she spends a lot of time with her civil servants about paying taxes and things like that and planning what she is going to do in the future. For example, if any of her children or sons and daughters were going to come to Ireland she would try to make sure that they would have all of the security that they would need. *[16-year-old Catholic female]*

Anne, like Seamus, is Catholic. She also realizes that the queen is not important for the national identity of Northern Irish Catholics. She is fully aware of the limitations of the queen's political power, and in a later response, she says that the prime minister is more important for Northern Ireland because "he has more a say in the way things are run."

As predicted, the fifth-year students reported a significantly greater weakness in the role of the monarch than did the first-year pupils (appendix 2, table 14). In the present population, the older-age peers seemed more aware of the limitations in the queen's role in Northern Ireland. These results support the findings of previous research emphasizing different stages in development regarding images of the queen (Greenstein and Tarrow 1970a, 1970b, Greenstein 1975; Irwin 1991; Piaget 1976).[1]

Children in the older-age-groups at the integrated school think of the queen as a mere figurehead, reflecting a high level of political awareness (appendix 2, table 15). In general, first-year pupils in the integrated school do not have very coherent views about the queen's actual role in British society. The integrated fifth-year schoolchildren showed themselves to be better informed than did the first-year integrated school children about the actual role of the British monarch. This indicates a considerable overlap between the age groups associated with the stages of cognitive development.

In summary, twelve of the first-year sample appear to lack an abstract distinction of the head of state's role; however, four of the young pupils from the nonintegrated school seem to have a more balanced interpretation of the queen's actual political position. This may reflect the fact that the streaming of these middle-class children into a grammar school environment allows them to develop, at a faster rate, attitudes, values, and cognitions that are not evident in their working-class counterparts from the integrated school.

Children's Images of the Queen and the Prime Minister

The story in which the schoolchildren are asked to compare the roles of the head of state and the head of government shows the distribution of political themes that emerge regarding their cognitive and evaluative images of the queen and the prime minister. This story goes right to the center of a number of theoretical issues that arise in analyzing these Belfast schoolchildren's political images of the interrelationship of the political roles of the queen and the prime minister.

The following examples of respondents' views are important elements of these Belfast schoolchildren's perceptions of the political roles of these public authority figures. Three themes emerged from our sample of first-year pupils. Examples of the first political theme indicate that the younger children's age group at the integrated school believe that the queen has more political power than the prime minister. The queen is thought of as an effective leader.

Confused Perceptions of the Queen and Prime Minister: Younger Children at the Nonintegrated School

A similar pattern emerges from some of the responses of the nonintegrated school's first-year schoolchildren. The second theme that emerged from this study illustrates that Doug and Tracey speculate in a rather confused fashion regarding the political imagery of both the head of state and the head of government. Doug confuses the queen and prime minister's roles, not realizing that the monarch can advise and try to influence the prime minister but has no real power to initiate or change policies within the political system.

In his story Doug expresses a confused understanding of the political roles of the queen and the prime minister. Also, he believes that Margaret Thatcher is still the prime minister of Britain. However, he does recognize that the prime minister is elected and can be replaced by the electorate, whereas the queen is a member of an aristocratic family:

INTERVIEWER: *Who is more important for Northern Ireland, the queen or the prime minister?*

DOUG: The prime minister is probably more important, 'cause he comes up with all the ideas of what to do. Well, he doesn't have much power, but he can think of the things to do. She has to ask the prime minister and get his advice, the same as the prime minister has to ask the queen for advice.

INTERVIEWER: *So is that the one you like best?*

DOUG: Yes, I like the prime minister best, because he's been elected and people must like him. But people don't necessarily like the queen because she's a member of the family. She has a right, but nobody has voted for her, so she can be in that position all the time. *[12-year-old Protestant boy]*

Similarly, Tracey's description of who is the effective ruler of the nation is rather blurred, and she is unable to clearly distinguish between both political roles. Tracey refers to the benevolent behavior of the monarch toward all of her subjects, looking after their basic needs, the homeless, the elderly, and poverty.

INTERVIEWER: *Who is more important for Northern Ireland, the queen or the prime minister?*

TRACEY: The prime minister, he helps our country to get along, but the queen is more important, because she thinks of England more as her country. She travels here and she sends Princess Diana here quite a lot to visit hospitals and Prince Charles as well to visit hospitals. So I'd probably say the queen.

INTERVIEWER: *Why would that be important that members of the royal family come to visit Northern Ireland?*

TRACEY: Because I think they need to know about Northern Ireland. Know what the people's in it needs are, because there's a lot of homeless people in England. But there are a lot of homeless people and elderly people in Northern Ireland who need our help as well. So I think it's good that she sends members of the royal family to see what the same variation is in both countries.

INTERVIEWER: *What kind of powers would the queen have other than the prime minister, and how would that be important to Northern Ireland?*

TRACEY: The queen has no power, but the prime minister, he does take over in the North. They both sort of help Ulster in their own ways. They don't do the same thing, but they mean what they do in their own ways. The prime minister, I don't think he does very much. He decides who's going to be Chancellor and takes over what party that the members of parliament say.

INTERVIEWER: *So is the queen the one you like best?*

TRACEY: Aye. She doesn't joke very much, but I think if you got to know her she would have a very good personality. With their family and grandchildren, I think the royal family is growing, and that's good because then, if something happens you always have something to fall back on. I think that's good because the royal family are always helping each other. They're always thinking what needs they need and what needs the country needs, and I think that's good. *[12-year-old Protestant female]*

While Doug mildly approves of the queen, Tracey realizes that Protestants, who want to preserve the link with Britain, hold the queen and the royal family in high esteem as the symbol of their patriotism and allegiance and loyalty to the crown. She also goes on to describe the monarch as head of the British Commonwealth, accurately depicts how her patronage assists charities in helping the poor, and suggests that as head of the armed services the queen can send British troops to Northern Ireland.

PERCEPTIONS OF THE PRIME MINISTER AS EFFECTIVE LEADER
OF NORTHERN IRELAND: YOUNGER CHILDREN AT THE
NONINTEGRATED SCHOOL

The third theme, examining the functions of both political incumbents, shows that some first-year children at the nonintegrated school are well-informed politically, realizing that the prime minister makes laws and is elected and has political powers that surpass those of the monarch. However, they are not fully aware that the linchpin holding the British cabinet system together is the collective responsibility of all cabinet members to make unilateral decisions. The British prime minister, who is primus inter pares, pledges the collective responsibility of his cabinet colleagues to serve as Her Majesty's government (Norton 1984). They are all equals who come under the party whipping system preserving party loyalty and strict party discipline. For example, a government minister cannot announce a new policy or ridicule his or her colleagues without cabinet discussion and consent, and a minister or backbencher cannot express private opinions in public through the media.

We now turn to statements made by Hazel and Teddy regarding the political roles of the incumbents. They both demonstrate an incipient awareness of the prime minister's powers and the queen's more figurehead nonpolitical status. They are still a little bit confused, however, by the importance of the political party system in Britain. Although Hazel believes that the prime minister is the more powerful political figure, she has not fully grasped the subtleties of the prime minister's actions:

INTERVIEWER: *Who is more important for Northern Ireland, the queen or the prime minister?*

HAZEL: The prime minister is more important in my view because the queen is based mainly in Britain itself and in Northern Ireland as well. Sometimes she would come over here on state visits, but the prime minister, although he doesn't come over here, he seems to want to help us, and he can do something about it rather than the queen has to go to the government and say do something to change this if they could.

INTERVIEWER: *So is that the one you like best?*

HAZEL: I don't know really. I don't know enough to say really. But at the minute the prime minister seems to be doing more than the queen could. That's because he has more power and he could do that. *[12-year-old Protestant female]*

Teddy believes that the queen can make important decisions so long as they do not contradict those of the prime minister:

INTERVIEWER: *Who is more important for Northern Ireland, the queen or the prime minister?*

TEDDY: Probably the prime minister because he is more important for Britain for actually what happens, well in some things. He would govern everything that happens in Northern Ireland. Whereas the queen would play a part in that, but most of all what happens in Northern Ireland, he makes the changes in laws, or whatever.

INTERVIEWER: *What kind of powers would the prime minister have that the queen doesn't have?*

TEDDY: A lot of changes in policies and laws and things. The queen doesn't have much of a say in.

INTERVIEWER: *What do you think would be the big differences between the queen and the prime minister?*

TEDDY: The prime minister is elected by polls and things. Then there are different rulers of each political party and everything but the queen. It's always the same family.

INTERVIEWER: *So is that the one you like best?*

TEDDY: That's a difficult question. I don't really know. Maybe the prime minister, but I'm not sure. The prime minister probably has more say in what happens. He wants to hear what everybody else in the country thinks, but sometimes the queen doesn't take any important decisions which are made by the prime minister. *[12-year-old Protestant male]*

Teddy has a pretty clear understanding of the prime minister's role as head of government, whereas Hazel seems a trifle confuzed between the political roles of both incumbents.

PERCEPTIONS OF THE MONARCH AS AN EFFECTIVE LEADER OF NORTHERN IRELAND: YOUNGER CHILDREN AT THE INTEGRATED SCHOOL

Responses by first-year boys at the integrated school regarding the second story-completion question, an episode in which they describe the effective powers of the queen and the prime minister, are especially interesting because they focus on why the prime minister and the queen do not introduce policies to alleviate poverty in Northern Ireland.

Margaret Thatcher was not a very popular figure with the Protestant community in Northern Ireland because as prime minister, she introduced the 1985 Anglo-Irish Accord giving the southern Irish government a political role in the running of politics within the province. I found it interesting that Richard said that he did not like "Maggie:"

INTERVIEWER: *Who is more important for Northern Ireland, the queen or the prime minister?*

RICHARD: Och. The prime minister, because, not because he's more higher up, but because he's more important to us.

INTERVIEWER: *Why would you think that?*

RICHARD: If the queen didn't have a prime minister going round to tell people what to do, then the country wouldn't run very good.

INTERVIEWER: *So is the prime minister the one you like best?*

RICHARD: Aye. The current prime minister is nice, but we didn't like the other prime minister, 'cause Margaret Thatcher made lots of taxes and didn't want to help Northern Ireland. *[12-year-old Protestant boy]*

Although Patrick is confused about the queen's actual political role, clearly he prefers the queen than an inefficient prime minister who does not care about the underprivileged:

INTERVIEWER: *Why is the queen more important for Northern Ireland?*

PATRICK: Because whenever the prime minister wants to do something he has to get her word on it first, I think, whatever he does. I'm not too sure about Northern Ireland, but that is the way it is in the United Kingdom. You see, she is royalty and he isn't. He is the leader in politics. I think the queen would be as I said; see, if he wants to get anything changed or whatever he'd have to get her word on it first.

INTERVIEWER: *Is that the one you like best?*

PATRICK: Well, I think I'd rather have the queen because you see, all the prime ministers, they are all the same. They say they'll do this and that, but they never do it. They say they'll help the poor and stop the poll tax, but, see, they all say that but they never get around to doing it. So you see, I'd rather have the queen. *[12-year-old Catholic boy]*

Richard and Patrick believe that royalty is more important than the prime minister, because the queen is above politics. They perceived the monarchy as politically neutral and nonpartisan because the queen is outside the decision-making process, serving as a central political figure embodying the political loyalty of the citizens of Northern Ireland and the rest of the United Kingdom.

Diana, a 12-year-old Protestant girl, is unable to supply a detailed and concrete description of the prime minister's political role. Her perception of the head of state as a benevolent and kind person is evident in her explanation of why the queen is more important than the prime minister in changing politics to the betterment of the poor:

INTERVIEWER: *Who is more important for Northern Ireland, the queen or the prime minister?*

DIANA: Aye. The queen because she rules over the prime minister.

INTERVIEWER: *Why?*

DIANA: If he did something that the people didn't like, she would be able to change it. She looks after the sick people, say, people who couldn't afford, if they can't afford food or anything she can change it.

INTERVIEWER: *Is that the one you like best?*

DIANA: Aye. The queen, yes, because the prime minister is boring. *[11-year-old Protestant female]*

The appearance of the prime minister's subservient political relationship to the queen also bears a striking similarity to Joanie's colloquy with the interviewer. Joanie believes that the queen can make prime minister John Major reduce political violence in Northern Ireland; she also goes on to describe the peacefulness and tranquility of the Northern Irish landscape:

INTERVIEWER: *Why is the queen more important than the prime minister?*

JOANIE: The queen has more power. Just say she tried to get the killing stopped over religion. So John Major would get put to work straight away. So she'd make the ideas and tell him what to do and he'd get it done for her, so he would.

INTERVIEWER: *So is the prime minister the one you like best?*

JOANIE: I don't know very much about them so I couldn't say which I like best, I couldn't. You tell him about the countryside and how nice and how the River Lagan used to be nice and clean. It's a lovely walk through the countryside, plenty of land and fields and animals.

INTERVIEWER: *Would the queen do anything else in the society?*

JOANIE: The government pays for the books in the schools. I don't know what the queen does. *[12-year-old Catholic female]*

In general, the similarities in cognitive orientations found here appear to be an indication that the level of political information and awareness is lower in this sample of first-year pupils. These children have a generally low degree of accurate information to distinguish between the roles of the queen and the prime minister and clearly fit into the third stage of the Piaget and Weil (1970) model of gradual development.

The underlying political assumptions of the majority of first-year pupils at both schools have not yet quite reached the final stage of cognitive efficiency and intricacy. They do not realize that a variety of powers and political influence wielded by the prime minister make the position a very formidable and important one. For example, the party leader can appoint or sack members of the cabinet at will and also monopolize political patronage. These powerful political mechanisms allow the prime minister a considerable leverage in the political spectrum and are important political clubs to whip dissenters within their own parties into shape (Birch 1990).

PERCEPTIONS OF THE PRIME MINISTER AS THE EFFECTIVE
LEADER OF NORTHERN IRELAND: OLDER CHILDREN AT THE
NONINTEGRATED SCHOOL

While the younger children emphasized various interesting political themes about the actual nature of both political roles, one clear illustration of political imagery emerges from the older sample of children—a concrete awareness of the prime minister's status as effective ruler of Britain and of Northern Ireland.

Nabeel and Jessica outline why they perceive the prime minister as the effective leader of Britain's political system. Here is Nabeel's picturesque description of the prime minister's political role:

INTERVIEWER: *What kind of powers does the prime minister have that are more important other than the queen has?*

NABEEL: Really the queen hasn't any power at all, she can't even vote, for a start. The prime minister can make decisions about matters of government, things like the health service.

INTERVIEWER: *So is that the one you like best?*

NABEEL: When you say the prime minister, the prime minister could be whoever's elected, so, but yeah. I don't think the queen or the royal family is a particularly good system at all. I don't think it's right that people should be ruled or have any respect for someone just because they come from a certain family, and that family's been ruling for a long time. And attached to the royal family you've things like class system and things like that and people going to public schools, getting their jobs, and having their lives mapped out for them like that and other people being excluded from the system.

INTERVIEWER: *In the context of Northern Ireland, some people would like the queen and other people would see the symbolism of it as being distasteful. How about the prime minister, how would he figure in this?*

NABEEL: The emotions aroused by the prime minister would be less strong than those aroused by the queen, because people in Northern Ireland really don't have much say because of the political system and the political parties. They know who the prime minister is. He is chosen by the rest of the country which makes some people warm to him. But although people would feel they have some choice deciding who their prime minister was, they wouldn't feel antagonistic towards him. Also the prime minister does change and you don't really know who the prime minister is going to be. He might be somebody who supports your views or doesn't support your views. Because of that there is an ambivalent feeling towards the prime minister. The queen has been there 20–30 years so people have ingrained feelings about the queen.

INTERVIEWER: *How do you see that symbolism as being important? What does it mean? You're saying that it's important to one side of the community and is more antagonistic to another section of the community?*

NABEEL: I suppose the people in Northern Ireland, if you look at the Unionists or the Protestants, if you want to put it that way, they've lived in Northern Ireland a lot. Their way of life is being threatened by being part of Ireland by people who want them to be part of Ireland. A lot of their wealth and the imposition of the Catholic Church on them, and they don't want this. They want to stay where they are. The queen is a symbol of the British government and they want the British government to stay and protect them and to protect their livelihoods. And the way they see it is anything that takes away the British government is taking away the queen and would be a threat to them. And they also respect the British government and the queen because it is a symbol of their heritage as well and their links with Britain. And for the Catholic community, or the nationalist community, they'd see the queen as someone who had control over their state against their will. I think an American child would be very confused by this, you just can't understand straightaway everything that people would feel here. But if you stay in Northern Ireland for a while, you start to understand.
[16-year-old Hindu male]

Nabeel attacks the institution of the monarchy as costly, anachronistic, and bourgeois. He is cognizant of structural inequalities and outlines in a very thoughtful manner how the class system in Northern Ireland, represented by the monarch, segregates young people into different employment opportunities. An explicit question on the significance of the queen's role in Northern Ireland suggests the importance of the symbolic leadership of the monarch for Northern Irish Protestants. Interest in the monarchy and the royal family still abound in Northern Ireland as a vital component of the Protestant cultural tradition.

Nabeel's perceptions of the symbolism of the monarchy in Northern Ireland clearly demonstrate that the apparent neutrality or impartiality of the queen stimulates loyalty to the crown among the Protestant community as a symbol of their identity and unity of the nation and disloyalty to the queen's government, who cannot be trusted. Northern Irish Protestants are pragmatic in their distrust of central government, fearing a sellout of Northern Ireland to the Irish Republic by either a Tory or a Labor government, so that the impact of government in the province is much the same regardless of officeholders. The government and the prime minister are not perceived as representative of or responsible to the majority of people in Northern Ireland.

Jessica emphasizes that the prime minister is closer to the ordinary working person than the queen, who remains aloof from the public. Of the prime minister, Jessica says:

INTERVIEWER: *Who is more important for Northern Ireland, the queen or the prime minister?*

JESSICA: The prime minister is more important because he makes the laws. The idea of having a queen is nice, but she's too rich. It's a nice idea to have a queen. I think it's nice, but the prime minister is definitely more important politically.

INTERVIEWER: *What would be the main differences between the prime minister and the queen for people living in Northern Ireland?*

JESSICA: The prime minister is the one who goes to the European Community and things like that and the queen doesn't. The prime minister is really important for lawmaking and stuff like that. He's not really a figurehead.

INTERVIEWER: *So is that the one you like best?*

JESSICA: I don't know, but I suppose the prime minister is better in respect to being a lonely person. I sort of like them both, but the prime minister makes the laws and the queen appears sometimes to be distant from the people, whereas the prime minister doesn't stay away from the people.

INTERVIEWER: *Would the people see the queen as being more important for Northern Ireland, and if so, why?*

JESSICA: She's not loved by everybody; some people like her and some people don't. The queen is sort of special because not many countries have a monarchy. *[15-year-old Protestant female]*

Jessica's description of the prime minister shows a clear understanding of the control and power exercised by the head of government. Similarly, Nabeel's treatment of both the queen and the prime minister reflects both textbook accuracy and political cynicism in distinguishing between their roles. Older children at the nonintegrated school depict a stoic understanding, clarity, and knowledge of the way in which the prime minister may be the key political actor in the British political system but the queen has important symbolic significance for Northern Irish Protestants.

PERCEPTIONS OF THE PRIME MINISTER AS EFFECTIVE LEADER OF NORTHERN IRELAND: OLDER CHILDREN AT THE INTEGRATED SCHOOL

Similarly, fifth-year pupils at the integrated school demonstrate an incipient awareness about the actual roles of both political incumbents. The responses of Tiffany, a middle-class pupil from the integrated school, describe how the main British political parties, the Conservatives and Labor, do not run candidates in general elections in Northern Ireland. She also reflects an awareness of the queen's symbolic stature for Northern Irish Protestants but to a lesser degree than Nabeel's dynamic and colorful description:

INTERVIEWER: *Who is more important for Northern Ireland, the queen or the prime minister?*

TIFFANY: If you think about it, it depends if you're a Loyalist. He'd say the queen's more important, because the prime ministers don't really do much for Northern Ireland. But the prime ministers do a lot because we can't vote directly for the Conservative Party or whatever. We have the Workers Party or whatever. I think there's like the Northern Ireland Conservative Party coming up now. They're not really worried with us because we don't have as much voting power as the people on the mainland so they're not that concerned we can't put them out of power. I think if you were to ask me that question politically, that the prime minister's more important because he's the person who can get laws changed, whereas the queen is a sort of an ornament. She doesn't have that kind of power. *[16-year-old Protestant female]*

The personality of the prime minister becomes crucial in Tiffany's choice of political figures. The Unionists believe that when Mrs. Thatcher was prime minister, she tried to force Northern Ireland into a united Ireland by signing the 1985 Hillsborough Accord, allowing the Irish government a sort of consultative status in the internal affairs of the Six Counties.

Thatcherism tried to modify deep-rooted social values and political attitudes within Britain and thus to reinforce core conservative values in future decades of British young persons through intergenerational change. The former prime minister, Mrs. Thatcher, is not described in affectionate terms, but democratic traditions are preferred over a dictator:

INTERVIEWER: *So is the prime minister the one you like best?*

TIFFANY: As a person? The queen's sweet, smiles a lot, you can't help but like her. There are times when you hate the prime minister but other times you really like the prime minister. I know John Major's in now, but when Margaret Thatcher was in, she was doing one thing one day and something else another day. You could do worse, you could have Pol-Pot in power, a dictator. *[16-year-old Protestant female]*

Seamus's portrayal of the advisory capacity of the monarch suggests a vivid and subtle awareness of the intricate political activities of the prime minister:

INTERVIEWER: *So is the prime minister the one you like best?*

SEAMUS: The queen can suggest, and her suggestion would carry a lot of weight. But the prime minister would be far more important because he decides the policies. So the prime minister and the Houses of Parliament are more important as the queen doesn't have much of a say in the running of Northern Ireland. *[16-year-old Catholic male]*

The queen, who knows the secrets of past governments, has the wisdom, knowledge, and experience to advise the current prime minister, John Major, but the prime minister as the head of government embodies the power of Parliaments. Seamus appears to be suggesting that this pretence of the queen as the real ruler of Britain preserves the unity of the United Kingdom. When the interviewer presses him further on this issue, Seamus simply adds:

INTERVIEWER: *What does she really do?*

SEAMUS: She's trying to give England a bit of structure. Somebody really important that other countries can be jealous of. *[16-year-old Catholic male]*

The monarch is the great anachronism of twentieth-century British culture, history, and politics. The traditions and symbols of monarchy lead to an acceptance of the queen's political authority, thereby leading to consensus in society (Rose 1986).

Anne no longer believes in the myth of the monarch as the effective ruler of Northern Ireland but exhibits a precocious level of political awareness by choosing the secretary of state for Northern Ireland over the prime minister as the most important political figure in the province:

INTERVIEWER: *Who is more important for Northern Ireland, the queen or the prime minister?*

ANNE: I suppose the prime minister. He has more say in the way things are run. He would get on to his secretaries, for example, Tom King coming to Ireland or other things that they're going to do like bringing in more soldiers over here to stop all the bombs and tighten up security. I suppose the prime minister would be the best.

INTERVIEWER: *Is that the one you like best?*

ANNE: Och. No, not the one I like the best. I don't like him, but I don't hate him either. When I'm older and I'm more outspoken, maybe I'll understand it a bit more, but because you're 15 or 16, you don't understand what's going on or you don't take much heed of what he says. I suppose he's trying to stop violence and the bombings, which I agree with, but I suppose he could do it in better ways. *[16-year-old Catholic female]*

Anne's comments indicate her disparagement of the weak political conduct of the current prime minister, John Major, in preventing political violence in Northern Ireland. She goes on to say:

INTERVIEWER: *Who would you say is more important in making politicians help the people, the queen or the prime minister?*

ANNE: I don't think John Major has a lot to say. He doesn't seem to be really the best, whereas Margaret Thatcher would have had more power over the situation. But then again, if the queen wants anything done, he's not going to turn her down. But it's very lucky that she would not get into much views about politics, than say, the prime minister would. *[16-year-old Catholic female]*

Anne wants to trust and admire the actions and political behavior of the prime minister but suggests that the electorate will not hesitate to try to replace the head of government and the governing party in a general election if his or her leadership does not live up to the high standards demanded by the people of Northern Ireland. Over the course of her storytelling, Anne seems to suggest that the prime minister at the apex of the governmental power structure controls the movement of the party machine, decides the political agenda of the cabinet, and controls the civil service and government.

Ronnie recognizes how important Prime Minister John Major is in preventing an escalation of violence in Northern Ireland and in building a relationship with the then southern Irish government of former Prime Minister Albert Reynolds. He portrays a prime minister whom one should acknowledge with respect and admiration. Here is how Ronnie responds to the second of the information questions about the queen and the prime minister:

INTERVIEWER: *Why is the prime minister more important for Northern Ireland than the queen?*

RONNIE: He is the guy who does things, the queen kind of looks good. The prime minister is right in there doing things, passing bills and all that kind of stuff. But the queen does nothing in particular.

INTERVIEWER: *Is that the one you like best?*

RONNIE: Yes, because he is a pretty cool guy and a "man of action." The queen opens the Parliament, where John is the leader of the Parliament. Like he is doing the stuff and she is for show really. He is actually after setting up talks with the prime minister in the south of Ireland, every six weeks or something. They are having talks which is a very good thing, improving relations and stuff. And his government is the one who financed our school here so that hasn't been a bad thing. In general he is trying to get the whole thing sorted out. He also has the troops here instead of civil war. But then again, it wasn't him who started that. All the policies go through him. It all basically revolves around him. He is the man in charge. *[16-year-old Protestant male]*

It is reasonable to conclude that these older children seem more aware of the effective role of both the queen and prime minister than any of the younger children from the integrated school. It can also be seen that the older children in both school systems showed more knowledge of these political positions than their younger peers, reflecting differences in their stages of development.

Fifth-year pupils in this sample explicitly assert that the prime minister is the effective ruler of the nation (appendix 2, table 16).[2] At every age group in both school systems, many more children described the prime minister as a very powerful political figure (appendix 2, table 16). This fits the basic pattern, noted in the previous section, of increased awareness among the older children of the actual role of the head of government. This would appear to be another general indication that the level of political information is higher among the older age group than in the younger age group.

However, when the possible effects of the prime minister's role in the political imagery of children in both school systems is investigated, more children from the nonintegrated school think of the prime minister's role as weak (appendix 2, table 17). A relationship exists between parapolitical perceptions of the prime minister's noneffective role and pupils in the nonintegrated school. This would seem to suggest that the imagery of the queen is more important in these children's political reality. This may be explained in part by the fact that these middle-class children do not believe that the prime minister has proved to be an effective political instrument in eliminating the PIRA, which attempts to destroy the status quo in Northern Ireland.

It has been asserted that there may be certain differences in partisan orientations between Protestant children in the two school systems. More Protestants in the nonintegrated school mention the weak role of the prime minister (appendix 2, table 18). This is surprising, considering that most of their students appear to be aware of the noneffective role of the queen.

It might be speculated that the attachment of Protestant children in the nonintegrated school to the crown, as protector of their ethnoreligious identity, religious faith, liberty, and privileges, has something to do with their disparagement of the queen's government and total commitment in their loyalty and support of the monarchy. The positive political imagery of the queen is an indication of the political importance of the crown for Northern Irish Protestants.

The Queen Imagined in Action

We now present children's responses on the outcome of the story-completion episode in which a traffic policeman stops the head of state's car for speeding and violating one of her own laws. This episode concentrates on children's expectations about how the queen would behave in this situation: whether the queen should be punished or admonished under such circumstances, whether the queen is benign or malign, whether she is viewed in a positive manner, or whether there are some behavioral indications of deference in the interaction between the characters in the story. The Greenstein and Tarrow (1970a, 1970b) study findings indicated that (1) English children are less likely than American or French children to envision the head of state being punished for breaking the law, (2) English children do imagine that the queen should be gently admonished, and (3) overt evaluations of the queen are more balanced.

We turn now to the distribution of three political themes that emerged among the younger age peers in this study: whether deference is revealed in the meeting between the policeman and the head of state, whether the monarch is viewed in a favorable light, and whether the queen should be punished for a traffic violation.

OVERVIEW OF THE OUTCOME AND EVALUATION OF THE HEAD OF STATE—POLICEMAN EPISODES

YOUNGER PROTESTANTS AT THE NONINTEGRATED SCHOOL

First-year pupils at the nonintegrated school exhibit a degree of effective attachment to the monarch. When the queen exceeds the speed limit, these Protestant children declare that the head of state should not be punished for a traffic violation. Their deferential evaluation of the queen and the policeman story speaks for itself. Here is how Doug, Tracey, and Teddy account for the behavior of the queen and the police officer.

Doug's policeman displays deference toward the monarch in his story. He believes that the queen should not be punished for a traffic violation:

INTERVIEWER: *One day the queen was driving to a meeting. Because she was driving very fast, the police stop the car. Finish the story.*

DOUG: Well, the driver of the car the queen was in said that they had to go to the meeting quickly. And the policeman doesn't want to charge them for speeding because it's the queen, but the driver of the car says that they really have to get to the meeting very quickly and the policeman lets them drive on and doesn't charge them with anything. But he makes sure they don't speed anymore. He tells them not to. The next time they won't be so lucky.

INTERVIEWER: *What do you think the police would say?*

DOUG: "Do you realize that you're breaking the speed limit at the minute?" The driver might say, "Oh yes, but we're going to a meeting; we have to go there very quickly or we'll be late if we don't turn up." The policeman said, "That's okay, but just keep it in the speed limit and don't speed."

INTERVIEWER: *What does the queen say?*

DOUG: She doesn't say anything. She just stays at the back and lets the driver talk to them.

INTERVIEWER: *What do you think they'd finally decide?*

DOUG: The policeman would probably let them go, 'cause he won't risk getting sacked or fired. *[12-year-old Protestant boy]*

Tracey expresses a positive attitude toward the queen in her story, believing that the monarch should not be punished by the police officer. She also suggests that the police officer would behave in a deferential manner if he stopped the queen's car:

INTERVIEWER: *One day, the queen was driving to a meeting. Because she was driving very fast, the police stop the car. Finish the story.*

TRACEY: If they saw the queen they'd probably have a nervous breakdown. She could really go wild if the policeman stopped her, and I'm sure she probably would feel guilty for driving fast, anyway. I think the police are pretty foolish for stopping her. I don't think I could really imagine the police stopping the queen. The queen would probably say, "I can't stop here, I have to get to this very important meeting, and if I'm late I'll be the laughing stock of England." And the police say, "Sorry, ma'am, sorry for stopping, we didn't realize who it was. But you were driving pretty fast, and you shouldn't have been because it's dangerous on the roads." So she starts off at five miles an hour and she bombs it the rest of the way when she can't see the police anymore. The police feel like kicking their shins; that would be embarrassing to stop the queen.

INTERVIEWER: *What do you think the police would say?*

TRACEY: They'd probably say, "'Scuse me, Ma'am, you are going pretty fast on the roads." She says, "But I have to get to a meeting." But then he'd say, "But you are dangerous on the road traveling at that speed." He would probably say then, "As long as you drive slowly from here to the meeting it would be excused, and we won't say more about it."

INTERVIEWER: *What does the queen say?*

TRACEY: She would probably be very snappy because she's in a rush to this meeting and if it's important she'd probably want to get there pretty fast. She would probably say that I could press charges against you. I think it would be pretty funny.

INTERVIEWER: *What do you think they'd finally decide?*

TRACEY: The police would probably decide to let her go as long as she promised to drive slowly to the meeting or as long as they didn't catch her driving that fast again. But they couldn't do anything, I don't think, because the queen can't get sued or get charges pressed against her because she is really important and everybody respects her as well. And at the end of everything we all have to sing the royal anthem for her. So they probably would have to let her go on her way. *[12-year-old Protestant girl]*

In the following story Teddy's police officer behaves in a very deferential way toward the monarch. He articulates that the queen should not be punished for breaking the law:

INTERVIEWER: *One day, the queen was driving to a meeting. Because she was driving very fast, the police stop the car. Finish the story.*

TEDDY: They probably wouldn't press charges. They would sort of look in and be about to charge her for a ticket and they'd see she was the queen. They'd probably actually apologize and they'd say, "Try not to drive too fast again." And they'd probably just let her off the charge of speedy driving.

INTERVIEWER: *What do you think the police would say?*

TEDDY: "Well, we're awfully sorry, sorry about that; we didn't realize, but could you try not to drive just as fast in future? Slow down a bit, but it's okay, you can go on now, but don't do it again."

INTERVIEWER: *What does the queen say?*

TEDDY: She'd probably let it pass at that and not say anything else and just drive off. She might be a bit cross, it depends, at being just stopped. You're going to get a ticket or a driving charge.

INTERVIEWER: *What do you think they'd finally decide?*

TEDDY: They'd probably finally decide to just let her go and not mention it again, but then again she might bring it up, about stopping her, and some action might be taken against him or something.

INTERVIEWER: *What kind of action do you think they might take against him?*

TEDDY: They could be suspended from duty for a certain amount of

time or whatever. They would probably be suspended from duty or
that's all, probably. *[12-year-old Protestant boy]*

There is a commitment to liberty and justice and an acceptance
within the rest of the United Kingdom to work within the rules of
the game. However, Doug's, Tracey's and Teddy's narratives show
a pattern consistent with the impression left by the younger age
group of Protestants at the integrated school. The political and
religious symbolism that the queen invokes is an important factor
in the British heritage of these Protestant children. Not only is
the queen important constitutionally for these children, but their
descriptions of a deferential policeman account for class differences in the society. It is noteworthy that for these three first-year
pupils, the head of state is more likely not to be punished by a
deferential policeman for violating the traffic law. According to
these three children, the queen is above and beyond the law of
the land.

Hazel lives in the "Holy Land" neighborhood nearby Queen's
University. Her description of the queen and traffic policeman
story is reasonably conventional, although the norm of public
safety, missing in the aforementioned stories, is very evident in
her account of the queen's interaction with the policeman. Although the policeman is deferential toward the queen, Hazel believes that the monarch should be punished for speeding:

INTERVIEWER: *One day, the queen was driving to a meeting. Because she was driving very fast, the police stop the car. Finish the story.*

HAZEL: Well, once the police realize it was the queen, they'd be very
apologetic. If it were someone else they'd fine them immediately. Just
because the queen's more important, they'd let her off. But just because
she's the queen it doesn't mean she has any more right to break the
law. Royalty, it doesn't make any difference. Even if you and I were
doing it, they'd fine us, but they wouldn't fine her. But they should fine
her just the same if she was going too fast.

INTERVIEWER: *What do you think the police would say?*

HAZEL: They'd probably say, "We're terribly sorry Your Majesty."
They'd be very worried that she was going to say something to them
and then they'd be apologetic to the queen. Then if somebody else was
coming along they'd probably say, "You're fined such and such an
amount of money," which I don't think is very fair.

INTERVIEWER: *What does the queen say?*

HAZEL: She would probably be rather, "I don't think you should fine me because I'm the queen." But then she'd probably turn around and fine somebody else for doing something wrong. She probably would try not to be getting fined, depending on how much the fine, so that people wouldn't think it's not right. Just because she's royalty, she doesn't have to pay the fine. She'll probably be more inclined to pay the fine than somebody else because for whatever reason.

INTERVIEWER: *What do you think they'd finally decide?*

HAZEL: I think they should fine her, but whether they would or not, I don't know really, because any other person, they would fine them. But they probably wouldn't fine her. Yet if she said, "I want to pay the fine, because it's not right," then she'd be excused. Then they'd probably let her pay the fine. But then they might not make her pay as much. *[12-year-old Protestant girl]*

In Hazel's answer to the confrontation between the queen and the policeman, the illegal behavior of the leader of Britain must be punished. She believes that everybody is equal before the law and the queen should not warrant any special privileges or favors from the police. However, Hazel seems to be of the opinion that the policeman would not punish the monarch, suggesting perhaps that there is one law for the rich and another for the poor. This tendency to punish people who violate societal laws, norms, and values stems from the conservative nature of Northern Ireland's political culture. Stable and responsible government is reflected in how people are socialized into their political system (Punnett 1980).

YOUNGER CATHOLICS AT THE INTEGRATED SCHOOL

Here is how Gerry and Joanie, two first-year Catholic children at the integrated school, describe in a lively and picturesque fashion the interaction between the queen and the traffic policeman when the royal car is stopped.

Gerry describes the Queen in a negative manner because he feels that she should be punished for breaking the law. His policeman shows respect toward the queen but is certainly not cowed or embarrassed by the encounter:

INTERVIEWER: *One day, the queen was driving her car to a meeting. Because she was driving very fast, the police stop the car. Finish the story.*

GERRY: Just said, "Excuse me, could you get out of the car please," and the window comes down and he says, "Oh, it's you Miss, I was just going to get you to blow in this wee bag here to see how much you had to drink." So she goes, "Excuse me, I am the queen here; you are not allowed to do things like this to me," and he says, "Well, but you are way over the speed limit there, you know," and she goes, "Well I'm trying to get away from here, you know," and he says, "Sure, if you just blow in this wee bag here, sure I'll let you go if you're all right so." She goes, "Well, I don't want to press on anything," and she blows in the bag, and he goes, "Oh you're way over the limit, Miss, you have had way too many. Where have you been? Where were you before this?" She goes, "I was at the airport, I'm just home from the airport, I'm going to this meeting," and he says, "Was it just from the airport to here?" And she says, "Yes," and he says, "First-class flight?" And she says, "Yes," and he goes, "Did you have anything to drink on the plane?" And she said, "Yes, I had a glass of wine, and two glasses of wine," and he goes, "Well, what kind of wine was it, Miss?" And she said, "It was a sweet white wine," and he goes, "Well, I will have to see about this. Could you come down to the station?" And she goes, "I'm not going to the station and I will sort you out after, but I have to go to this meeting now," and he says, "But I am afraid I can't do that now" and she says, "Well is that the way you want to play with me or something? I'll have you fired." And he goes, "Well, I'm going to give you a ticket," and he gives her a ticket and he says, "I want this paid and I want you down at the station later on to straighten out this," and she goes, "Very well, then," and she goes off.

INTERVIEWER: *What do the police say?*

GERRY: I don't think that they would be a bit pleased, because she is the queen and maybe they'd be embarrassed, the papers getting on to it and on the front page and all, "Police Arresting Queen."

INTERVIEWER: *What does the queen say?*

GERRY: She'd be very annoyed and embarrassed as well, like come along, the most important woman in the North and getting stopped by the police and getting a ticket and just getting the breathalizer done and all. Just funny, you know.

INTERVIEWER: *What do they finally decide?*

GERRY: They may have gone a bit far and maybe let her off with it and tell her, "As loads of people are complaining to you about speed limits and kids getting knocked down and you're supposed to be doing something for the thing and you're actually speeding yourself." The police were sorry for the breathalizer thing done and the ticket and that, but maybe she could slow down a wee bit, and take more heed, "More heed less speed." *[12-year-old Catholic boy]*

Similarly, Joanie portrays the queen's behavior negatively: breaking the law and wanting to punish the police officer for stopping her. She believes that the queen should be cautioned by the police officer because every person is equal before the law. Her policeman does not display any deference whatsoever toward the queen:

INTERVIEWER: *One day the queen was driving her car to a meeting. Because she was driving very fast, the police stop the car. Finish the story.*

JOANIE: The police have to do their job no matter how important they are. Just say it was me daddy that was driving too fast, then he'd be brought in by the police. But just say it was the queen, then they'd do nothing. Then they're not going to be fair and stick to their own job and say, "Excuse me, can I see your license?" But the queen doesn't drive, somebody else drives it for her. Then she gets her license out and he goes, "Could you pull over?" Then he checks it and he goes, "That's okay." "But there's a sign further on down the road that says you're only allowed to drive 19 miles per hour. Could you please stick to that." And the queen says, "Excuse me, do you know who you're talking to?" And he says, "Yes, but I have to keep to my job." And then there's an argument and he's brought to court and the magistrate says, "Why were you giving cheek to the queen?" And he answers, "No, I wasn't giving cheek, I was only keeping to my job, because if it was an ordinary person, then I would do the same, and not only to the queen." So you can't do your job differently just because she's royalty.

INTERVIEWER: *What do you think the police would say?*

JOANIE: The sergeant would probably stand up and say, "Yes, I agree with this man." But the queen's solicitor stands up and says, "I don't agree with this man, he shouldn't have given cheek to her." Then the policeman says, "I didn't give cheek to her, I was only doing my job. I spoke to her nicely, and what I did, I do to other people. And I only give her a bit of advice about the 19 miles per hour down the road and could she please stick to that." And he says, "I don't think that's being cheeky." Then it's all solved and the policeman's free and the queen's furious.

INTERVIEWER: *What does the queen say?*

JOANIE: She says it's ridiculous. The policemen are going to have to be changed. And she's very angry and just walks out.

INTERVIEWER: *What do you think they'd finally decide?*

JOANIE: The sergeant goes up to the queen and the guard says, "Stop." And he goes, "I'd like to speak to the queen." But the guard goes, "Sorry, that can't be possible." One of the guards goes and asks her all about it and he goes up himself. "They'll be no cheek given."

And she goes, "That's fine with me." She says, "I'll have to give you a punishment," and he says, "That's not fair. I came up here to make a truce, to make up." And she goes, "OK, fair's fair," and they make up. So he goes back and tells them about it 'cause he thought he was going to get the sack and he was really frightened and all. But the sergeant says, "Yes, it's okay you still have your job." *[12-year-old Catholic girl]*

Both of these stories are animated and colorful accounts of the political leader imagined in action. Gerry and Joanie imagined that (1) the policeman did not project an explicit manifestation of deference to the queen, (2) the queen behaved in an unfavorable manner, and (3) the monarch should be admonished for breaking the law. Even though the crown is the epitome of the judicial and political processes within the United Kingdom, both of these Catholic children realize that equality before the law for every citizen and the norm of public safety are part of a much larger scheme of things in Northern Ireland, reflecting the fact that no special privileges or favors should be handed out to members of a higher social standing: the law is the law.

YOUNGER PROTESTANTS AT THE INTEGRATED SCHOOL

In contrast, the following first-year Protestant children at the integrated school appear cynical about the possibility of the police punishing the queen for a traffic violation. Richard and Alexis also exhibit deference toward the monarch and imagine that the queen is not punished for speeding.

Richard believes that the police officer would not punish the queen because he would understand that she was speeding to avoid an attack by PIRA terrorists. His policeman behaves in a deferential way to the queen:

INTERVIEWER: *One day, the queen was driving her car to a meeting. Because she was driving very fast, the police stop the car. Finish the story.*

RICHARD: The policeman sort of strolls over and stops the car and takes out his pencil and book and the window opens up and this voice says, "What do you think you're playing at?" As the policeman moves to the window, he jumps back in shock because he recognizes the queen. He says, "Oh, I beg your pardon, miss," and he runs off. At least that's what I'd do if I met the queen.

INTERVIEWER: *What do you think the police would say?*

RICHARD: "I'm very sorry, Your Majesty; because you were traveling very fast we were afraid you would have an accident." But he wouldn't book her or anything. They probably would ask her if she wants a police escort to her meeting 'cause of the terrorists.

INTERVIEWER: *What does the queen say?*

RICHARD: Not in these exact words, but she'd probably say, "Get on your bike." She would probably tell him to go off and catch other people that are speeding around town apart from her. But he should have realized from the start that there were royal flags on the front of the car. Like even Maggie Thatcher would have flags on her car.

INTERVIEWER: *What do you think they'd finally decide?*

RICHARD: They wouldn't book the queen or bring her to court. They would be embarrassed and want to help her get safely to her meeting. They would stutter and say, "I'm S-S-S-Sergeant B-B-Buchanan." And he'd tell the other policeman, "It was the queen! It was the queen!" And they'd try and protect the queen from any attacks by the IRA. So they would have in the escort two motorbikes in the front and two motorbikes in the back. *[12-year-old Protestant boy]*

Alexis is from the coastal town of Portrush. Implicit in her story is the view that the queen should not be punished for a traffic violation. Alexis's policeman behaves in a positive and a deferential manner toward the monarch:

INTERVIEWER: *One day, the queen was driving her car to a meeting. Beause she was driving very fast, the police stop the car. Finish the story.*

ALEXIS: When the police stopped the car, she rolls down her window just a wee bit so she could hear, and the police charge her for driving fast. When she rolled down her window all the way, the policeman jumped back in shock. She'd say, "I'm driving so fast and it's against the law, but I'm rushing for a very important meeting, and if you want you can fine me if you want because I'm going against my own laws." But the policeman loves to meet the queen on duty, and he doesn't fine her. And the queen tells him she'll tell the sergeant to put a rise up in his pay.

INTERVIEWER: *What do you think the police would say?*

ALEXIS: He's happy to see her and he's just started his job and he's met the queen. At first he wasn't sure about the job, but now he is, having met one of the royal family. And that the sergeant would be very thrilled about it and all.

INTERVIEWER: *What does the queen say?*

ALEXIS: "Thank you, I know that I'm going against my own law, but I'm rushing to an important meeting, so fine me four pounds, because I shouldn't have been driving so fast anyway." She's glad that the police obey her rules and laws and she's very glad to meet the young policeman and all. She's very sad about it and hopes he does very well on his job in the future.

INTERVIEWER: *What do you think they'd finally decide?*

ALEXIS: The queen would like to pay for it, but because it's her own law, and the policeman says, "It's all right now." "I'll put a rise up in your pay and see you don't pay your tax for a month." *[11-year-old Protestant girl]*

These replies given by first-year pupils at the integrated school are clearly representative of separate patterns of political socialization particular to Protestant and Catholic children in Belfast. The respondents are illustrative of the various political and religious cleavages dividing the communities. Some of these patterns, however, may not represent varieties of children in other parts of the United Kingdom, since Northern Ireland represents a distinct historical and cultural regional context distinct from the rest of the United Kingdom.

Older Protestants at the Nonintegrated School

The theme of deference is also exhibited by fifth-year Protestant pupils in the nonintegrated school. However, compared with the first-year Protestant pupils, these children were more likely to view the monarch in a more favorable light. Jessica and Nabeel emphasize that the queen is both human and law-abiding, portraying the monarch as a very real person. Here is how these two middle-class fifth-year pupils from the nonintegrated school respond to the episode in which the child describes the interaction between the head of state and the traffic policeman.

Jessica portrays the queen in a positive manner. Although not actually praising the policeman for doing his duty, she shows a pattern quite consistent with that of Hazel, a first-year female at the same school—that the queen must be punished because everybody is equal before the law:

INTERVIEWER: *One day, the queen was driving her car to a meeting. Because she was driving very fast, the police stop the car. Finish the story.*

JESSICA: I didn't think the queen drove her own car. The police stop her, she was breaking the law, she must have been driving too fast. She should be booked for it. All right, she's the queen, but that doesn't give her the right to break the law.

INTERVIEWER: *What do you think the police would say?*

JESSICA: I don't think I'd go for that particular policeman, because you don't convict the queen the first time you meet her. I think the queen is lucky to meet a proper policeman, and she wouldn't object to that if she was law-abiding.

INTERVIEWER: *What does the queen say?*

JESSICA: I don't know what she'd say. She is law-abiding, so she would say, "Young man, I know how you feel, but you have to book me because I was speeding."

INTERVIEWER: *What do you think they'd finally decide?*

JESSICA: There'd be a big scandal if it got out. I don't know what the fine is for speeding, I think they'd try and keep it quiet if they could. She'd pay the fine and that would be my solution, because the people could see that the queen is human and she can speed and so on. They might destroy this fantasy of the queen, that she's above in a castle, or whatever. *[15-year-old Protestant girl]*

On the other hand, the norm that the national leader is above the law is expressed in Nabeel's statements with regard to the queen's violation of a traffic law. Clearly he believes that the monarch should not be punished and he portrays the queen in a very positive light:

INTERVIEWER: *One day, the queen was driving her car to a meeting. Because she was driving very fast, the police stop the car. Finish the story.*

NABEEL: The queen is difficult, it's happened to other members of the royal family. I think it would depend a lot on the policeman. I don't think the queen would do anything to try to get out of it or say, "I'm the queen and let me go." But a lot of policemen would feel that way about it. And I suppose even if the policeman who stopped her wanted to give her a speeding ticket, it would get higher and higher up the police organization. Eventually somebody would say, "Oh, it's the queen, we're not going to do anything about it," and even then if it did get to court, it would be one of these things that they'd wave around the side and forget about it, really.

INTERVIEWER: *What do you think the police would say?*

NABEEL: They'd be very polite to her and unlike perhaps they would be to other speeding motorists. If the policeman didn't like the queen and he felt she should be prosecuted for speeding, he would still be very polite to her but very firm. The policeman might say, "Oh, Your Majesty, you were speeding, you shouldn't be doing that. Go home, please."

INTERVIEWER: *What does the queen say?*

NABEEL: The queen doesn't really have much choice about what she says because she does have to sort of do her job and she wouldn't be able to do anything like say, "I'm the queen, you can't prosecute me for speeding." She would sort of sit down and let things happen. More than anything else she might get a bit annoyed in private and sort of say to somebody, "I'm very irritated because I was stopped for speeding today." But she'd also try to be nice to the police and things. I don't think she'd make any comment at all to the press or anything like that, she'd be completely quiet about that. It'd be pretty difficult for her, a bit of a scandal if the queen was caught speeding. Just to sort of protect her not to mention names.

INTERVIEWER: *What do you think they'd finally decide?*

NABEEL: It probably wouldn't come to court at all 'cause that sort of thing can happen. [*16-year-old Hindu boy*]

Further images reveal positive evaluations of the head of state, manifestations of deference by the police, and the exoneration of the queen from any form of punishment, illustrating Nabeel's positive feelings toward the monarch. In summary, Nabeel and Jessica are representative of the variety of fifth-year pupils at the nonintegrated school. Both children also clearly exhibit patterns of political socialization that are evident among fifth-year counterparts at the integrated school—political authority is respected but is not above admonition or punishment as a traffic violator.

Three themes also emerged from fifth-year children in the nonintegrated school: (1) deference is exhibited to the queen by the traffic policeman, (2) the monarch is evaluated in a neutral to favorable manner, and (3) the head of state is not punished for a traffic misdemeanor. This pattern is consistent with the impression left by the first-year group suggesting an awareness of class differences where you do not punish somebody in authority, especially where that personage is an important political and religious symbol of the state.

OLDER PROTESTANT AND CATHOLIC CHILDREN AT THE INTEGRATED SCHOOL

The following statements exhibit interesting findings among Protestant and Catholic fifth-year pupils at the integrated school regarding the queen and the traffic policeman story. Deborah, James, and Ronnie describe the relationship between the queen and the policeman in terms of a hierarchical relationship where the queen does not have to obey the rules or the police.

Deborah is from a middle-class Protestant neighborhood in Newtownards outside the city of Belfast. She moved there from the city of Londonderry with her family when she was very young. Deborah describes in an imaginative, sarcastic, and lively fashion the queen as a person who could successfully co-opt a groveling policeman by taking him away on an all-expenses-paid vacation in Jamaica. She demonstrates deference toward the monarch, and firmly believes that the police officer would never dream of giving the queen a ticket for speeding:

INTERVIEWER: *One day, the queen was driving her car to a meeting. Because she was driving very fast, the police stop the car. Finish the story.*

DEBORAH: She gets her chauffeur to get out of the car to explain the situation. The policeman started groveling and started saying, "Sorry, I didn't realize who you were," and all that kind of stuff. And she says, "Why don't you get in and go for a ride with me?" And then he says, "Sure, you are the boss!" And he gets in and they go for a drive around London. The queen then decides that she doesn't want to go to the meeting after all because she had been to so many of these things and they are all totally boring, so they decide to go to Jamaica for a few weeks. So they get one of her private planes and they fly over and decide that they like it and they stay there forever after. And they are there for the rest of their lives.

INTERVIEWER: *What do the police say?*

DEBORAH: They would probably start groveling and say that he didn't realize who it was and say that she could go ahead.

INTERVIEWER: *What does the queen say?*

DEBORAH: She would probably tell her chauffeur to apologize or something.

INTERVIEWER: *What do they finally decide?*

DEBORAH: It would probably be all forgotten about in the end because they have gone off to Jamaica and they are just trying to forget about it. They would probably be too embarrassed to charge her. *[16-year-old Protestant girl]*

Clearly, James is intolerant of the queen and government ministers breaking the laws that are made in parliament. He portrays the monarch in a cynical and unfavorable way and assumes that the police officer would punish the queen for breaking the traffic rules and regulations:

INTERVIEWER: *One day, the queen was driving to a meeting. Because she was driving very fast, the police stop the car. Finish the story.*

JAMES: That has happened, sort of but not with the queen. It's happened with ministers of Parliament. About six months ago they introduced a law about wearing safety belts, and none of the ministers wear safety belts and they all got caught, and some of the ministers didn't own up to this. They denied everything. Not all of them were caught by the police; some of them were photographed by newspapers, and were published. Some of them volunteered to pay the fine who weren't caught by the police, and said, "That's fair enough. We introduced the law, so we should do it." Well, the queen, she wouldn't have been driving for a start anyway, but she should pay as well. She has to be seen to be abiding by the laws that she's brought about; if she's not seen to do that then everything sort of breaks down. Even though it's one small situation, the people would say, "If the queen doesn't abide by the laws, then why should we?" It has to work all of the way then.

INTERVIEWER: *What do the police say?*

JAMES: The policeman wouldn't stop the car at the start. They would probably know that she can't wear seat belts for security reasons and try to cover it up. But she would still have to make a statement about it and try to explain what was going on. If it did sort of look that she was breaking her own law, it would look a bit careless. The papers would have a field day.

INTERVIEWER: *What does the queen say in that sort of situation?*

JAMES: I would probably say she would take it quite well. She would pay the fine even if the situation was to her advantage and make a statement of what was going on and show that she had already paid the fine so that people should obey by the rules. That's really all she could do. *[16-year-old Catholic boy]*

It may appear from the following story that Ronnie's policeman is behaving in a deferential way toward the queen. Also, he seems to articulate that the policeman would not punish the queen for a traffic violation. However, when the content and tone of his story is reflected upon, it is clear that Ronnie is in fact portraying the monarch in a cynical and unfavorable light:

INTERVIEWER: *One day, the queen was driving to a meeting. Because she was driving very fast, the police stop the car. Finish the story.*

RONNIE: The policeman obviously doesn't go to the passenger, he would go to the driver. The driver winds down his window. They have a big kind of thing in the back so you can't see the queen. He is giving the driver bad vibes. He is saying, "You went 200 mph and you have got a back taillight broken as well." He is really getting at the driver. The queen kind of winds down the window and says, "Excuse me," just like a queen does, you know, and the policeman is like a changed man and he goes down on his knees and starts groveling and starts crying and stuff and is extremely apologetic, and he says, "Well, don't mind what I said, just go on ahead. I'll give you a police escort."

INTERVIEWER: *What do the police say?*

RONNIE: They would be very sorry and they would probably repeat that about twenty times. "I'm really, really sorry, so sorry, it is my fault, I'm really sorry," and they would keep going on and on until the queen gets bored.

INTERVIEWER: *What does the queen say?*

RONNIE: The queen would give him a knighthood, I reckon. She wouldn't be at all worried about it really. She would say, "Oh, no problem, no problem," because the queen is a nice person.

INTERVIEWER: *What do they finally decide?*

RONNIE: They would finally decide that the queen was in the right and the policeman was definitely in the wrong. No doubt about it, and the queen would go on to her meeting without any more hassle and nothing more said, that kind of thing. *[16-year-old Protestant boy]*

It is noteworthy that the adult theme of political sarcasm and cynicism toward the monarch evidently has developed among all three young people. Negative political orientations directed toward the queen are a result of a feeling that everybody must abide by the laws (James), that the queen can in fact bribe a policeman (Deborah), and that the supposed social position of the queen allows her to get away with breaking the law (Ronnie).

Noreen's response, on the other hand, shows a pattern which is quite consistent with the impression left by James's political imagery. Noreen, a Catholic from the coastal town of Larne, believes that the queen should be punished for breaking the law. She speaks about the monarch in a very unfavorable way:

INTERVIEWER: *One day, the queen was driving to a meeting. Because she was driving very fast, the police stop the car. Finish the story.*

NOREEN: I'm sure the police would be shocked and say, "Sorry, Ma'am, and I think it would be best if you would slow down," and she would probably say, "Well, sorry, I'm in a hurry and I'm going to a meeting," and they would say, "Well, sorry, Ma'am, we can't let you off with that, even though you are in royalty, so I will have to give you a ticket." But then again, it all depends on who it is. He might turn around and say, "Oh, sorry, ma'am, away you go there," I don't know. They would probably give her a warning to tell her to slow down and let her go.

INTERVIEWER: *What do the police say?*

NOREEN: "Oh, I think it would be best for you to slow down or take your helicopter the next time if you are in a hurry in case you would knock someone down."

INTERVIEWER: *What does the queen say?*

NOREEN: She would probably agree and say that she was very sorry and she would remember the next time, or something like that.

INTERVIEWER: *What do they finally decide?*

NOREEN: They would probably just give her a wee warning and just tell her to watch out the next time and do nothing serious about it because people tend to do that. Like even higher police, if they were speeding like that they would kind of say, "Well, away you go there," so they would probably say to her, "Just slow down a wee bit and take care," and say nothing to her again. They don't want to embarrass her or themselves by saying, "Well, here, I want to give you a ticket." *[16-year-old Catholic girl]*

It is reasonable to conclude that older and younger Protestants in both schools are less likely than Catholic children to envision the queen being punished for a traffic violation. Regarding manifestations of deference to the head of state, the proportion of unfavorable evaluations of the monarch is lower among first-year Catholics and higher among fifth-year pupils and first-year Protestants.

An interesting finding of the study captures how the older age groups in both schools show negative evaluative assumptions about the head of state (appendix 2, table 19). Among the younger age peers, negative evaluations[3] of the queen among the nonintegrated school's pupils also outweigh the integrated school's first-year pupils' evaluations.

While it might be assumed that the younger age group would display a more positive evaluation of the monarch like their counterparts in the integrated school, this is not the case (appendix 2, table 19). These differences in affective orientations were unexpected.[4] Several explanations of the differences might be given. An awareness of the moral consequences of breaking the law, in addition to parental values of obedience and respect for public authority, may have had a marked effect on these children's perceptions of "right and wrong." The conservative nature of Northern Ireland's society also reinforces such value systems. The illegal activities of lawbreakers are not tolerated in the overall society.

In summary, first-year pupils from the nonintegrated school were less likely to use the "queen above the law" theme than were the rest of the age peers in the study. In contrast, first-year respondents from the integrated school hold a more positive perception of the queen's behavior toward the policeman. Catholic children show none of the deference that exudes from Protestant children in their portrayal of both the monarch and the policeman. Also, James, Ronnie, and Deborah from the integrated school, despite their religious differences, have by age sixteen developed a cynical orientation toward the possibility of the policeman actually punishing the queen, reflecting the salience of class differences in affecting political behavior.

Conclusions

The findings for children in both schools conformed to the Greenstein and Tarrow (1970a, 1970b) model with a high concentration of pupils in favor of the queen located in the nonintegrated school. An emphasis on monarchical symbolism reflects the fact that Protestant pupils in the nonintegrated school identify with the queen.[5]

These results suggest we need to incorporate a better understanding of children's images of political authority in political flash point areas into political development theory. To better understand the political world of children, we need to know about their knowledge and feelings about political authority and how these political images are related with cultural and historical factors particular to that conflict region. The political lives of children in Northern Ireland are very different from perceptions of political leaders and institutions in the rest of the United Kingdom. In Northern Ireland in recent years there has been a tendency in the integrated schools toward a reciprocal understanding and acceptance of the respective politics of both traditions (Irwin 1991, 1994; Moffat 1993). This behavior is reflected in the integrated schoolchildren's more balanced interpretation of the queen and the prime minister.

The perceptions of the evaluative aspects of the roles of the political incumbents are very different for both schools and for the four school years under consideration in this study. More differences in political imagery are evident among fifth-year pupils in the integrated school, which may reflect the fact that the openness of the school environment permits the pupils to grasp a more balanced interpretation of the differences between the queen and the prime minister and between the ethnoreligious groups at the school. Fifth-year Catholic and Protestant students from the integrated school tend to adopt a more cynical attitude toward the monarch than the fifth-year pupils from the other school. First- and fifth-year pupils from the nonintegrated school hold an idealized image of the crown, perceiving the prime minister's role as less important even though they clearly recognize the separation of powers.

Piaget and Weil (1970) found that some dramatic changes took place in the psychological development of children as they moved from a more abstract stage to a more concrete knowledge of political phenomena. I found differences in the political orientations of first- and fifth-year pupils to the queen and the prime minister. Further, fifth-year pupils from the nonintegrated school hold benign views of the queen compared to their counterparts in the integrated school. This may be due in part to the fact that the majority of fifth-year pupils at the nonintegrated school are middle-class Protestants, whereas the religious, gender, and class structures of the integrated school are mixed. Furthermore, the continuity of the constitutional monarchy has led to a stability in the political culture of Northern Ireland as values and norms are transmitted from one generation to the next. In other words, the deferential nature of British society leads to a consensus in political attitudes (Birch 1990; Jennings 1965; Norton 1984; Punnett 1980; Rose 1986).

Supporting evidence was found for Greenstein's (1975) assertions on the emergence of more balanced views of the British prime minister. Evidence can be found in the concentration of fifth-year pupils' knowledge about the actual political functioning of the head of government compared to the less salient political role of the monarch. Further evidence for this difference can be seen in the benign orientations of first-year children toward the head of state and much less balanced views of the prime minister. The younger-age peers are in the early stages of cognitive development (Kohlberg 1981; Piaget 1976). The movement into the final stages of increasing complexity and sophistication has not yet been achieved.

Distinctive patterns are evident for both schools when the queen was imagined in action. Equality before the law and the norm of public safety were prevalent images of the queen's behavior; however, more students at the nonintegrated school believed that the queen should be neither cautioned nor punished for violating the law. In contrast, equality before the law was the most vocal norm among the integrated school's pupils, who perceived the queen as not being above the law. In other words, class position and status should not procure punishment for illegal behavior, as the queen is not above the laws of the land (Greenstein and Tarrow 1970a, 1970b; Greenstein 1975).

In conclusion, the main differences in political imagery are between schools. The nonintegrated school's pupils have a slightly more positive image of the head of state than of the head of government. First-year pupils from this school also exhibit more sophistication in their cognitive constructions and reconstructions of images of political authority. The integrated school's first-year students, on the other hand, have more flux in comparison. The pattern of children's images of political leaders and the links between different levels of children's cognitive political development and class background fit into the findings of previous scholarly research.

It can be observed that at all four-year age groups in both school systems, many more children display a substantial degree of knowledge about the political roles and behavior of the queen and the prime minister. Several reasons can be suggested to explain the pattern described above (Crossman 1972; Punnett 1980; Sampson 1973).

First, the parliamentary system in Britain gives rise to the leadership role of the prime minister being the equivalent of primus inter pares, so that the prime minister's political role within the cabinet has developed to overshadow other ministers and the members of his or her political party (Richards 1983; Rose 1986). Children watching the news on television begin to notice that it is the prime minister who influences what political road the party must take (Connell 1971). The collective responsibility of the cabinet is affected by the control that party leaders exercise over party members in Parliament (Bogdanor 1981; Norton 1984).

Children begin to understand as they get older that government is unlikely to act effectively unless it is led by the prime minister (Greenstein and Tarrow 1970a, 1970b; Greenstein 1975). Older children in this study seemed to recognize that there is tension between the idea that government should represent the political interests of the people and the need for ministers to take effective political action by enacting legislation and following the lead of the prime minister (Birch 1990; Crossman 1972). Also, they appeared to recognize that the British cabinet remains basically ambivalent about the relative merits of the traditional amateur member of parliament who services the needs of his or her constituents, and the modern technocratic European specialist who advocates for a tighter union with the European Union. Indeed, Britain's role in the European Union is a lively one, working to promote political interests contrary to the Maastricht Treaty; John Major has not shied away from publicity and strong stands on core sovereignty issues.

Although the prime minister is at the very heart of British politics, the queen is at the core of Britain's political culture and stable democracy (Coles 1986; Greenstein and Tarrow 1970a, 1970b). Consequently, the picture painted by the media of the queen opening Parliament and appearing on television as an intrinsic part of the British national anthem catches the attention of children (Sampson 1973). Children accept the legitimacy of the queen's political authority as part of Britain's traditional link with the historical and cultural past, which provides continuity and stability for the British political system (Crossman 1972; Martin 1963; Sampson 1973). In Northern Ireland, the queen is an object of loyalty within a constitutional monarchy (Miller 1978). For most children in this study, we see remarkable detail in their descriptions of the queen and the prime minister. Thus, if we really want to understand who is relating to what political leaders and why, and, why traditional, well-established links between children and nation are enduring, we need to understand the role of political development, political culture, and political socialization in the political life of children. Politics plays a key role in explaining the links between children and nation and may play a greater role in the future study of intractable conflicts as ethnoregional conflicts continue to escalate around the world.

7

Putting Children's Wisdom into Practice

Introduction

With the end of the cold war, ethnic conflicts involving clashes of intercommunity identity are now reasserting themselves on the world stage. It is likely that these conflicts are caused, maintained, and defined by a multiplicity of political, economic, geographic, historical, cultural, and psychological factors. Thus, enduring and just conflict resolution is a long-term process of social change. This study explores one possible avenue of movement toward conflict resolution and social change in Belfast, Northern Ireland: integrated education.

This study contributes to our understanding of integrated education and the political world of Belfast children by reviewing these schoolchildren's political imagery of violence and peaceful change. Northern Ireland will serve as an important model of success or failure for other societies also trying to heal from the collective trauma of sustained intercommunity conflict and/or violence. For example, the violence in Lebanon, South Africa, Israel, and Rwanda has de-escalated as of the time of this writing but what kind of policies and institutions are necessary to ensure that these societies achieve a positive and just peace? It is also important to be able to assess whether or not and, if so, how young children will be able to adapt to peace despite their exposure to a culture of political violence. It is possible integrated schooling may promote intergroup tolerance and understanding in war-weary societies and help bring about intergenerational change.

A Next Step Toward Peace?

What can we learn from what these young persons have to say about the Northern Ireland conflict and their political world? As

181

described above, the children interviewed for this study included younger (11-to 12-year olds) and older (15- to 16-year olds) groups in both an integrated and nonintegrated (predominantly Protestant) school. These children were individuals with different perspectives, but some common themes emerged in their discussions. As discussed in chapters 5 and 6, children from both schools and both age-groups mentioned several different factors influencing the Northern Ireland conflict.

Some mentioned terrorism: "get the IRA out because they are just causing nonstop trouble" *[Jennifer, 11-year-old Protestant, nonintegrated school]*. Some mentioned socioeconomic factors: "Maybe the prime minister is not doing very much about the economy and the way people have to live here. The poor people only get so much to live on every week and they are not coping too well and their stomachs empty" *[Gerry, 12-year-old, Catholic, integrated school]*. Some mentioned social class: "I think class is part of the conflict. There are some middle-class people who are prejudiced but I haven't come across it. I think it would be predominantly working-class" *[Jessica, 15-year-old, Protestant, nonintegrated school]*. Some mentioned religious factors: "Well it's just about the religion, Catholics and Protestants" *[Joanie, 12-year-old Catholic, integrated school]*. One student said the conflict was not so much political, but rather the activity of criminal gangs: "If you look at other countries that are having trouble, like Italy, they have people like the Mafia and they kill more people in one year than we do here, it's just that it's publicized different. It's publicized as a war here. It's like two wee gangs and that's the bit that needs to be stopped *[James, 16-year-old, Catholic, integrated school]*.

The most salient theme that emerged in talk about the political milieu and the regional conflict for all children in all groups was national identity. However, the images of national identity differed among the children. For example, a Protestant boy from the older group at the nonintegrated school articulated, "The people in Ulster are patriotic, and the queen is the head of the state for them. Northern Ireland is part of Great Britain and the people in the South of Ireland think that Northern Ireland should become part of Ireland" *[Stan, 16-year-old, Protestant]*. This description of the intercommunity conflict is put forth matter-of-factly and describes an either-or, zero-sum position of national identity (Fisher and Ury 1981).

Several students linked images of national identity to issues of political power and political security. Speaking of the queen, a Protestant boy from the older group at the nonintegrated school said,

"The Loyalists look up to her. I don't particularly think they do. I think it's just because they don't want the south invading. They don't want Catholic rulership" *[Russell, 15-year-old, Protestant]*. A Hindu boy from the older age group at the nonintegrated school also speaks about the symbolism of the monarch for Northern Ireland's Protestant community. "I suppose the people in Northern Ireland if you look at the Unionists or the Protestants if you want to put it that way, they've lived in Northern Ireland a lot. Their way of life is being threatened by people who want them to be part of Ireland." *[Nabeel, 16-year-old, Hindu]*. Thus, national identity is a pathway to political power, but perhaps, more importantly, a protection from threat, suggesting that the attachment to national identity is fueled by fear. For Protestants, the queen, rather than the prime minister, is an enduring symbol of their British identity, heritage, and security.

A Catholic boy in the younger group at the integrated school expressed an emphatic image of national identity. "Northern Ireland is a part of the United Kingdom where the Republic of Ireland is not. So I think the prime minister has more of a say for to get a stop to everything and just tell everyone it is going to be stopped, that's it, and maybe take all the Protestants out of Northern Ireland. Which I would like to see like" *[Patrick, 12-year-old, Catholic]*. Interestingly, however, his one-dimensional perspective is complicated by his experience at the integrated school. "But I'm a Catholic, like, but my best mate is a Protestant so I wouldn't like to see that" *[Patrick]*

A Protestant girl in the older group at the integrated school described ironies in how the groups see each other. "If you ask them why do they hate them, then they just go, 'Well, they go around blowing up people.' We're doing that as well, why do you hate them? They say, 'But that's different,' and you say, 'No, it's not different, it's just the same'" *[Donna, 15-year-old, Protestant]*. This student from a Loyalist enclave said that she speaks about these things with extremists in her community. In this way, though young and perhaps unpersuasive for now, she is acting as an agent of social change.

A Catholic girl from a mixed marriage is in the older group at the integrated school. She said that the integrated school had not particularly changed the way she thinks about the two communities. "I come from a mixed background, so I never really noticed any difference" *[Anne, 16-year-old, Catholic]*. However, she said that she observed changes in other children. "First year students come to this school from the Donegall Pass and the Falls Road and they said, 'I never realized that Catholics are nice and they didn't beat me up. I always thought their eyes were closer together.' These are the wee stories you hear." Children are aware of the perspectives of their peers. They can also observe change when it occurs. "It's funny listening to some first years and then the way they change their views. After the first year, people don't really care less, it doesn't matter. Religion doesn't really come into it now." *[Anne]*

These comments suggest that the experience of the integrated school may impact upon some of the older children's understandings of national and religious identity. Or, it may be that these comments reflect a preselection process whereby eccentric parents deviated outside the established educational system (Wright 1991). Anne, above, may be one example. From a mixed marriage, she said she was unaffected by the integrated school. However, she said that she observed children with different perspectives and that these perspectives changed. Also, her viewpoints may impact on others with more sectarian views. When I asked the children in this study why they went to the integrated school, the answers varied: The children came from a mixed marriage or neighborhood, their parents and/or grandparents had decided to send them, their friends were going to the school, or the child decided to try something new.

Several of these older students at the integrated school were reflective about integrated education as a policy for change. "It's [integrated education] extremely important because it's the future of everything that's happening here because it's going to be a next step toward peace" *[Ronnie, 16-year-old, Protestant]*. "I just think it's the atmosphere here. You come in and you think that Catholics will stay on this side and Protestants will stay on that side. This is what they expect, but if you throw all of them in together, you can't tell by looking at someone whether they're Catholic or Protestant" *[Anne, 16-year-old, Catholic]*. "If every school in this country was integrated, it would change a hell of a lot of people's attitudes" *[Niall, 16-year-old, Catholic]*.

Integrated education may have affected the children's understandings of their identity and the other group. Images of identity form for the individual from early childhood as part of the process of political socialization. Understanding of the "other" can be encoded in the identity and world view of a community (Northrup 1989). In Northern Ireland, segregation or limited intercommunity contact allows for unidimensional, or even fictional images, of the other to go unchallenged by experience. In this way, identity and conflict can be sustained through generations. Further, in the Northern Ireland conflict, national and religious identity is seen as nonnegotiable and zero-sum. This makes the conflict more intractable and a win-win solution difficult to imagine.

However, I want to suggest that integrated education seems to create an opportunity for moving the identity conflict for these children from a win-lose situation to a win-win situation by expanding the identity pie. For these children, the Protestant-Catholic divide is bridged by the broader identity of attending an integrated Christian school. One fact that is essential for this expanded identity to be possible is that the school's academic, religious, and athletic curriculum encompasses the particular culture of each community. For example, the academic curricula includes both British and Irish history as well as an emphasis on Northern Ireland's wider global context. Courses in the Gaelic language are offered. There are religious instruction classes that emphasize a common Christian tradition, but there are clerics and nuns with offices in the school who represent almost all of Northern Ireland's religious denominations. The athletic curriculum reflects both traditionally Protestant and Catholic sports which all children have a chance to play.

Another factor that may also be crucial for the success of this process, is that integrated education is not a top-down, government-enforced policy. The forcible integration of the whole education system would likely be resisted by the clergy, extremist local politicians, paramilitary organizations, and some families, and would thus escalate intercommunity conflict. The existence of integrated schooling, however, gives parents and young people, Protestants and Catholics, and middle- and working-class people the choice and opportunity of breaking out of a sectarian and static culture (Moffat 1993; Wright 1991).

The integrated school environment provides a neutral environment, in which Protestant and Catholic children learn about each other's cultures: how they are different, but also how they are the same (Irwin 1994). The children begin to hear each other's stories, and there is a widening and a sharing of identity that may lead to structural change. Also, the integrated sector is a new voice, forging a dialogue with the nonintegrated sector and prompting the introduction by the British government of the Education for Mutual Understanding (1989) curriculum in all schools in Northern Ireland. Also, there is a commitment on behalf of families, teachers, and children to come up with a common curriculum to solve each community's needs. Importantly, neither group has been assimilated. The curriculum has instead preserved each group's distinct cultures and identities.

People in the local community are committed to promoting social change in Northern Ireland. There have been physical threats against such people working for peace and reconciliation, including the founding members of the integrated school in our study. They are perceived by extremists as a potential threat in shifting the power balance in Northern Ireland. Teachers in nonintegrated schools who advocate integrated education have not been promoted, parents who send their children to integrated schools have been harassed and intimidated, and businessmen lose contracts or have their premises bombed if they carry out work for the integrated school sector.[1]

However, people in both communities want to create a new experience and are prepared to suffer such opposition in order to move society forward toward a positive peace and just reconciliation. As a Belfast history teacher in the integrated school put it, "People need the conflict to keep their identities, but they don't need to resolve it by cutting the heads off of each other."[2] Finally, this study has suggested that not all of these young people mirror society or use old rhetoric when looking at their political world. Some of the political perceptions from the integrated school-children suggest that positive new ideas are beginning to bear fruit in this next generational group, reflecting a more shared and meaningful experience.

How can this expanding of the identity pie for children in the integrated school relate to the larger society? Many persons have suggested that the European nation-state is being superseded by a federation of equal and democratic regions that will foster minority and regional cultures within each of the European nations (Byrne 1994a, 1995; Dixon 1994a, 1994b; Hayes 1990; Hume 1988; Kearney 1988). I would suggest that such a dynamic could serve to expand the national identity pie for Catholics and Protestants in Northern Ireland by preserving the interests and security of both parties within a larger supranational identity.

A local region, Northern Ireland, firmly entrenched within the context of a federal Europe could provide a political context that protects the local cultural heritages of Protestants and Catholics within a supranational setting that would propel Northern Ireland forward into the twenty-first century (Byrne 1995; Dixon 1994a, 1994b; Kearney 1988). With the 21 February 1995 joint publication by the British and Irish governments of the "Frameworks for the Future" document to promote a just and final peace in Northern

Ireland, both communities have now to face a common future together.

However, such an expanded vision of a wider, shared identity may not readily develop in Northern Ireland where national identity is so deeply entrenched. Mutual fear and distrust limits interaction and contact between the Catholic and Protestant communities. Other political feelings about the European Union may also provide obstacles to such a process. Asked if a European identity would help a process of peace and reconciliation, a boy from the nonintegrated school said, "I think it would be stupid to force the European community on people. I think there should be a referendum to decide whether they should go into Europe or not. I personally believe that they shouldn't. I believe it should stay the way it is. It's quite useful now. It would change it totally if they did and national identity would totally decrease. People wouldn't associate England with things, they'd associate Europe with things eventually" [Russell, 15-year-old, Protestant]. However, a boy from the nonintegrated school was more hopeful. "The European thing, that could work. There are quite a few M.E.P.s, and if they could get together in Europe. It could be a common ground. But it's all going to have to start from education because how do politicians start thinking the way they do?" [James, 15-year-old, Catholic].

However, in order to promote and sustain a liberal and pluralistic democracy in Northern Ireland, the integrative educational structure, political tolerance and cooperation, and the rate of economic development and growth must be increased to a level comparable to richer regions within the European Union (Kearney 1988). The fundamental problem facing any movement towards a lasting and just peace and reconciliation for everyone in Northern Ireland is that integrated education alone cannot change the base and mode of the present conflict when the underlying structural dimensions remain static (Stephen 1990b).

At the European regional level, a lasting solution to the Northern Ireland conflict and other ethnoregional conflicts in Europe could be overcome as these countries enter a larger culturally diverse European community where specific ethnic differences and identities were respected and multiple heritages were cherished, and encouraged to develop within a larger supranational setting (Byrne 1995; Hayes 1990; Kearney 1988).

Recommendations for Future Research

This book attempts to bring forth the perspectives and wisdom of children who otherwise would not be heard. They speak about their political world, including political authority figures and the Northern Ireland conflict and its possible resolution. Their discussions are relevant to possible avenues for movement toward peace.

Governmental Policies

British and Irish governmental policy formulation and what mixtures of policy they adopt are also vital considerations for building a just peace in Northern Ireland (Byrne 1994a, 1995; McGarry and O'Leary 1990; O'Leary and McGarry 1993). Many scholars have theorized that major political, social, and economic structural changes will be necessary to promote tolerance and understanding (Bew et al. 1995; Byrne 1995; Byrne and Carter 1994; Guelke 1988; O'Leary and McGarry 1993; Whyte 1990; Wright 1987). Hence, further study is necessary to investigate the effects of educational and political policies on intercommunal relations in Northern Ireland.

I propose that parallel political structures promoting just and egalitarian policies, based on grassroots participation, are needed to sustain and promote the growth of the integrated school sector in Northern Ireland (Byrne 1995). The educational and political forums diverge in Northern Ireland so much that educational policy recommendations could not be successful unless there is a convergence between the educational and political sectors to create a peaceful solution within the political system (Byrne and Carter 1994). Switzerland and the Netherlands provide concrete European examples of such convergence between sectors. Unfortunately, this important dimension falls outside the scope of this research project but scholars need to address this issue in their research. They need to examine and learn from the conflict resolution mechanisms that communities in other divided societies have employed to resolve differences between groups. Also, scholars need to understand that political and educational policies are not mutually exclusive: they complement each other on the path toward promoting grassroots peacebuilding.

School Peace Programs

If trends in Africa and Eastern Europe in 1995 are indicative of the future, then more efforts should be made to build a coherent peace program into the education systems in the United Kingdom,

Northern Ireland, and the Republic of Ireland. Efforts to promote a better understanding of conflict and peace-building among the children who will be tomorrow's leaders in all dimensions of socio-economic and political life would augur well for the future local civic societies in these regions.

For example, delegates from all branches of education in Ireland, North and South, who attended the Irish Peace Institute-sponsored international conference on "Education for Peace," which took place at the University of Limerick, Ireland, in October 1991, were acutely aware of the vital necessity for a positive and coordinated effort by educationalists and policy makers, north and south of the border, to integrate a consistent peace dimension into the second-level curriculum. The Chairman of the Irish Peace Institute (IPI), Mr. Tom O'Donnell, who was joint chair of the conference organizing committee said that:

> The conference was of great value to the educationalists from Ireland, Europe, the United States, and Japan who have professed interest in a follow-up conference. The IPI would also like to commission a study of the present situation of peace education in Ireland, North and South, with a view to determining the most logical way forward.[3]

The development and introduction of a peace-building and conflict-resolution database could prove to be a very important, interesting, and educational instrument in providing children with the necessary skills and knowledge of what conflict is and how to intervene, negotiate, facilitate, and mediate parties to a particular dispute.

Peace Organizations, Nongovernmental Organizations, and Universities

We need further research on independent nongovernmental and nonpolitical organizations, such as the IPI, and the Center for the Study of Conflict at the University of Ulster at Coleraine, which are in ideal positions to promote convergence between educational research centers and grassroots activists. These organizations would also be in a position to sponsor ongoing programs of research between and among Irish, British, European, and American universities and local peace organizations and groups, such as the Tipperary Peace People or the Corrymeela Peace Community, involved in peace-building in educational and community relations at the grassroots level in Britain, Northern Ireland, Europe, the United States and the Irish Republic.[4]

A coordinated and collaborative problem-solving approach would allow for the formulation and implementation of policies between the institutional, educational, and grass-roots sectors. Also, the unified cooperation of peace organizations, such as Families Against Intimidation and Terrorism, and Widows Against Violence Empowerment, in Northern Ireland, would provide a more realistic challenge to the sectarianism and violence mounted by the paramilitaries and extremists, and permit a more structured and united peacebuilding and reconciliation program to develop.

Regional Identity

A secular third pillar provides the balancing act which relegates, in importance, the ethnoreligious cleavage in Dutch society (Lijphart 1968, 1975). Also, within western Europe, San Marino, Monaco, Gibraltar, and the Papal State are clear-cut examples of independent, sovereign republics and principalities that have persisted despite ethnolinguistic, ethnopolitical, ethnocultural, and geographic submersion within a larger geographical entity (Thompson and Ronen 1986). These ethnoterritorial states have developed distinctive national characteristics and have traditionally been devoted to peace and social equality (Gottlieb 1993; Smith 1982; Vayrynen 1984). These pluralistic and nonviolent ideals have not conflicted with the interests of their larger neighbors (Lijphart 1968; Rokkan and Urwin 1982, 1983). Northern Ireland could not, however, go down the road of a Unilateral Declaration of Independence (UDI) because a sizeable minority of the nationalist population, whose allegiance is to a united Ireland would make such a political conglomerate totally ungovernable, opposing the reemergence of a Unionist populist state (Guelke 1988; Wright 1987). However, Northern Ireland could become a local canton/region within a larger community setting.

Another research avenue, therefore, would be to focus on placing Northern Ireland within the context of a wider community. The geographical proximity and cultural relatedness of Scotland, for example, suggests that a regional arrangement could be reached between the British and Irish governments within the European Union (Nairn 1977). An examination of ties between Scotland and Northern Ireland may assist in our understanding of how many Scots would align themselves with the paramilitary groupings on both sides of the bicommunal divide if a civil war ever erupted in Northern Ireland.

The European Connection

The growing socioeconomic and political complexity of post-Maastricht European society necessitates the facilitation and encouragement of ordinary people to open up more integrated schools to meet the rising demand in Northern Ireland and to assist in creating a more pluralistic and tolerant society. Because the present educational system continues to raise barriers to communication between the two traditions in Northern Ireland, the introduction of such schools would give students common social skills that are both universal and simple (Hayes 1990). Change is favored as more students from both sides of the communal divide travel to Europe and the United States via school or college exchange programs, or learn new scientific and cultural ideas that link them to the ever wider, changing European and American societies (Hayes 1990). Hence, the recruitment of teachers at all levels could be expanded to include the Irish Republic, Great Britain, the United States, and the wider European market, imparting diverse and new perspectives to Northern Ireland's students.

More research is needed, therefore, on the exchange of European ideas as a positive contribution to conflict resolution and peace-building in strife-ridden regions within the European Union. Hayes (1990) has concluded that the federal framework of the European Union will synergize regional cultures, thereby accommodating ethnocultural diversity in Northern Ireland. The process of European economic and political integration means that the nation state is dispersing power both upwards to Strasbourg and Brussels and downwards to the regional level (Byrne 1994a, 1995; Dixon 1994a, 1994b; Hume 1988; Kearney 1988). These regional identities will simultaneously coexist with national identities expressed through art, literature, sports, and customs and with the secularizing influences associated with the rest of industrialized Europe (Kearney 1988; Keogh and Haltzel 1994).

Northern Ireland—The Future?

While conflict persists in Northern Ireland, integrated schools may be one of the most important factors to help build peace in the region. Integrated schools are creating a new social group that bridges the sectarian divide between the Catholic and Protestant communities and will be an important force in helping to expand the identity pie. For example, the integration of Protestant and

Catholic children in the integrated school in our study seemed to reduce prejudice and mistrust by reframing or expanding the students' understndings of identity. The integrated school curriculum weaves together the Protestant and Catholic narratives in a way that respects and maintains each cultural identity while developing a broader, shared identity.

This widening of understandings of identity is congruent with the context of the European Union, where European Union laws and policy are being developed to accommodate ethnocultural diversity. Multinationalization and the greater movement of people within the European Union will create greater employment opportunities and different cultural experiences for the people of Northern Ireland. Integrated education will be congruent with a changing economic and cultural region.

Also, we must continue to explore the ways in which adult conflicts do social, psychological, and emotional damage, especially to children, but really to all of humanity. Integrated education may be a way to heal from and reverse this process. Learning to transform these conflicts is essential for social society's future. And we can learn from our children. As one child said, "integrated education is the next step toward peace." The current changing political context within Northern Ireland reflects that a process of peace-building has begun and that integrated schooling is just one more step on a long, arduous journey toward a lasting settlement.

Appendix 1
History of Education in Northern Ireland

Londonderry, the Ecumenist

THE Northern Ireland government made attempts in 1857 and 1922 to introduce integrated schools in which Protestants and Catholics would learn a common curriculum side by side. Both attempts failed because of the intransigence of the Protestant and Catholic churches (Gallagher and Worrall 1982). Lord Londonderry's Education Act of 1923 was a further attempt to end segregated education in Northern Ireland by providing public elementary schools for all young people. Religious instruction along denominational lines would be permitted outside school hours. However, this legislation was opposed by both Catholic and Protestant churches and populist governmental ministers, who felt that mixed education would promote secularism instead of the separate religious experiences, values, norms, and ethos that existed (Darby 1976).

The sectarian policies of the populist governmental ministers contrasted with pluralistic efforts by Lord Londonderry in 1923 to create a nonsectarian education system throughout Northern Ireland (Akenson 1973; Birrell and Murie 1980). Lord Londonderry wanted religious neutrality and an impartial education system to prevent religious cleavage and sectarianism (Wilson 1989). The system was to be open to both Protestant and Catholic children, with Protestants appointed as teaching staff to Catholic schools and vice versa (Buckland 1979).

Agitation for compulsory Bible teaching in all schools by the United Educational Committee of Protestant Churches (UECP) and the Orange Order brought about the capitulation of Lord Londonderry. In a flurry of new political activity, both interest groups, demanding that religious ministers should sit on regional educational committees, used the general election of May 1929 as a caveat to force government responsiveness (Wilson 1989). Prime

Minister William Craig's government surrendered to the wily poli-
ticking of the UECP and the Orange Order because the ever-
looming general election dictated that it would be political suicide
not to amend the 1923 Education Act (Buckland 1979; Wilson
1989).

The 1930 and 1947 Education Acts
and the Power-Sharing Executive

The 1930 Education Act made Bible class an integral part of the
curriculum for all primary and secondary schools. This amend-
ment alienated the Catholic clergy, who perceived Bible teaching
and public schools as strictly Protestant (Watt 1980). The minister
of education, Lord Londonderry, and Prime Minister Craig then
totally abandoned the integrated school idea. In the aftermath of
this fiasco, Protestants attended state schools and Catholics set up
their own private schools (Murray 1985). Important studies of the
school system in the province have demonstrated the almost total
segregation of the education system (Barrit and Carter 1962; Darby
1976; Darby and Dunn 1987; Murray 1985; Rose 1971).

The Northern Ireland 1947 Education Act increased by 65 percent the amount of capital expenditure by the government on
Catholic schools (Wilson 1989). In January 1968 the Catholic clergy
accepted the four-and-two category, whereby four persons would
be appointed to the management committee by the Church and
two by the local educational authority (Whyte 1990). In 1972, when
Direct Rule was imposed by the British government, political responsibility for education reverted to London. The 1973 Sunningdale Agreement set up a devolved power-sharing executive in
Northern Ireland between moderate political parties on both sides
of the bicommunal divide. The new Northern Irish Minister of
Education, Basil McIver, was supported by the Presbyterian
Church and the Church of Ireland in his efforts to introduce inte-
grated education, but he was opposed by both an uncompromising
Catholic hierarchy and a reactionary Free Presbyterian Church.

Militant actions in 1975 by the Ulster Workers Council (UWC)
brought about the collapse of the power-sharing executive (Arthur
1987). The Catholic and Free Presbyterian hierarchies were re-
lieved that the militant actions of the UWC prevented enactment
of any progressive legislation by Basil McIver. The reaction of the
Presbyterian and Methodist Churches was to seek to change the

status quo by promoting integration at all levels of society, including the schools (Wilson 1989).

The Integrated Education Sector

Efforts for integrated religious education by the All Children Together (ACT) movement of liberal parents from both communities in 1978 reduced barriers to integrated education in the province. This secular movement was initially an important development in establishing the first two integrated secondary schools in the greater Belfast area. In 1986, the Belfast Charitable Trust for Integrated Education (BELTIE) opened two more integrated schools. Since 1981, seventeen new primary and over five new secondary integrated schools have been set up in Northern Ireland (Moffat 1993; NICIE 1991a, 1991b, 1991c). The progressiveness of both ACT and BELTIE and the Northern Ireland Council for Integrated Education (NICIE) in assisting the development of integrated schooling in Northern Ireland for the public good clearly demonstrate liberal Catholic and Protestant assertiveness in the face of vigorous opposition. These groups seek to provide integrated education to eradicate traditional ethnoreligious antagonisms. The commitment of the Catholic clergy to maintaining the Catholic ethos of their schools in Northern Ireland has become threatened by integrated schooling (Murray 1985; Whyte 1990).

A grassroots increase in demand for integrated primary and secondary schools in the Province and recent policy efforts by the British government to allow for that choice suggest that integrated education is providing new opportunities for more positive communication and understanding (Hughes 1994; Irwin 1991, 1994; McEwen 1990; Moffat 1993). Darby (1976) notes that Catholic clerical control of secondary schools is threatened by the falloff in vocations and the increasingly aggressive demands of the Catholic laity for access to the role of headmaster in the schools. The primary impetus for integrated education in the province has come not from the Northern Ireland Office, the British government, the clergy, or the political elites but from grassroots constituents. In response to this demand, the Department of Education for Northern Ireland (DENI) introduced legislation in 1988 to promote integrated education (Dunn 1989).

Also, some grassroots organizations have attempted to promote contact between adults on both sides of the communal divide. The

Ulster People's College, for example, is an independent antisectarian community educational college that tries to develop a common agenda, identify causes of sectarianism, and promote social change (Lovett 1990). Also, an expansion of university education, as a result of the British Labor Party's 1948 Butler Education Act, resulted in more Protestant-Catholic elite contact at the university level in Northern Ireland (Coakley 1985). The choice of integrated schooling must now be provided for all of the people in Northern Ireland, regardless of class or religious background.

The Education Program

Does the separate school system foster a different education program? Different histories and cultures are taught through segregated education, shaping the cultural, political, ethnoreligious, and national identities of Protestants and Catholics (Jahoda and Harrison 1985; Magee 1974; Murray 1983, 1985). Barritt and Carter (1972), Devlin (1969), and Murray (1983, 1985) note how different religious instruction, sports, and history classes socialize schoolchildren into different sociopolitical worlds.

Protestant and Catholic children in separate schools belong to different social, cultural, and sports organizations (Whyte 1986, 1990). Thus, even game activities are different: Gaelic football and hurling are played at Catholic schools, while cricket and rugby are played at Protestant state schools (Murray 1983). Although soccer attracts support from both communities, it is fiercely divisive because the communities support different clubs that are generally sectarian (Murray 1985). For example, Catholics go to Derry city games and support the Republic of Ireland team, while Glentoran fans sing "The Orange Sash," "God Save the Queen," and "Come On, Northern Ireland" in supporting the national side.

Attitudes and stereotypes are passed on by parents to their children from each generation to the next (Hughes 1994). Coles (1986) recognized that grown-ups reinforce cultural stereotypes among their children, who try to imitate their elders. This process perpetuates the sectarian nature of Northern Irish society. Family traditions and peer group pressure influence what schoolchildren think and what organizations, clubs, and churches they join, giving rise to a kind of "us-versus-them" outlook based on the disparagement of the other ethnic group coexisting in the Province.

Teachers and educators have an important role to play, according to O'Donnell (1977), in reframing the context that influences stereotypical behavior and in establishing new behaviors, especially in primary schools where pupils are beginning to formulate sectarian stereotypes. Integrated schools could help to change this process by helping to move young people away from traditional prejudices and stereotypes.

A Common Educational System?

The two separate educational systems are similar in structure, organization, staffing, and examinations (Darby and Dunn 1987; Dunn 1986; Murray 1983). Protestant and Catholic children also have some elements of a common Northern Irish identity. Dunn (1989) and Darby (1978) note the existence of a shared Northern Irish culture; local schools make excursions to such venues as the Ulster Museum and the Ulster Folk Museum. The many elements of shared heritage could assist in the gradual building of an integrated education system and a consensual common culture (Byrne 1994a; Byrne and Carter 1994; Robinson 1971).

For integrated education to spread throughout the Province (Irwin 1991, 1995; Moffat 1993), the fears and objections of the Catholic Church will have to be overcome (Murray 1985; Wilson 1989). Increased communication between schools, especially those in segregated residential areas, and between schools and statutory bodies will also be necessary if integration proponents are to succeed (Darby 1976, 1983; Dunne and Smith 1989). Loyalist and Republican paramilitaries, as well as a majority of the political elites, would probably favor the status quo because it ensures their control in flashpoint residential areas.

The teacher plays a significant role in the socialization of young men and women, empowering students to make important and strategic choices and arrange their ideas, attitudes, and beliefs (Lynch 1987). Teachers indirectly reinforce values acquired at home, in school, and among friends that are an instrumental part of children's conceptual bases (Banks 1986). Therefore, teaching has paramount implications for the socialization process in Northern Ireland because teachers reflect the attitudes of the broader society in the classroom.

Murray (1985) found in his analysis of teachers, however, that Protestant teachers emphasized the importance of British identity whereas Catholic teachers stressed the significance of Irish symbols and national emblems. Protestant and Catholic schoolchildren internalize the norms and values promoted by their teachers, thus reinforcing those already stored in their schemata from parents, media, and peers.

Conclusions

What we find in the literature on education in Northern Ireland is mostly speculation about the effects of integration, with little empirical evidence to support the views. In my view, integrated schools will be one of the most important forces in redefining Northern Irish society in the next twenty years; thus it is of vital importance to document this development in detail.

The literature on education in Northern Ireland examines either the integrated (Irwin 1991; Moffat 1993; McEwen 1990) or the non-integrated (Murray 1983, 1985) educational sectors without drawing connections between the two. In this study I have attempted to fill the void in the literature by comparing the political imagery of children in both sets of schools, linking children's political perceptions to age differences and similarities. I have responded to some of the criticisms of integrated education by incorporating an understanding of the history and culture of the two communities in Belfast, Northern Ireland, and by proposing some educational and political policy possibilities.

Appendix 2

Table 1
Children's Evaluation of Religion as a Cause of the Conflict, by School and by Age

Percentage of Children Mentioning Religion as a Cause of the Conflict					
Integrated School			Nonintegrated School		
Age	No Mentions	One or More Mentions	Age	No Mentions	One or More Mentions
11–12	50	50	11–12	50	50
15–16	64	36	15–16	88	12
Phi = .14 ($\underline{N}$ = 19)			Phi = .41 ($\underline{N}$ = 16)		

Table 2
Children's Evaluation of Religion as a Cause of the Conflict, by Religious Affiliation

Percentage of Children Mentioning Religion as a Cause of the Conflict		
Both Integrated and Nonintegrated Schools		
Religion	No Mentions	One or More Mentions
Protestant	71	29
Catholic	40	60
Phi = .29 ($\underline{N}$ = 34)		

Table 3
Children's Suggestions that Terrorists Should Be Punished,
by School and by Age

Percentage of Children Mentioning that Terrorists Should be Punished					
Integrated School			Nonintegrated School		
Age	No Mentions	One or More Mentions	Age	No Mentions	One or More Mentions
11–12	75	25	11–12	50	50
15–16	36	64	15–16	50	50
Phi = .38 ($\underline{N}$ = 19)			Phi = 0.0 ($\underline{N}$ = 16)		

Table 4
Protestant Children's Suggestions
that Terrorists Should Be Punished,
by School

Percentage of Protestant Children Mentioning that Terrorists Should Be Punished		
School	No Mentions	One or More Mentions
Integrated	44	56
Nonintegrated	53	47
Phi = .29 ($\underline{N}$ = 34)		

Table 5
Protestant Children's Evaluation of the
Queen as a Symbol of Identity,
by School

Percentage of Protestant Children Mentioning the Queen as a Symbol of Identity		
School	No Mentions	One or More Mentions
Integrated	56	44
Nonintegrated	27	73
Phi = .29 ($\underline{N}$ = 34)		

Table 6
Children's Evaluation of Partition as a Cause of the Conflict,
by School and by Age

Percentage of Children Mentioning Partition as a Cause of the Conflict					
Integrated School			Nonintegrated School		
Age	No Mentions	One or More Mentions	Age	No Mentions	One or More Mentions
11–12	87	13	11–12	75	25
15–16	64	36	15–16	25	75
Phi = .27 ($\underline{N}$ = 19)			Phi = .50 ($\underline{N}$ = 16)		

Table 7
Protestant Children's Evaluation
of Partition as a Cause of the Conflict,
by Religion

Percentage of Children Mentioning Partition as a Cause of the Conflict		
Religion	No Mentions	One or More Mentions
Protestant	54	46
Catholic	90	10
Phi = .34 (N = 34)		

Table 8
Children's Evaluation of Prejudice as a Cause of the Conflict,
by School and by Age

Percentage of Children Mentioning Prejudice as a Cause of the Conflict					
Integrated School			Nonintegrated School		
Age	No Mentions	One or More Mentions	Age	No Mentions	One or More Mentions
11–12	87	13	11–12	100	0
15–16	45	55	15–16	75	25
Phi = .43 (N = 19)			Phi = .38 (N = 16)		

Table 9
Protestant Children's Evaluation
of Prejudice as a Cause of the Conflict,
by School

Percentage of Protestant Children Mentioning Prejudice as a Cause of the Conflict		
School	No Mentions	One or More Mentions
Integrated	56	44
Nonintegrated	93	7
Phi = .45 (N = 24)		

Table 10
Children's Interpretation of the Conflict as Inevitable, by School and by Age

Percentage of Children Interpreting the Conflict as Inevitable, by School and by Age					
Integrated School			Nonintegrated School		
Age	No Mentions	One or More Mentions	Age	No Mentions	One or More Mentions
11–12	37	63	11–12	25	75
15–16	36	64	15–16	75	25
Phi = .01 (N = 19)			Phi = .50 (N = 16)		

Table 11
Children's Interpretation of the Conflict as Environmental Violence, by School and by Age

Percentage of Children Mentioning Environmental Violence					
Integrated School			Nonintegrated School		
Age	No Mentions	One or More Mentions	Age	No Mentions	One or More Mentions
11–12	0	100	11–12	25	75
15–16	33	67	15–16	63	37
Phi = .44 (N = 19)			Phi = .38 (N = 16)		

Table 12
Children's Negative Mentions of Political Authority, by Religion

Percentage of Children Mentioning Nonsupport for Public Authority		
Religion	No Mentions	One or More Mentions
Protestant	37	63
Catholic	0	100
Phi = .39 (N = 34)		

Table 13
Children's Solutions to the Conflict
as Integrated Education,
by Religion and by School

Percentage of Children Mentioning Integrated Education as a Solution to the Conflict		
School	No Mentions	One or More Mentions
Integrated Protestant Catholic	89 50	11 50
Nonintegrated Protestant	100	0
Phi = .55 ($\underline{N}$ = 34)		

Table 14
Children's Evaluations of
the Queen's Role as Weak,
by Age

Percentage of Children Mentioning Queen's Weak Role		
Age	No Mentions	One or More Mentions
11–12	31	69
15–16	0	100
Phi = .45 ($\underline{N}$ = 35)		

Table 15
Children's Evaluation of the Queen's Role as Weak, by School and by Age

Percentage of Children Mentioning Queen's Weak Role					
Integrated School			Non-integrated School		
Age	No Mentions	One or More Mentions	Age	No Mentions	One or More Mentions
11–12	50	50	11–12	12	88
15–16	0	100	15–16	0	100
Phi = .61 ($\underline{N}$ = 19)			Phi = .26 ($\underline{N}$ = 16)		

Table 16
Children's Evaluation of the Prime Minister's Role as Powerful, by Age

Percentage of Children Mentioning the Prime Minister's Powerful Role				
Age	No Mentions	One or More Mentions	Group	Mentions
11–12	12	88	English Children	51
15–16	0	100		
Phi = .27 ($\underline{N}$ = 35)			Phi = .66 ($\underline{N}$ = 80) Greenstein (1975)	

Table 17
Children's Evaluation of the Prime Minister's Role as Weak, by School

Children Mentioning the Prime Minister's Weak Role		
School	No Mentions	One or More Mentions
Integrated	84	16
Nonintegrated	44	56
Phi = .43 ($\underline{N}$ = 35)		

Table 18
Protestant Children's Evaluation of the
Prime Minister's Role as Weak,
by School

Protestant Children Mentioning the Prime Minister's Role as Weak		
School	No Mentions	One or More Mentions
Integrated	78	22
Nonintegrated	47	53
Phi = .31 ($\underline{N}$ = 24)		

Table 19
The Queen and the Policeman: Children's
Negative Evaluation of the Queen,
by School and by Age

The Queen and the Policeman: Percentage of Children Negatively Mentioning the Queen					
Integrated School			Non-integrated School		
Age	No Mentions	One or More Mentions	Age	No Mentions	One or More Mentions
11–12	63	37	11–12	0	100
15–16	45	55	15–16	36	64
Phi = .64 ($\underline{N}$ = 19)			Phi = .53 ($\underline{N}$ = 16)		

Appendix 3
Research Instrument

1. Two children are playing in their room. Their parents are out. When the parents return, they notice that there is a window broken in the kitchen. Finish the story any way you like.

2. To go to school, Jack (Janet) must cross a dangerous road. His (her) parents have told him (her) always to walk across and never to run. One day, while he (she) is crossing the road, a policeman tells him (her) to run instead of walking. What does he (she) do? Finish the story.

3. Now here is a different kind of story. A new child comes to your school. S/he comes from another country. S/he says to you: "There are some things about Northern Ireland that I don't understand. Tell me what they are." For example: Suppose s/he says: "Tell me what the queen is?" What would you say?

4. Who is more important for Northern Ireland, the queen or the prime minister? Why?

5. One day, the queen was driving her car to a meeting. Because she was driving very fast, the police stop the car. Finish the story.

6. How old are you?

7. Tell me, why did you decide to come to this school?

Notes

Chapter 1. Children in a Global Context

1. To prevent any kind of harassment of pupils, parents, or staff, the schools will not be identified. The integrated school will be referred to simply as the integrated school, and the nonintegrated school will be referred to as the nonintegrated school.

Chapter 2. The Historical World of Children in Belfast, Northern Ireland

1. The Scottish highland Catholic Gaels were originally Irish Gaels from Ulster who invaded the highlands in the fifth century, conquering and integrating the indigenous Pique population.
2. The Land League was founded in 1789 by Michael Davitt to lower rents and increase peasant proprietorship by means of peaceful demonstrations, boycotting, and some violence.
3. The Home Rule League was founded in 1873 by Issac Butt and Joseph Biggar to obtain home rule for Ireland. Charles Stewart Parnell became leader in 1880 in an attempt to gain tenant support for the party's political aganda.
4. Started in December 1994, the Framework for Peace has been instrumental in creating a Republican and Loyalist cease-fire and in setting up the possibility of future roundtable constitutional discussions among the various political parties in Northern Ireland, mediated by both the British and Irish governments.
5. "Spotting" refers to determining to which group a person belongs based on their physiological traits, cultural habits, or other characteristics.

Chapter 3. Political Learning and Children

1. Irwin (1991) studied integrated schooling in Belfast, Northern Ireland, and Jerusalem, Israel.

Chapter 4. Children in a Troubled City

1. For excellent discussions of combining both research paradigms, see Ashworth et al. 1986; Babbie 1986; Bailey 1982; Bogdan and Taylor 1975; Bogdan and Biklen 1985; Creswell 1994; Kirk and Miller 1986; Krippendorf 1980; Peshkin 1993, Poling and Fuqua 1986; Strauss and Corbin 1990; Van Maanen et al. 1982.
2. There are five secondary all-ability and coeducational integrated schools

to date in Northern Ireland. There are over seventeen primary schools in Northern Ireland.

3. The enrollment of pupils at the integrated school ensures that an equal number of Catholics and Protestants are working class, middle class, academically weak, academically strong, boys, and girls. The criteria that select pupils for the nonintegrated school differ, since middle-class boys and girls attend an academically strong school that prepares its pupils for entry to the professions and university. The composition of the pupils and staff at the integrated school is a 47 percent Catholic, 3 percent other, and a 50 percent Protestant ratio. The composition at the nonintegrated school is a 5 percent Catholic, 5 percent other, and a 90 percent Protestant ratio.

4. Both staff rooms in the integrated school are mixed by religion and gender.

5. In Northern Ireland, Catholics are called Taigs, Papists, or Fenians, and Protestants are called Jaffas, Orangies, or Prods. The ethnoreligious affiliation of the individual is determined by the soccer team he or she supports—Glasgow Rangers in the case of Protestants and Glasgow Celtic for Catholics.

6. The child refused to take part in the study because he was afraid to be interviewed by a stranger.

7. In the nonintegrated grammar school, preselection is determined by academic ability as well as by economic and religious choice. In order to determine why the children attended the integrated school the researcher asked each respondent why he or she chose to go to this particular school. The responses varied; the parents chose to send the child, the child wanted to try something different, the grandparents wanted the child to go to the school, or the child's best friend was going (*See* Morgan et al. 1992; Wilson and Dunn 1989). The researcher also asked each child in the integrated school about their parents: whether they were liberal or conservative, peace activists, from a mixed marriage, or involved with paramilitary groupings. The political behavior of each parent varied from case to case.

8. The Montgomery and Crittenden (1977) test took the weighted average from three coders who independently coded responses according to quantitative principles. They obtained the reliability coefficients of .65.

Chapter 5. How Children Think and Feel about Conflict and Its Resolution

1. A platform introduced in 1991, during the course of the field research, by both the British and Irish governments to formulate discussions leading to a power-sharing agreement between Northern Ireland's constitutional political parties.

2. All of the children in the nonintegrated school offered interesting and thoughtful insights into the intractable nature of the bicommunal conflict. However, half of the integrated school's first-year sample, who come from very different social backgrounds, were either too shy or too afraid to discuss their perceptions of the Northern Ireland scenario. My own experience of group behaviors in Northern Ireland suggests that the escalation of sectarian violence in 1991 added to the polarization of the communities, resulting in the persistent fear, suspicion, and mistrust of strangers or outsiders held by most people (Harris 1972). This can explain, in part, the reaction of these very young children to the researcher, whom they did not know and, therefore did not trust.

3. The pronunciation of the letter "H" reveals the ethnoreligious identity of the individual. See Coles (1987) and Fields (1976) for more discussion on the topic.

4. Opposition to the PIRA has been found in previous research to be an important component in Protestant adults' political behavior (Bruce 1992; Dunn and Morgan 1994; Moxon-Browne 1983). Therefore, Protestant children are compared to see if there are any substantial differences between these children in both types of schools. However, in this example differences between the schools are not significant.

5. This respondent is suggesting that the initial cause of the present-day intercommunal strife in Northern Ireland was the effort, in 1601, by the British monarch James I to colonize, or "plant," the province of Ulster.

6. During the course of my stay, the integrated school was evacuated because of a telephoned bomb threat.

7. Negative mentions of political authority would include statements such as "The police would give you a kicking" "We don't trust the RUC" "They [the police] are a pack of traitors."

8. However, outright support for law and order issues in Northern Ireland is reflected in orientations toward public authority by Protestant pupils in both schools. The results are not presented in tabular form, because statistical calculations were not possible as a result of zero figures. Protestant students in both schools overwhelmingly support the security forces in Northern Ireland. As the RUC and UDR are predominantly Protestant, it is not surprising that Protestant schoolchildren would be more willing to accept their counterterrorist activities. Previous studies indicate that the security forces are popular among the majority community (Moxon-Browne 1983) but not among the minority community (Boyle et al. 1980; Stalker 1988).

9. For example, Protestant first-year children in the nonintegrated school mentioned en masse that the queen should be punished for a traffic violation.

10. The major focus of this study is in the realm of developmental psychology; it is less an examination of the impact of religion or school type on children's political orientations.

Chapter 6. How Children Think and Feel about Authority Figures

1. The phi of .45 calculated above indicates a moderate to perfect relationship between the queen's weak role as a political leader and age. In contrast, Greenstein's (1975) sample of 80 ten- to fourteen-year-old English children provided a phi of .66 between weak role and age.

2. We can see from Table 19 that the phi of .27 signifies a weak relationship between the prime minister's powerful political role and the students' age. A phi of .66, on the other hand, indicates a strong relationship between these variables for Greenstein's (1975) sample of 80 ten- to fourteen-year-old English children when compared with 106 French and 111 U.S. children. Greenstein (1975) did not, however, divide his sample into two separate age groups.

3. Children's story completions are treated as negative in which the queen is annoyed, unfriendly, pulls rank arrogantly, threatens to sack the policeman, or drives off in a huff.

4. A phi of .64 for the integrated school and .53 for the nonintegrated school,

when compared to Greenstein's (1975) finding of .84, indicates a perfect association between these variables.

5. Although the focus of this particular small sample study is in the realm of developmental psychology, political attitudes toward the queen appear to be identical for both sets of Protestant students. In other words, there appears to be no significant difference in Protestant children's attitudes toward the symbolic significance of the monarch, indicating that the integrated school may not be totally affecting the ingrained beliefs and feelings of these children regarding the queen. Protestant children possess deeply held convictions that uphold the political and religious significance of the monarch as the source of their ethnoreligious identity (Miller 1978).

Chapter 7. Putting Children's Wisdom into Practice

1. In an interview with Mr. X, one of the "founding fathers" of the integrated school.

2. In an interview with a history teacher at the integrated school, Belfast, Northern Ireland, December 1991.

3. In an interview with Tom O'Donnell, Chairman of IPI, former Irish Minister for the Gaeltacht and member of both the Irish and European Parliaments, University of Limerick, 11 January 1992.

4. An example of such powerful collaboration is the recent efforts by Professor John Darby at the Center for the Study of Conflict, University of Ulster at Coleraine, Professor Ted Robert Gurr of the University of Maryland, and Professors Fred Pearson and Otto Feinstein of the Center for Peace and Conflict Studies, Wayne State University, to develop a global data bank on early warning indicators and models of ethnic conflict to help practitioners and international institutions to anticipate and respond to crisis situations before they become too violent.

Bibliography

Agnew, J. 1989. Beyond reason: Spatial and temporal sources of ethnic conflicts. In *Intractable conflicts and their transformation,* edited by L. Kriesberg, T. Northrup, and S. Thorson, 41–53. Syracuse, N.Y.: Syracuse University Press.

Akenson, D. H. 1973. *Education and enmity: The control of schooling in Northern Ireland, 1920–50.* Newton and Abbot: David and Charles.

Allison, G. T. 1971. *Essence of decision: Exploring the Cuban missile crisis.* Boston: Little, Brown and Co.

Almond, G., and S. Verba. 1965. *The civic culture.* Boston: Little, Brown and Co.

Amir, Y., S. Shlomo, and R. Ben-Ari, eds. 1984. *School desegregation: Cross-cultural perspectives.* London: Lawrence Erlbaum.

Arthur, P. 1974. *The people's democracy, 1968–73.* Belfast: Blackstaff.

———. 1986. The Anglo-Irish agreement: Conflict resolution or conflict regulation. Paper read at the International Conference on Peacebuilding. Derry: Magee College, University of Ulster.

———. 1987. The Anglo-Irish agreement: Conflict resolution or conflict regulation? *Bulletin of Peace Proposals* 18 (4):555–563.

———. 1987. *The government and politics of Northern Ireland.* (2d ed.). London: Longman.

Arthur, P., and K. Jeffrey. 1988. *Northern Ireland since 1968.* New York: Basil Blackwell Ltd.

Ashworth, P. D., A. Giorgi, and J. J. de Koning, eds. 1986. *Qualitative research in psychology: Proceedings of the international association for qualitative research in social science.* Atlantic Highlands, N.J.: Humanities Press.

Aughey, A. 1989. *Under siege: Ulster unionism and the Anglo-Irish agreement.* New York: St. Martins Press.

Aunger, E. A. 1975. Religion and occupational class in Northern Ireland. *Economic and Social Review* 7 (1):1–18.

———. 1983. Religion and class: An analysis of 1971 census data. In *Religion, education and employment: Aspects of equal opportunity in Northern Ireland,* edited by R. J. Cormack and R. D. Osborne, 32–57. Belfast: Appletree Press.

Babbie, E. 1986. *The practice of social research.* Belmont, Calif. Wadsworth Publishing Co.

Bagehot, W. 1873. *The English constitution.* Boston: Little, Brown and Co.

Bailey, K. 1982. *Methods of social research.* 2d ed. New York: Macmillan.

Banks, J. A. 1986. Multicultural education: Development paradigm and goals. In *Multicultural education in western societies,* by J. A. Banks and J. A. Lynch, (eds) 1–28. New York: Praeger.

Barritt, D. P., and C. F. Carter. 1972. *The Northern Ireland problem*. 2d ed. London: Oxford University Press.

Bell, G. 1976. *The Protestants of Ulster*. London: Pluto.

Beresford, D. 1987. *Ten men dead: The story of the 1981 Irish hunger strike*. London: Grafton Books.

Bew, P. 1977. The problem of Irish unionism. *Economy and Society* 6 (1):89–109.

———. 1979. *Land and the national question in Ireland, 1858–82*. New Jersey: Humanities Press.

———. 1983. A Protestant parliament and a Protestant state: Some reflections on government and minority in Ulster, 1921–43. In *Parliament and community*, edited by A. Cosgrove and J. I. McGuire, 40–72. Belfast: Appletree Press.

———. 1987. *Conflict and conciliation in Ireland, 1890–1910: Parnellities and radical agrarians*. Oxford: Clarendon Press.

Bew, P., and H. Patterson. 1985. *The British state and the Ulster crisis: From Wilson to Thatcher*. London: Verso.

———. 1987. The new stalemate: Unionism and the Anglo-Irish Agreement. In *Beyond the rhetoric: Politics, the economy, and social policy in Northern Ireland*, edited by P. Teague, 25–35. London: Lawrence and Wishart.

———. 1988. Ireland in the 1990s—north and south. In *Across the frontiers: Ireland in the 1990s, cultural-political-economic*, edited by R. Kearney, 78–91. Dublin: Wolfhound Press.

———. 1990. *Scenarios for progress in Northern Ireland*. London: Clarendon Press.

Bew, P., P. Gibbon, and H. Patterson. 1979. *The state in Northern Ireland, 1921–72: Political forces and social classes*. Manchester: Manchester University Press.

———. 1995. *Northern Ireland, 1921–1994: Political forces and social classes*. London: Serif.

Bilu, Y. 1989. The other as a nightmare: The Israeli-Arab encounter as reflected in children's dreams in Israel and the West Bank. *Journal of Political Psychology* 10 (3):365–89.

Birch, A. H. 1990. *The British system of government*. 8th ed. Boston: Unwin Hyman.

Birrell, D., and A. Murie. 1980. *Policy and government in Northern Ireland: Lessons of devolution*. Dublin: Gill and Macmillan.

Blondel, J. 1963. *Voters, parties and leaders*. Harmondsworth: Penguin.

Boal, F. W., and N. H. Douglas, eds. 1982. *Integration and division: Geographical perspectives on the Northern Ireland problem*. London: Academic Press.

Bogdan, R. 1972. *Participant observation in organizational settings*. Syracuse, N.Y.: Syracuse University Press.

Bogdan, R., and S. J. Taylor. 1975. *Introduction to qualitative research methods*. New York: Wiley.

Bogdan, R., and S. K. Biklen. 1982. *Qualitative research for education*. Boston: Allyn and Bacon.

Bogdanor, V. 1981. *The people and the party system*. Cambridge: Cambridge University Press.

Boserup, A. 1972. Contradictions and struggles in Northern Ireland. *Socialist Register* 5 (1):157–192.

Boyle, K., T. Hadden, and P. Hillyard. 1980. *Ten years in Northern Ireland: The legal control of political violence*. London: Cobden Trust.

Boyle, K., and T. Hadden. 1985. *Northern Ireland: A positive proposal*. London: Penguin Books.

Bowyer-Bell, J. 1974. *The secret army: A history of the IRA*. Cambridge: MIT Press.

Braungart, M. M., and R. G. Braunguart. 1990. The life-course development of left-and right-wing youth activist leaders from the 1960s. *Journal of Political Psychology* 11 (2):243–82.

Bruce, S. 1986. *God save Ulster! The religion and politics of Paisleyism*. Oxford: Clarendon Press.

———. 1992. *The red hand: Protestant paramilitaries in Northern Ireland*. New York: Oxford University Press.

Buchanan, R. H. 1976. The planter and the Gael: Cultural dimensions of the Northern Ireland problem. *Social Studies, Irish Journal of Sociology* 5 (1):1–22.

Buckland, P. 1979. *The factory of grievances: Devolved government in Northern Ireland, 1921–1939*. Dublin: Gill and Macmillan.

———. 1981. *A history of Northern Ireland*. Dublin: Gill and Macmillan.

Byrne, S. 1993. Conflict, complexity and children; integrated education in a segregated society: Northern Ireland, a case study. Ph.D. diss., Department of International Relations, Syracuse University, no. 6110, Ann Arbor, Mich., UMI Dissertation Services.

———. 1994a. Third parties in Northern Ireland: Exacerbation or amelioration. Occasional paper 9406, 1–54. Center for International Studies, University of Missouri-St. Louis.

———. 1994b. Patriot games revistied: How Northern Irish school children think and feel about conflict. Working paper series 39, 1–48. Program for the Analysis and Resolution of Conflicts, Syracuse University.

———. 1995. Conflict regulation or conflict resolution: Third-party intervention in the Northern Ireland conflict: Prospects for peace. *Journal of Terrorism and Political Violence*. 7(2): 1–24.

Byrne, S., and N. Carter. 1994. Shaping shared identities: Challenges for Quebec and Northern Ireland. Working paper series 38, 1–33. Program for the Analysis and Resolution of Conflicts, Syracuse University.

Cairns, E. 1980. The development of ethnic discrimination in children in Northern Ireland. In *A Society under stress: Children and young people in Northern Ireland,* edited by J. Harbinson and J. Harbinson, 69–84. Shepton Mallet: Open Books.

———. 1982. Intergroup conflict in Northern Ireland. In *Social identity and intergroup relations,* edited by H. Tajfel, 277–295. Cambridge: Cambridge University Press.

———. 1987. *Caught in a crossfire: Children and the Northern Ireland conflict*. Syracuse, N.Y.: Syracuse University Press.

Cairns, E., S. Dunn, V. Morgan, and M. Giles. 1989. *Attitudes toward integrated education in Northern Ireland: The impact of real choice*. Coleraine: Centre for the Study of Conflict, University of Ulster.

Cairns, E., C. Mc Clenhahan, S. Dunn, and V. Morgan. 1991. Preface for geographical location as a measure of ethnic/national identity in children in Northern Ireland. *Irish Journal of Psychology* 12 (3):346–54.

Canavan, P. 1989. Appraisal in the primary school: A case study. Master's thesis, Department of Pre-Service Education, University of Ulster at Jordanstown.

Cancian, F. M., and J. W. Gibson. 1990. *Making war/making peace: The social foundations of violent conflict.* Belmont, Calif: Wadsworth.

Coakley, J. 1985. *The Ethnic revival in modern industrialised societies: Implications of the Northern Ireland evidence.* Limerick: University of Limerick Press.

Coles, R. 1986. *The political life of children.* Boston: Houghton Mifflin Co.

Connell, R. W. 1971. *The child's construction of politics.* Melbourne: Melbourne University Press.

Cormack, R. J., and R. D. Osborne. 1983. *Religion, education and employment: Aspects of equal opportunity in Northern Ireland.* Belfast: Appletree Press.

Cox, W. H. 1987. Managing Northern Ireland intergovernmentally: An appraisal of the Anglo-Irish Agreement. *Parliamentary Affairs* 40 (1):80–97.

Creswell, J. W. 1994. *Research design: Qualitative and quantitative approaches.* Thousand Oaks, Calif.: Sage.

Crossman, R. H. S. 1972. *The myths of cabinet government.* Cambridge: Harvard University Press

Cunningham, M. J. 1991. *British government policy in Northern Ireland, 1969–89.* Manchester: Manchester University Press.

———. 1994. *British government and the Northern Ireland question: Governing a divided community.* Sheffield: PAVIC

Curtis, L. 1984. *Ireland, the propaganda War: The British media and the 'battle for hearts and minds'.* London: Pluto Press.

Darby, J. 1976. *Conflict in Northern Ireland: The development of a polarised community.* Dublin: Gill and Macmillan.

———. 1983 *Northern Ireland: The background to the conflict.* Belfast: Appletree Press.

Darby, J., and S. Dunn. 1987. Segregated schools: The research evidence. In *Education and policy in Northern Ireland,* edited by R. D. Osborne and R.L. Miller, 21–47. Belfast: Queen's University and the University of Ulster Policy Institute.

Darby, J., D. Murray, D. Batts, S. Dunn, S. Farren, and J. Harris, 1977. *Education and community in Northern Ireland: Schools apart?* Coleraine: New University of Ulster.

Dawes, A. 1990. The effects of political violence on children: A consideration of South Africa and related studies. *International Journal of Psychology* 25 (1):13–31.

Dawson, R. E., and K. Prewitt. 1969. *Political socialization.* Boston: Little, Brown and Co.

Devlin, B. 1969. *The price of my soul.* London: Pan.

Dixon, P. 1994a. European integration, modernisation and Northern Ireland, 1961–75. *Etudes Irlandaises* 19 (1):167–82.

———. 1994b. The usual English doubletalk: The British political parties and the Ulster Unionists, 1979–94. *Irish Political Studies* 9 (1):25–40.

Dixon, P., and P. Bew. 1994. Labour party policy in Northern Ireland. In *The*

Northern Ireland question: Perspectives and policies, edited by B. Barton and P. Roche, 151–165. Avebury: Aldershot.

Dodge, C. P., and M. Raundalen. 1987. *War, violence and children in Uganda.* Oslo: Norwegian University Press.

———. 1991. *Reaching children in war: Sudan, Uganda, and Mozambique.* Bergen, Norway: Sigma Forlag.

Duffy, G., and N. Frensley. 1991. Community conflict processes: Mobilization and demobilization in Northern Ireland. In *International crisis and domestic politics: Major political conflicts in the 1980s* edited by James Q. Lamare, 81–125. New York: Praeger.

Dunn, S. 1986. The role of education in the Northern Ireland conflict. *Oxford Review of Education* 12 (3):233–242.

———. 1989. Integrated schools in Northern Ireland. *Oxford Review of Education,* 15 (2):121–128.

———. and A. Smith. 1989. *Inter school links.* Coleraine: Centre for the Study of Conflict, University of Ulster.

———. 1994. *Protestant alienation in Northern Ireland: A preliminary survey.* Coleraine: Center for the Study of Conflict, University of Ulster.

Easton, D., and J. Dennis. 1969. *Children in the political system: Origins of political legitimacy.* New York: McGraw Hill.

Evenson, K. 1994. Specialized cognition: A pact for the future. Unpublished paper.

Fairleigh, J., ed. 1975. *Sectarianism—roads to reconciliation: Papers read at the 22nd annual summer school of the social study conference, St. Augustine's College, Dungarvan, 3–10 August 1974.* Dublin: Three Candles.

Farrell, M. 1980. *Northern Ireland: The orange state.* 2d ed. London: Pluto.

———. 1983. *Arming the Protestants: The formation of the Ulster special constabulary and the Royal Ulster Constabulary, 1920–27.* London: Pluto.

Feehan, J. M. 1986. *Bobby Sands and the tragedy of Northern Ireland.* Dublin: The Permanent Press.

Fields, R. M. 1975. Psychological genocide: The children of Northern Ireland. *History of Childhood Quarterly: The Journal of Psychohistory* 3 (1):201–224

———. 1976. *Society under siege: A psychology of Northern Ireland.* Philadelphia: Temple University Press.

Fisher, R., and W. Ury. 1981. *Getting to YES: Negotiating agreement without giving in.* New York: Penguin Books.

Fraser, T.G. 1986. *Partition in Ireland, India and Palestine: Theory and practice.* London: Macmillan.

Fraser, M. 1973. *Children in conflict.* London: Secker and Walton.

Gaffikin, F., and M. Morrisey. 1990. *Northern Ireland: The Thatcher years.* Atlantic Highlands, N.J.: Zed Books.

Gallagher, E., and S. Worrall. 1982. *Christians in Ulster, 1968–80.* Oxford: Oxford University Press.

Gallagher, T. 1987. *Bridging the divide? Education and the Northern Ireland communities.* Belfast: National Council for Educational Research, Queen's University.

Galliher, J. F., and J. L. Degregory. 1985. *Violence in Ireland: Understanding Protestant perspectives.* Dublin: Gill and Macmillan.

Garbarino, J., K. Kostelny, and N. Dubrow. 1991. What children can tell us about living in danger. *American Psychologist.* 46 (4):376–83.

Garvin, T. 1987. *National revolutionaries in Ireland, 1858–1928.* Oxford: Clarendon Press.

Gibbon, P. 1975. *The origins of Ulster Unionism: The formation of popular Protestant politics and ideology in nineteenth-century Ireland.* Manchester: Manchester University Press.

Girvin, B. 1986. National identity and conflict in Northern Ireland. In *Politics and society in contemporary Ireland,* edited by B. Girvin and R. Sturm, 65–84. Aldershot: Gower.

Gottlieb, G. 1993. *Nation against state: A new approach to ethnic conflicts and the decline of sovereignty.* Washington, D.C.: Council on Foreign Relations.

Greenstein, F. I. 1960. The benevolent leader: Children's images of political authority. *American Political Science Review* 54 (1):934–943.

———. 1961. More on children's images of the president. *Public Opinion Quarterly* 25 (Winter):648–654.

———. 1965. *Children and politics.* New Haven: Yale University Press.

———. 1975. The benevolent leader revisited: Children's images in three democracies. *American Political Science Review* 69 (1): 1371–1398.

Greenstein, F. I., and S. Tarrow. 1970a. Children and politics in Britain, France and the United States. *Youth and Society* 2 (1):234–246.

———. 1970b. *Political orientations of children: The use of a semi-projective technique in three nations.* Beverly Hills, Calif.: Sage Publications.

Greenstein, F. I., V. Herman, R. N. Stradling, and E. Zurick, 1969. Queen and prime minister—The child's eye view. *New Society* (23 October):50–61.

———. 1974. The child's conception of the queen and the prime minister. *British Journal of Political Science* 4 (July):257-287.

Greer, J. E. 1980. The persistence of religion: A study of adolescents in Northern Ireland. *Character Potential* 9 (2):139–149.

Greer, J. E., and J. Long. 1989. Religion in rural Ulster. *Education North* 1 (2):15–19.

Guelke, A. 1988. *Northern Ireland: The international perspective.* Dublin: Gill and Macmillan.

———. 1991. The political impasse in South Africa and Northern Ireland: A comparative perspective. *Comparative Politics* 23 (2):143–162.

———. ed. 1994. *New perspectives on the Northern Ireland conflict.* Aldershot: Avebury.

Gurr, T. R. 1993. *Minorities at risk: A global view of ethnopolitical conflicts.* Washington, D.C.: United States Institute of Peace Press.

Harris, R. 1972. *Prejudice and tolerance in Ulster: A study of neighbours and 'strangers' in a border community.* Manchester: Manchester University Press.

Haufmann, E., and J. W. Getzels. 1955. Interpersonal attitudes of former Soviet citizens, as studied by a semi-projective method. *Psychology Monographs* 69 (4):22–46.

Hayes, M. 1990. Whither cultural diversity? A speech delivered on 29th November to the MSSc Irish Studies Forum at Queens University, Belfast. Pamphlet no. 2. Belfast: Community Relations Council.

Hepburn, A.C. 1983. Employment and religion in Belfast, 1901–1951. In *Religion, education and employment: aspects of equal opportunity in Northern Ireland,* edited by R. J. Cormack and R. D. Osborne, 105–140. Belfast: Appletree Press.

Hermann, M. G., and J. T. Preston. 1994. Presidents, advisers, and foreign policy: The effects of leadership style on executive arrangements. *Journal of Political Psychology* 15 (1):75–97.

Hermann, M. G. 1994. Presidential leadership style, advisory systems, and policy making: Bill Clinton's administration after seven months. *Journal of Political Psychology* 15 (2):363–75.

Heskin, K. 1980. *Northern Ireland: A psychological analysis.* Dublin: Gill and Macmillan.

Hess, R. D., and J. V. Torney. 1967. *The development of political attitudes in children.* Chicago: Aldine Publishing Co.

Hewitt, C. 1981. Catholic grievances, Catholic nationalism and violence in Northern Ireland during the civil rights period: A reconsideration. *British Journal of Sociology* 23 (3):362–380.

Hickey, J. 1984. *Religion and the Northern Ireland problem.* Dublin: Gill and Macmillan.

Hill, G. 1970. *An historical account of the plantation in Ulster at the commencement of the seventeenth century, 1608–1620.* Shannon: Irish University Press.

Hughes, J. 1994. Prejudice and identity in a mixed environment. In *New perspectives on the Northern Ireland conflict,* edited by A. Guelke, 86–104. Aldershot: Avebury.

Hunter, J. 1982. An analysis of the conflict in Northern Ireland. In *Political cooperation in divided societies: A series of papers relevant to the conflict in Northern Ireland,* edited by D. Rea, 9–59. Dublin: Gill and Macmillan.

———. 1996a. Northern Ireland civil rights assoiation. In *encyclopedia of nonviolent action,* edited by C. Kruegler and W. Voegle. New York: Garland Publishing.

Irvin, C. 1996b. From civil rights to hunger strikes: Transforming struggle in Northern Ireland. In *Nonviolent direct action: Transforming struggles,* edited by D. Bond. New York: Praeger. Forthcoming.

Irwin, C. 1991. Education and the development of social integration in divided societies. Department of Social Anthropology, Queen's University, Belfast.

———. 1994. The myths of segregation. In *New perspectives on the Northern Ireland conflict,* edited by A. Guelke, 104–119. Aldershot: Avebury.

Jackson, A. 1989. *The Ulster party: Irish Unionists in the House of Commons, 1884–1911.* Oxford: Clarendon Press.

Jackson, H., and A. McHardy. 1984. *The two Irelands: The problem of the double minority* 2, London: The Minority Rights Group.

Jahoda, G., and S. Harrison. 1975. Belfast children: Some effects of a conflict environment. *Irish Journal of Psychology* 3 (1):1–19.

Janis, I. L. 1982. *Victims of groupthink: A psychological study of foreign policy decisions and fiascoes.* 2d ed. Boston: Houghton Mifflin.

Jennings, I. 1965. *The British constitution.* 3rd ed. Cambridge: Cambridge University Press.

Jervis, R. 1976. *Perception and misperception in international politics.* Princeton: Princeton University Press.

Jordan, T. E., 1993. A ship of clever lads: Origins, occupations and physique of male British convicts transported to Australia, 1842–43. *International Journal of Comparative and Applied Criminal Justice* 17 (1):149–71.

———. 1994. Ireland and the quality of life: The famine era. Unpublished manuscript.

Kearney, R. 1988. Introduction: Thinking otherwise. In *Across the frontiers: Ireland in the 1990s: Cultural-political-economic,* edited by R. Kearney, 7–29. Dublin: Wolfhound Press.

Keil, F. 1979. *Semantic and conceptual development: An ontological perspective.* Cambridge: Harvard University Press.

Kelley, K. 1982. *The longest war: Northern Ireland and the IRA.* Dingle: Brandon Book Publishers.

Kenny, A. 1986. *The Road to hillsborough.* Oxford: Pergamon Press.

Keogh, D., and M. H. Haltzel. 1994. *Northern Ireland and the politics of reconciliation.* Washington, D.C.: Woodrow Wilson Center Press.

Kirk, J. 1986. *Reliability and validity in qualitative research.* Beverly Hills, Calif.: Sage.

Kohlberg, L. 1981. *The philosophy of moral development: Essays on moral development.* New York: Harper and Row.

Kriesberg, L. 1982. *Social conflicts.* 2d ed. Englewood Cliffs, N.J.: Prentice-Hall Inc.

———. 1992a. Intractable conflicts in the Middle East. Occasional Paper 34, 1–34, Program on the Analysis and Resolution of Conflicts, Syracuse University.

———. 1992b. Ethnicity, nationalism and violent conflict in the 1990s. Paper presented at the Annual Meeting of the Peace Studies Association, February, Boulder, Colorado.

Kriesberg, L., T. Northrup., and S. J. Thorson. eds. 1989. *Intractible conflicts and their transformations.* Syracuse: Syracuse University Press.

Krippendorff, K. 1980. *Content analysis: An introduction to its methodology.* Beverly Hills, Ca. Sage.

Lee, J. 1973. *The modernization of Irish society, 1848–1918.* Dublin: Gill and Macmillan.

Lijphart, A. 1968. *The politics of accommodation: Pluralism and democracy in the Netherlands.* Berkeley: University of California Press.

———. 1975. Review article: The Northern Ireland problem: Cases, theories, and solutions. *British Journal of Political Science* 5 (2):83–106.

Loughlin, J. 1987. *Gladstone, home rule, and the Ulster question, 1882–1893.* Atlantic Highlands, N.J.: Humanities Press.

Lovett, T. 1990. Community education and community division in Northern Ireland *Convergence* 23 (2):25–33.

Lynch, J. 1987. *Prejudice reduction and the schools.* London: Cassell Education Ltd.

Lyons, F. S. L. 1971. *Ireland since the famine.* London: Weidenfeld and Nicolson.

MacDonald, M. 1986. *Children of wrath: Political violence in Northern Ireland.* Cambridge, England: Polity.

MacLaughlin, J. G., and J. A. Agnew. 1986. Hegemony and the regional question: The political geography of regional industrial policy in Northern Ireland. *Annals of the Association of American Geographers* 76 (2):247–261.

Mair, P. 1987. Breaking the nationalist mould: The Irish Republic and the Anglo-Irish Agreement. In *Beyond the rhetoric: Politics, the economy, and social policy in Northern Ireland,* edited by P. Teague, 45–70. London: Lawrence and Wishart.

Manheim, J. B., and R. C. Rich. 1986. *Empirical political analysis: Research methods in political science.* 2d ed. New York: Longman.

Markman, E. 1989. *Categorization and naming in children: Problems of induction.* Cambridge: MIT Press.

Martin, K. 1963. *Britain in the sixties: The Crown and the establishment.* Harmondsworth: Penguin.

McAllister, I. 1977. *The Northern Ireland social democratic and labour party: Political opposition in a divided society.* London: Macmillan.

McCann, E. 1974. *War and an Irish town.* Harmondsworth: Penguin

McEwen, A. 1990. Segregation and integration in Northern Ireland's education system. In *Schools under scrutiny: The case of Northern Ireland,* edited by L. Caul, 15–36. London: Macmillan.

McEwen, A., U. Agnew, J. Salters, and M. Salters. 1993. *Integrated education: The views of parents.* Belfast: School of Education, Queen's University Press

McGarry, J. 1988. The Anglo-Irish Agreement and the prospects for power sharing in Northern Ireland. *The Political Quarterly* 59 (2):136–50.

McGarry, J., and B. O'Leary, eds. 1990. *The future of Northern Ireland.* Oxford: Clarendon Press.

———, eds. 1993. *The politics of ethnic conflict regulation: Case studies of protracted ethnic conflicts.* New York: Routledge.

McWhirter, L. 1983. Contact and conflict: The question of integrated education. *Irish Journal of Psychology* 6 (1):13–27.

Miller, D. 1978. *Queens rebels: Ulster loyalism in historical perspective.* Dublin: Gill and Macmillan.

Miller, R. L. 1983. Religion and occupational mobility. In *Religion, education and employment: Aspects of equal opportunity in Northern Ireland,* edited by R. J. Cormack, and R. R. Osborne, 156–185. Belfast: Appletree Press.

Miles, M. B., and M. A. Huberman. 1984. *Qualitative data analysis: A sourcebook of new methods.* London: Sage Publications.

Moffat, C., ed. 1991. *Education together for a change: Integrated education and community relations in Northern Ireland.* Belfast: Fortnight Educational Trust.

Montgomery, A. C., and K. S. Crittenden. 1977. Improving coding reliability for open-ended questions. *Public Opinion Quarterly* 41 (2):1–26.

Moore, J. 1991. Dean slates churches on segregated schooling. *Irish Times* September 1.

Morgan, A. 1980. Socialism in Ireland—red, orange and green. In *Ireland: Divided nation, divided class,* edited by A. Morgan and B. Purdie, 25–52. London: Ink Links.

Morgan, V., S. Dunn, E. Cairns, and G. F. Fraser. 1992. Parental involvement in education: How do parents want to become involved. *Educational Studies* 18 (1):11–20.

Moxon-Browne, E. 1983. *Nation, class and creed in Northern Ireland.* Aldershot: Gower.

Munck, R. 1985. *Ireland: Nation, state and class struggle.* London: Westview Press.

Murray, D. 1983. Schools and conflict. In *Northern Ireland: The background to the conflict,* edited by J. Darby, 136–151, Syracuse, N.Y.: Syracuse University Press.

————. 1985. *Worlds apart: Segregated schools in Northern Ireland.* Belfast: Appletree Press.

Nairn, T. 1977. *The break-up of Britain.* London: NLB.

Nelson, S. 1984. *Ulster's uncertain defenders: Protestant political paramilitary and community groups and the Northern Ireland conflict.* Belfast: Appletree Press.

Northern Ireland Council for Integrated Education. 1991a. *Statement of principles.* Belfast: NICIE Publications.

————. 1991b. *The NICIE model scheme of management, memorandum and articles of association: A rational and commentary.* Belfast: NICIE Publications.

————. 1991c. *Scheme for management of grant-maintained integrated schools: ABC school.* Belfast: NICIE Publications.

————. 1991d. *Annual report, 1989–90.* Belfast: NICIE Publications.

————. 1991e. *Memorandum of association of Omagh integrated primary school limited: The companies (Northern Ireland) Order 1986, company limited by guarantee and not having a share capital.* Belfast: NICIE Publications.

————. 1991f. *Education together in the 1990s.* Belfast: NICIE Publications.

Northern Ireland Curriculum Council. 1990a. *Cross-curricular themes: consultation report.* Belfast: Stranmillis College.

————. 1990b. *Cross-curricular themes: Consultation report.* Belfast: Stranmillis College.

Northern Ireland Department of Education. 1989a. *Education reform in Northern Ireland: Proposals for history in the Northern Ireland curriculum.* Bangor: DENI.

————. 1989b. *Cultural heritage: A cross-curricular theme.* Bangor: DENI.

————. 1989c. *Education for mutual understanding: A cross-curricular theme.* Bangor: DENI.

————. 1989d. *Northern Ireland education reform act.* Bangor: DENI.

Northrup, T. A. 1989. Dynamics of identity in personal and social conflict. In *Intractable conflicts and their transformation,* edited by L. Kriesberg, T. Northrup and S. Thorson, 55–83. Syracuse, N.Y.: Syracuse University Press.

Norton, P. 1984. *The British polity.* New York: Longman.

O'Brien, C. C. 1972. *States of Ireland.* London: Hutchinson.

————. 1986. Ireland: The mirage of peace. *The New York Review of Books* 33 (7):23–33.

O'Donnell, E. E. 1977. *Northern Irish stereotypes.* Dublin: College of Industrial Relations.

O'Dowd, L., B. Rolston, and M. Tomlinson. 1980. *Northern Ireland: Between civil rights and civil wars.* London: CSE Books.

O'Leary, B. 1986. The Anglo-Irish Agreement: Folly or statecraft? *West European Politics* 10 (1):5–32.

———. 1987. The Anglo-Irish agreement: Meanings, explanations, results, and a defence. In *Beyond the rhetoric: Politics, the Eeonomy, and social policy in Northern Ireland,* edited by P. Teague, 145–173. London: Lawrence and Wishart.

———. 1989. Coercive consociationalism in Northern Ireland. *Political Studies* 37 (4): 562–588.

O'Leary, B., and J. McGarry. 1993. *The politics of antagonism: Understanding Northern Ireland.* Atlantic Highlands, N.J.: Athlone Press.

O'Leary, C., S. Elliot, and R. A. Wilford. 1988. *The Northern Ireland assembly, 1982–86: A constitutional experiment.* New York: St. Martin's Press.

O'Malley, Padraig. 1983. *The Uncivil wars: Ireland today.* Belfast: Blackstaff Press.

O'Neill, T. 1969. *Ulster at the crossroads.* London: Faber and Faber.

Osborne, R. D., and R. L. Miller. 1987. *Education and policy in Northern Ireland.* Belfast: Policy Research Centre, Queen's University and University of Ulster.

O'Sears, D. 1968. Development of political attitudes in children. *Harvard Education Review* 38 (1):571–577.

Patterson, H. 1980. *Class conflict and sectarianism: The Protestant working class and the Belfast Labour movement, 1868–1920.* Belfast: Blackstaff Press.

Perceval-Maxwell, M. 1973. *The Scottish migration to Ulster in the reign of James I.* London: Rutledge and Kegan Paul.

Peshkin, A. 1993. The goodness of qualitative research. *Educational Researcher* 22 (2):24–30.

Piaget, J., and B. Inhelder. 1958. *The growth of logical thinking from childhood to adolescence.* New York: Basic Books.

———. 1969. *The Psychology of the child.* New York: Basic Books.

———. 1972. Intellectual evolution from adolescence to adulthood. *Human Development* 15 (3): 1–12.

———. 1976. *The grasp of consciousness: Action and concept in the young child.* Cambridge: Harvard University Press.

Piaget, J., and A. M. Weil. 1970. The development in children of the idea of the homeland and of relations with other countries. In *Learning about politics: A reader in political socialization,* edited by R. Sigel, 53–65. New York: Random House.

Poling, A., and R. W. Fuqua, eds. 1986. *Research methods in applied behavior analysis: Issues and advances.* New York: Plenum Press.

Probert, B. 1978. *Beyond orange and green: The political economy of the Northern Ireland crisis.* London: Zed.

Punamaki, R., and R. Suleiman. 1990. Predictors and effectiveness of coping with political violence among Palestinian children. *British Journal of Social Psychology* 29 (1):67–77.

Punnett, R. M. 1980. *British government and politics.* 4th ed. London: Heinemann.

Rapoport, D. 1971. *Assassination and terrorism.* Canada: TH Best Printing Co., Ltd.

Rea, D. 1982. *Political cooperation in divided societies: A series of papers relevant to the Northern Ireland conflict.* Dublin: Gill and Macmillan.

Richards, P. G. 1983. *Mackintosh's government and politics of Britain.* 6th ed. London: Hutchinson.

Roberts, H. 1986. *Northern Ireland and the Algerian analogy: A suitable case for Gaullism.* Belfast: Athol Books.

————. 1987. Sound stupidity: The British party system and the Northern Ireland question. *Government and Opposition* 22 (3):315–335.

Robinson, A. 1971. Education and sectarian conflict in Northern Ireland. *The New Era,* 52 (1):384–388.

Rokkan, S., and D. Urwin, eds. 1982. *The politics of territorial identity: Studies in European regionalism.* London: Sage.

————, eds. 1983. *Economy, territory and identity: Politics of western European peripheries.* London: Sage.

Rolston, B. 1987. Alienation or political awareness? The battle for the hearts and minds of Northern nationalists. In *Beyond the rhetoric: Politics, the economy and social policy in Northern Ireland,* edited by P. Teague, 58–91, London: Lawrence and Wishart.

Rose, R. 1971. *Governing without consensus: An Irish perspective.* London: Faber and Faber.

————. 1976. *Northern Ireland: A time of choice.* London: Macmillan.

————. 1986. *Politics in England.* 4th ed. Boston: Little, Brown and Co.

Rosenau, N. 1975. The sources of children's political concepts: An application of Piaget's theory. In *New direction in political socialization,* edited by D. C. Schwartz and S. K. Schwartz, 163–187. New York: Free Press

Russell, J., and J. A. Schellenburg. 1976. Political attitude structure of schoolboys in Northern Ireland. *Irish Journal of Psychology* 3 (2):73–86.

Sampson, A. 1973. *The new anatomy of Britain.* New York: Stein and Day.

Schank, R., and R. Abelson. 1977. *Scripts, plans, goals and understanding: An inquiry into human knowledge structures.* Hillsdale, N.J.: Lawrence Erlbaum Associates.

Schmitt, D. E. 1988. Bicommunialism in Northern Ireland. *Publius, the Journal of Federalism* 18 (Spring): 33–45.

Senehi, J. 1996. Conflict and Culture: Storytelling—a matter of life and death. *Mind and Human Interaction,* August, forthcoming.

Shea, P. 1981. *Voices and the sounds of drums.* Belfast: Appletree Press.

Sigel, R. S., ed. 1970. *Learning about politics: A reader in political socialization.* New York: Random House.

Sigel, R. S., and M. B. Hoskin. 1981. *The political involvement of adolescents.* New Brunswick, N.J.: Rutgers University Press.

Smith, A., and S. Dunn. 1990. *Extending school links: An evaluation of contact between Protestant and Catholic pupils in Northern Ireland.* University of Ulster at Coleraine: Centre for the Study of Conflict.

Smith, A., and A. Robinson. 1992. *Education for mutual understanding: Perceptions and policy.* Coleraine: Center for the Study of Conflict, University of Ulster.

Smith, A. D. 1982. Nationalism, ethnic separatism and the intelligentsia. In *National Separatism,* edited by C. H. Williams, 122–158. Vancouver: University of British Columbia Press.

Spencer, A. E. C. W. 1987. Arguements for an integrated school system. In *Education and policy in Northern Ireland*, edited by R. D. Osborne, R. J. Cormack, and R. L. Miller, 99–111. Belfast and Queen's University and University of Ulster: Policy Research Institute.

Stalker, J. 1988. *Stalker*. London: Harrap.

Stephen, F. 1990a. Integrated nursery education. *Child Care (Northern Ireland)* 15 (Nov./Dec.): 12–19.

———. 1990b. Integrated education in Northern Ireland. Paper presented at the Annual Meeting of the educate Together in the 1990s Conference, 12 May, University College Galway.

Stewart, A. T. Q. 1967. *The Ulster crisis*. London: Faber and Faber.

———. 1977. *The narrow ground: Aspects of Ulster, 1609–1969*. London: Faber and Faber.

Straker, G. 1992. *Faces in the revolution: The psychological effects of violence on township youth in South Africa*. Athens: Ohio University Press.

Strauss, A. L., and J. Corbin. 1990. *Basics of qualitative research: Grounded theory, procedures, and techniques*. Newbury Park, Ca.: Sage.

Stringer, M., and R. P. Watson. 1991. Intergroup violence and intergroup attribution, *British Journal of Social Psychology* 30 (1):261–66.

Synder, G. H., and P. Diesing. 1978. *Conflict among nations: Bargaining, decision-making, and system structure in international crises*. Princeton: Princeton University Press.

Thompson, D. L., and D. Ronen. 1986. *Ethnicity, politics, and development*. New York: Lynne Rienner Publisher Inc.

Todd, J. 1987. Two traditions in Unionist political culture. *Irish Political Studies* 2 (1):1–26.

Tolley, H. 1973. *Children and war: Political socialization to international conflict*. New York: Teachers College Press.

Tovey, H. 1975. Religious group membership and national identity systems. *Social Studies* 4 (20):124–43.

Trew, K. 1983. Group identification in divided society. In *Children of the troubles: Children in Northern Ireland*, edited by J. Harbinson, 109–119. Belfast: Learning Resource Centre, Stranmilis College.

———. 1986. Catholic-Protestant contact in Northern Ireland. In *Contact and conflict in intergroup encounters*, edited by M. Hewstone and R. Brown, 93–106. Oxford: Blackwell.

Van Maanen, J., J. Dabbs, and R. R. Faulkner. 1982. *Varieties of qualitative research*. Beverly Hills, Ca.: Sage.

Vayrynen, R. 1984. Regional conflict formations: An intractable problem of international relations. *Journal of Peace Research* 21 (4):337–359.

Volkan, V. 1985. The need to have enemies and allies: A developmental approach. *Journal of Political Psychology* 6 (2):219–47.

Waddell, N., and E. Cairns. 1986. Situational perspectives on social identity in Northern Ireland. *British Journal of Social Psychology* 25 (2):25–31.

Wallis, R., S. Bruce, and D. Taylor. 1986. No surrender: Paisleyism and the politics of ethnic identity in Northern Ireland. Unpublished paper. Published by the Department of Social Studies, Queen's University Belfast.

―――. 1987. Ethnicity and evangelicalism: Ian Paisley and protestant politics in Ulster. *Comparative Studies in Society and History* 29 (2):293–313.

Watt, D. 1981. *The constitution of Northern Ireland: Problems and prospects.* London: Heinemann.

Weber, M. 1968. *Economy and society.* New York: Bedminister Press.

Whyte, J. 1978. Interpretations of the Northern Ireland problem: An appraisal. *Economic and Social Review* 9 (1):257–282.

―――. 1981. Why is the Northern Ireland problem so intractable? *Parliamentary Affairs* 34 (4):422–435.

―――. 1983. How much discrimination was there under the Unionist regime, 1921-68? In *Contemporary Irish studies,* edited by T. Gallagher, and J. O'Connell, 34–59. Manchester: Manchester University Press.

―――. 1986. How is the boundary maintained between the two communities in Northern Ireland? *Ethnic and Racial Studies* 9 (2):219–234.

―――. 1990. *Interpreting Northern Ireland.* Oxford: Clarendon Press.

Williams, C. H., ed. 1982. *National separatism.* Cardiff: University of Wales Press.

Wilson, D., and S. Dunn. 1989. *Integrated education: Information for parents.* Coleraine: Centre for Conflict Studies, University of Ulster.

Wilson, T. 1989. *Ulster: Conflict and consent.* Oxford: Basil Blackwell.

Wright, F. 1973. Protestant ideology and politics in Ulster. *European Journal of Sociology* 14 (1):213–280.

―――. 1987. *Northern Ireland: A Comparative analysis.* Dublin: Gill and Macmillan.

―――. 1991. Integrated education and new beginnings in Northern Ireland. Working Paper 6, Center for the Study of Conflict, University of Ulster at Coleraine, Corrymeela Press.

Yogev, A., and N. S. Ben-Yehoshua. 1991. Determinants of readiness for contact with Jewish children among young Arab students in Israel. *Journal of Conflict Resolution* 35 (3):547–62.

Ziegler, D. W. 1990. *War, peace and international politics.* Boston: Scott, Foreman and Little, Brown Higher Education.

Index